G. Wood Hill

The law of real property in England;

A course of lectures delivered at the Institute of Actuaries, Staple Inn Hall, Holborn,

during the session 1896-97

G. Wood Hill

The law of real property in England;
A course of lectures delivered at the Institute of Actuaries, Staple Inn Hall, Holborn, during the session 1896-97

ISBN/EAN: 9783337732929

Printed in Europe, USA, Canada, Australia, Japan

Cover: Foto ©ninafisch / pixelio.de

More available books at **www.hansebooks.com**

THE LAW OF
REAL PROPERTY IN ENGLAND:

A COURSE OF LECTURES

BY

G. WOOD HILL,
Barrister-at-Law.

DELIVERED AT THE

Institute of Actuaries, Staple Inn Hall, Holborn,

During the Session 1896-97.

LONDON:
CHARLES & EDWIN LAYTON,
56, FARRINGDON STREET, E.C.

1898.

PREFACE.

THE education of an actuary covers a wide field of knowledge and research. He must be an efficient mathematician capable of applying his technical skill to the everyday problems of life; a practical financier possessing a comprehensive knowledge of the different classes of investment and of the causes which regulate and govern the value of money; and withal he must have a large and peculiar acquaintance with the law, embracing not only the ordinary commercial law, particularly the law of contracts, the law of joint stock companies, and especially the law relating to life assurance companies, to guide him in the discharge of his duties as a manager; but he must also have an intimate acquaintance with the principles of the law of real property in order that he may grasp the exact nature and bearing of the various forms of possession, and of the conditions and responsibilities arising out of the inheritance and disposition of property.

The actuary is in constant need of his knowledge of the law of real property. He has to advise on the purchase or mortgage of estates; life interests, contingent or in possession; and reversionary interests; and is frequently consulted on the financial adjustment of operations arising out of family or other arrangements. In fact, the actuary who is in full practice must have this law at his fingers' ends.

Although it is essential that he should know the law, the actuary is never expected to become a lawyer. The difference between knowing the law and being a lawyer is as wide as the difference between theory and practice; and the actuarial student in his studies will learn sufficient of the law to convince him of the danger of interfering in the practice of it.

The actuarial student proceeds to the study of the law in a different way to the legal student. He naturally, therefore, meets with many difficulties, arising most frequently from the want of a clear perception of the basis on which the whole fabric is built. The Council of the Institute of Actuaries, recognizing these difficulties, and being always anxious to assist the students in their studies, invited Mr. George Wood Hill to give a series of lectures in plain and simple language on the law of real property. These lectures were listened to with marked attention and interest, and were received with evident satisfaction and pleasure by those who were fortunately able to attend them; and their issue now in printed form will, it is reasonably hoped, supply the students with sufficient knowledge to serve as an introduction to the more complete study of the subject.

It should be clearly understood that these lectures do not contain all that it is necessary for the actuary to know on the subject. They are merely aids to study; and by presenting to the mental vision a kind of miniature photograph of the subject, they will serve to stimulate the student to investigate further, and with deeper interest, into the recesses of the law of real property.

H. W. M.

25 July 1898.

LECTURES

ON THE

LAW OF REAL PROPERTY IN ENGLAND.

BY

Mr. G. WOOD HILL.

1896–1897.

INDEX.

	PAGE
Actuary—	
education	iii
not a lawyer	iv
Agricultural Holdings Act, 1883	72
Appointment, general power of...	56
Chattel real	71
Contingent Remainders Act, 1877	48, 60
Conveyancing and Law of Property Acts	84
forfeiture of lease	80
mortgagee's interest passes to personal representatives	90
power to grant leases	92
power of sale	96
consolidation	105
Copyholds	63
De donis conditionalibus	19
Devises of land	57
Disentail	20
Emblements	72
Enfranchisement...	67
Entail	20
Equity of redemption	86, 88, 106

	PAGE
Escheat ...	... 10, 13
Estates—	
in fee simple	17
freehold, and less than freehold	17
in tail	18
for life	21
equitable estates ...	28
legal estate	31
Executory devises	... 51, 57
Fealty	7, 12
Fee—	
a feudal estate in land	6
originally inalienable	8
alienation by sale and by will	13
fee simple	17
fee tail	18
base fee	34
Feudal system	5
Fines and recoveries	20
Frauds, Statute of	74
Freehold ...	17
Gavelkind	39
Heir	24
Hereditaments, corporeal and incorporeal	38
Heriot	65
Homage ...	6
Inheritance Act, 1833 ...	24
Investiture	7
Judicature Act ...	... 31, 93
Knight Service ...	9, 12, 14
Leases—	
grant	73
assignment	76
covenants...	... 76, 79
underlease	78
mortgage...	78
forfeiture...	80
surrender...	84
Lectures, object and scope	iv, 1, 2

	PAGE
Limitations, Statute of	100
Locke King's Act, 1854 ...	93
Manor—	
mesne Lords, or Lords of the Manor ...	9, 63
Court Baron	10
Marriage—	
right of marriage	10
marriage settlement	54
Merger	50
Mortgage—	
of lease	78
of land	... 85
form	... 85, 91
at law and in equity	... 85, 87
equity of redemption ...	86, 88, 106
covenants...	91
reconveyance	100
priority	101
tacking	102
consolidation	103
second mortgages	103, 105
Mortgagee—	
in possession	87
legal estate passes to personal representative ...	90
right to sue	94
foreclosure ...	94
power of sale	... 95, 96
right to take possession ...	96
,, to appoint receiver ...	98
,, to grant leases ...	98
Mortgagor—	
right to grant leases ...	92
,, to bring actions	93
,, to repay after giving notice	99
Paramount, lord	8
Partition, writ of	... 36
Perpetuities ...	... 27, 60
Portions	26
Primogeniture ...	26

		PAGE
Property—		
in land	...	4, 14
real and personal	...	69
chattel real	...	71
Quia emptores, Statute of	...	8
Quit rent...	...	12
Real Property Act, 1845	...	49, 50, 74
Remainder—		
vested	...	40
contingent	...	44
Reversion	...	39
Seisin—		
livery of seisin	...	7
must never be without owner	...	46
Settled Land Acts	...	22
Shelley's case, rule in	...	43
Socage, free	...	11, 14
Subinfeudation	...	8
Tacking	...	102
Tenancy—		
in common and joint tenancy	...	34
at will	...	72
by sufferance	...	72
from year to year	...	72
for term of years	...	73
Tenure—		
knight service	...	9, 12, 14
free socage	...	11, 14
gavelkind	...	39
copyhold	...	63
Terms of years	...	73
Uses—		
Statute of Uses	...	14, 29, 52
shifting Uses	...	51
Wardship	...	10
Williams on Real Property	...	3
Wills Act, 1837	...	14

THE
LAW OF REAL PROPERTY IN ENGLAND.

FIRST LECTURE.

[*Delivered 14 January 1897.*]

THE PRESIDENT (Mr. T. E. Young, B.A.): Gentlemen, in extending a cordial welcome to Mr. Wood Hill this evening, I may briefly refer to the origin and purport of this course of lectures. The Institute of Actuaries has always gladly accepted the view that, besides constituting a scientific body, its position involves the responsibility of assuming educational functions, and of endeavouring to utilize every opportunity of aiding its members, and particularly its younger members, the students, by an appropriate course of training and instruction. Hence, in the past, the Institute appointed lecturers and classes of a practical character, with a view of bringing within the range of the students the most authentic and the most recent knowledge, and as the Institute fully recognizes the fact that technical study and book knowledge are absolutely incompetent as an equipment for professional life, they have been guided by this feeling to devising a method of securing a practical education for the younger members by practical men. The course of lectures, consequently, which we inaugurate this evening, is an extension of that original design, and I may be permitted to express the confident hope that it is simply the beginning of a larger and ampler scheme of practical education in various other modes. With these brief remarks, showing the purpose which the Institute has in view in instituting this course, I have very great pleasure in asking Mr. Wood Hill to address us. (Applause.)

MR. WOOD HILL: Mr. President and gentlemen, in introducing me to this Hall, your President has stated the purpose and object that the Council have in view in asking you to be present here to listen to a course of lectures, to begin with, upon legal subjects. When the Committee of this Institute did me the honour to ask me to deliver a series of lectures upon legal subjects in this Hall, I was informed, as you have heard to-day, that the main object of those lectures was the education of candidates for admission into the Institute of Actuaries, to assist them, and to encourage them by interesting them in working up for their examinations in the subjects of the lectures, and to induce them to acquire such a knowledge of those subjects as would enable them to deal, as actuaries, not as lawyers, with matters of business involving a knowledge of the law with which they might have to deal in the course of the practice of their profession as actuaries. So that you will see, gentlemen, the object I have in mind is not to make lawyers of you, but to make you a little more competent as actuaries than you would be without any knowledge of the legal subjects upon which I have been asked to lecture to you. Now, the first lecture, at the request of the Council, that I have to deliver is upon the Real Property Law of England, or rather the principles of it. Into the details of it it would be impossible to go in the course of a series of three or four lectures, and I do not think it would be wise to do so, because as your intention is not to become lawyers, it is not necessary you should have that precise and accurate knowledge of the law which is required of a person who has to carry out, as a lawyer, legal transactions. I shall, therefore, only deal with the principles of any subject upon which I shall have to lecture, and certainly only with the leading principles of the Law of Real Property in England. What you want to know, and what I hope you will learn, is what the Law of Real Property is at the present day. But let me say this at the outset. It is impossible, or at least I think so, for any man to have an intelligent appreciation or understanding of the Law of Real Property in England as it is, unless he knows how it came to be what it is. And I have no doubt whatever that, in learning how the Law of Real Property in England came to be what it is, you will also, at the same time, learn what it is; so that you only have to learn how it came to be what it is to know what it is. Well, in the first place, it is an artificial subject, and there is, fortunately for you, and, I think, more fortunately for me, for

I am essentially an advocate, and not a professor, I am not in the habit of delivering lectures, and therefore I say, particularly fortunate for myself, there is an excellent text-book upon the subject, of which, I have no doubt, many of you are aware. It is the late Joshua Williams on " The Law of Real Property ", and I should advise every student of law, whether he intends to be an actuary, or a barrister, or a solicitor, or county magistrate, or to hold any other position of eminence or prominence in this country, to master the leading principles of the law of this country, and especially of the Law of Real Property, and he can do so from that book, if he only studies it. It is an interesting book, and it is really not a large book. This is the last edition, and if you master that book—or even the principal parts of it—you will know as much of Real Property Law as you are ever likely to want to know in practising your profession as an actuary. I do not think I can follow any other method better than the method which has been pursued by Mr. Joshua Williams in that book which is now a classic work. The matter has been re-arranged from time to time in the different editions, but I advise you to give it away if you happen to have an old edition, and to buy a new one, because it brings the Law of Real Property up to the present time, or very nearly to the present time. The last edition, I think, is dated in the year 1896. It is not an expensive book. It is published at the price of one guinea, and I think you can get it at some stationers for 15s. or 16s., and it is a book you will always be glad to have in your library, for if you don't often read it, you will often want to refer to it to refresh your memory, and as a book of reference it will always be of use to you, and the money would not be lost. So I strongly advise you to get this book, and to supplement, or rather fill in, the gaps which I must necessarily leave in a course of lectures. To begin with, you ought to get rid of all preconceived notions about law, and I don't think I can do better at the outset than read to you what Williams says in one of the earlier editions with reference to that matter. The passage does not appear, so far as I am aware, in the later editions, but I cannot tell you why. It seems to me pregnant with good sense, and I ask you to give me your attention while I read it. It is not long. You will find it in the old editions at the very beginning of the book. On page 16, in the tenth edition, Chapter I, he says this: "It seldom happens that any " subject is brought frequently to a person's notice without his

"forming, concerning it, opinions of some kind, and such
"opinions, carelessly picked up, are often carefully retained,
"though in many cases wrong, and in most inadequate. The
"subject of property is so generally interesting, that few persons
"are without some notions as to the legal rights appertaining to
"its possession. These notions, however, as entertained by
"unprofessional persons, are mostly of a wrong kind; they
"consider that what is a man's own is what he may do what he
"likes with. And, with this broad principle, they generally set
"out on such legal adventures as may happen to lie before them.
"They begin at a point at which the lawyer stops, or at
"which, indeed, the law has not yet arrived, nor ever will, but
"to which it is still continually approximating. Now, the
"student of law must forget for a time that if he has land he may
"let it or leave it by his will, or mortgage it, or sell it, or settle
"it; he must humble himself to believe that he knows as yet
"nothing about it, and he will find that the attainment of the
"ample power which is now possessed over real property has been
"the work of a long period of time, and that even now a common
"purchase deed of a piece of freehold land cannot be explained
"without going back to the reign of Henry VIII, or an ordinary
"settlement of land without recourse to the laws of Henry I.
"That such should be the case is certainly a matter of regret.
"History and antiquities are no doubt interesting and delightful
"studies in their place, but their perpetual intrusion into modern
"practice, and the absolute necessity of some acquaintance with
"them gives rise to much of the difficulty experienced in the
"study of the law, and to many of the errors of its less studious
"practitioners. The first thing then the student has to do is to
"get rid of the idea of absolute ownership. Such an idea is quite
"unknown to the English law. No man is in law the absolute
"owner of lands; he can only hold an estate in them." Now,
gentlemen, those words are not applicable to some of you, but I
have no doubt they are applicable in every sense to many of you.
I happen to know that some gentlemen who present themselves as
candidates for admission into this Institute have studied law, and
studied it carefully, and that they are really students of the law
in the best sense. They have not just looked at it and got up
enough, say, to pass the examination which the Council requires
every member of this Institute to have passed, but they have an
intelligent knowledge of the subject. But to the majority, no
doubt, of the gentlemen here present it is evident every word that

Mr. Joshua Williams has there said, is applicable, and I hope you will follow his advice, and assume that you know nothing about it, that you come here to learn, that I am going to do my best that you should learn, and to assist you to learn the law of England upon the subject of real property. Now, gentlemen, at the present day the whole of the form of our law with regard to real property, is based upon what is known as the Feudal System, and without a knowledge of that Feudal System, you cannot appreciate the present state of our law with regard to real property. I say "the form" emphatically, because the substance of the feudal tenures has happily gone. A very little remains of the substance, so little, indeed, that a lawyer very rarely hears anything about it, and a man who is not a lawyer, but is a mere man of business, hears nothing about it, except when, in his own experience, it is actually brought to his notice. Well, gentlemen, as I say, I do not think you can understand the present state of our law without having some knowledge, I do not mean to say a knowledge of all the details, but some knowledge, and an intelligent knowledge, of the Feudal System. With regard to the Feudal System, if you want to know—and I hope you will have the curiosity to want to know—the full details of the system, you will find them in a book which I think every gentleman ought to read, whether he intends to be an actuary, or a lawyer, or anything else—Hallam's "Middle Ages", Chapter ii, part I, is practically devoted to the history of the Feudal System. It is necessary that you should have this knowledge, because whatever may have been the Anglo-Saxon tenures, those of the Feudal System were completely established, with some variations and additions to which I need not direct your particular attention, in this country during the 11th and 12th centuries, that is, during the time of William the Conqueror and his successors on the throne, commonly known as the Norman kings. Now what was this Feudal System? It did not arise in this country. It came over, to put it shortly, with the Conqueror, but it existed in France and other countries in a form, not in the same form as it was established here exactly as I have said, but practically in the same form. The essence of this Feudal System was to establish between the grantor of what was called a fee, and the grantee of that fee, a relation of a personal character. You will see how different that is from our present notion; but that was the essential principle of the Feudal System. The relation was, as I say, of a personal character. It was this: the grantor, called the lord, afforded to the grantee, called his vassal, protection; and, on the other hand, the vassal owed to his lord certain services, generally, and at first, almost entirely, military service. In those days there was no settled order of government, and this Feudal System was a substitute, or something in the place of, a settled order of government. That you may thoroughly get into your minds how personal this relation was between the grantor who was called the lord, and the grantee, whom I have already said, was called the vassal, I will read to you from Hallam the ceremonies of investiture by a lord of his vassal in a fee, but before doing so, I think you ought to have a notion of what is meant by the word "fee." It is a feudal estate in land, either of one tract of land, or more; it may be a very large territory, it may be a very small territory. Abroad they were called feus, or fiefs, but in England we have used the word fee, and we still use the word fee. The word fee is in use to the present day. In the very last Act of Parliament relating to the Law of Real Property, I think you have the expression "in fee simple." You cannot understand what "in fee simple" means in that Act of Parliament, unless you know what a fee was under the Feudal System. Now, that you may understand, as I have said, fully, the personal character of the relation between the lord and the vassal, I will read to you from Hallam. At page 169, you will find the passage I am about to read. "The ceremonies, in conferring a fief upon a vassal"— he uses the word fief, I prefer to use the word fee, because the word fee is a word in daily use, and the word fief is not—"the "ceremonies used in conferring a fief were principally these, "homage, fealty, and investiture. The first—that is, homage— "was designed as a significant expression of the submission and "devotedness of the vassal towards his lord. In performing "homage, his head was uncovered, his belt ungirt, his sword and "spurs removed. He placed his hands, kneeling, between those of "the lord, and promised to become his man from thenceforward"— notice that expression, gentlemen—to be "his man from thence- "forward, to serve him with life and limb and worldly honour, "faithfully and loyally, in consideration of the lands which he held "under him. None but the lord in person could accept homage, "which was commonly concluded by a kiss." I do not know whether you have ever seen an undergraduate at one of the Universities take his degree. But I remember being very much in that position when the Vice-Chancellor conferred upon me my degree, and if you have ever seen a degree conferred, you will have a very vivid idea of the actual ceremony. The next thing is "an oath of " fealty was indispensable in every fief, but the ceremony was less " peculiar than that of homage, and it might be received by proxy. " It was taken by ecclesiastics, but not by minors, and in language " differed little from the form of homage. Investiture"—what we should now call a conveyance—"investiture, or the actual con- " veyance of feudal land, was of two kinds, proper and improper. " The first was an actual putting in possession upon the ground, " either by the lord or his deputy"—it is called in our law "livery of seisin." That is an expression you will often come across in reading Williams, and it is just as well that at the very outset you should know what it means. In plain English it means, actual delivery of possession, nothing more or less. "The second was " symbolical, and consisted in the delivery of a turf, a stone, a " wand, a branch, or whatever else might be made usual by the " caprice of local custom. Du Cange enumerates not less than 98 " varieties of investiture." If that presents any picture to your minds, it will be a picture of an intimate personal relationship between the lord and the vassal, between the lord who had the dominion over the territory out of which the fee was carved, and the vassal to whom possession of a portion of the territory, the fee, was delivered under the investiture. That being, speaking generally, the nature of a fee, one has to see what its incidents were. The principal incidents of a fee were aids, reliefs, and other matters to which I shall have to draw your more particular attention hereafter. You will find them, I think, stated in Hallam on the following pages, and you will also find them in Williams. But the main object of the Feudal System was to secure to the lord the military service of the vassal. The vassal was bound to serve his lord in war. That was the military system by which a local militia, if one may use a modern term with reference to anything so ancient as the Feudal System, was provided for the defence of the lord, to enable the lord to protect others, and generally to carry on the business of depredation, as it then was carried on—there is no other word for it. This Feudal System was the origin of our present system of tenures, and you will see, and I lay great stress upon it, established a personal relationship between the lord and the tenant. When the fee was first conferred, when the system was first established, the tenant could not determine that personal relation between himself and his lord without the consent of both parties. It is doubtful whether, in the first instance, the interest, or as we now say the estate of the vassal, in the land descended to his heirs. It is clear that at the outset he could not part with it during his lifetime, but we know, or at least the historians tell us, that shortly after the Feudal System was established in this country, a fee became descendible to the heirs of the tenant, that is, upon his death it went to some other person who was called his heir, and that by degrees, step by step, the power of disposing of that estate became very nearly, or almost, complete. But it was not until an important statute was passed, to which I shall have to draw your attention, known as the statute of "Quia emptores", was passed that every holder of a fee became entitled as of right, without the consent of his lord to alienate, that is, to dispose of, his fee. That statute created an epoch in the law relating to real property in England, and it is very short, and I should like to show you how very clearly our ancestors could put things. The whole statute consists of three very short chapters, and the part of the statute which relates to this matter is called the first chapter. It was a statute passed at Westminster, and it was passed in the 18th year of the reign of Edward I, in the year 1290. I will now read to you the enacting part of that statute. "That "from henceforth it shall be lawful to every freeman to sell at his "own pleasure his land and tenements, or part of them, so that "the feoffee shall hold the same lands or tenements of the chief "lord of the same fee by such service and customs as the feoffor "held before." That is extremely short and extremely simple. It gives the right to the tenant in fee to dispose of his lands in his lifetime to anyone he thinks fit, but subject to this, he cannot grant his estate in fee to another to be held of himself as the lord. You see the words are "so that the feoffee"—that is the grantee—"shall hold the same lands or tenements of the chief "lord at the same fee by such service and customs as the feoffor "held before." Now that had an enormous effect upon the law in England—that simple statute in those few words. I must here explain that William the Conqueror assumed to be the chief lord, or the lord paramount, of all the land in England. What happened? The persons to whom the king granted fees, or who were assumed to hold their fees of the king, from time to time granted to other persons fees to be held of themselves, and that was called subinfeudation, and this went on from time to time until the chief, or mesne, lord was unable to enforce, or was

obstructed in enforcing, his rights against his own vassal, and that statute was passed with the object of putting an end to that state of things. It did so effectually, because that statute has been in force from the day it was passed until the present day, and it is part of the Law of the Real Property in England at the present moment. No man can grant an estate in fee, as it is called, to be held of himself. He can substitute another in his place, but he cannot create the relation of lord and vassal between himself and his tenant; he can only, as I said, substitute another in his place who is the vassal of the lord from whom he holds, and in the absence of evidence to the contrary, in this country that lord is the Queen. There still exist certain manors in this country which are held by mesne lords called lords of the manor, and if a fee is part of such a manor, and the freeholder, the owner, as we say now, of that fee sells it to a purchaser, the purchaser holds that land of the lord of the manor. But unless something of that kind can be shown, and it is rather difficult nowadays to show it, because from the time that statute was passed it has been absolutely impossible to create a manor, and every manor, therefore, dates from before that time. All land in this country is assumed to be held from Her Majesty the Queen. She is the chief lord, or lady, or lady paramount. I think it would be right even to speak of the Queen as the lord, because it is a word used technically. It has nothing to do with sex, it has only to do with the person who has dominion over the land and the person who holds it. I will now direct your attention, more particularly than I have done, to the chief incidents of a feudal estate. You will find them stated, and, I think, more concisely stated, in Williams than in Hallam, and I would refer you to page 45 of the last edition of Williams: "The incidents of
" tenure by knight service, which was the most honourable
" species of free tenure, were these—First, the tenant was bound
" to discharge the obligation of military service annexed to his
" holding. The feudal obligation of military service was a royal
" service due to the king from his immediate military tenants,
" and the tenants of knight service of a mesne lord would
" generally be bound to perform this service, and to acquit his
" lord thereof to an extent proportionate to the value of his
" holding. In and after the reign of Henry II, the obligation
" of personal military service seems to have become generally
" commuted in the case of the tenants of mesne lords, for a money

" payment called scutage or escuage, and assessed first by the
" Crown, and afterwards by the authority of Parliament. But
" scutage and the feudal obligation for military service became
" obsolete after the reign of Richard II, if not earlier. The
" military tenant was first, moreover, expected, and afterwards
" obliged, to render to his lord pecuniary aids to ransom his
" person "—the lord's person—" if taken prisoner, and to help
" him in the expense of making his son a knight, and in
" providing a portion for his eldest daughter on her marriage.
" On entering upon his estate, the tenant was bound to do
" homage to his lord, kneeling to him and professing to become
" his man. He was also bound to take an oath of fealty." I
draw your attention to that, because every tenant now is bound
to take that. " An heir of full age was required to pay a fine on
" succeeding to his estate. If the heir were under age, the lord
" had, under the names of wardship, the custody of the body and
" lands of his heir, without accounting for the profits, to the age
" of 21 in males, and 16 in females. In addition to this, the
" lord possessed the right of marriage, or of disposing of his
" infant wards in matrimony. And if a male heir refused a
" suitable match, he was to forfeit a sum of money equal to the
" value of the marriage, that is, what the suitor was willing to
" pay down to the lord as the price of marrying his ward; and
" double the market value was to be forfeited if a male ward
" presumed to marry without his lord's consent. If a female
" heir refused the match tendered by her lord, he might hold her
" lands until she attained 21, and further, until he had taken the
" value of the marriage "—and the value was what he could
squeeze out of one of the nobles for his ward's hand.—" The
" king's tenants were, moreover, subject to many burdens and
" exactions, from which the tenants of other lords were exempt.
" Again, every lord who had two or more free tenants, had
" a right to compel them to do suit at Court, that is, duly to
" attend and to aid in transacting the business of the lord's
" Court or Court baron, wherein his freeholders were judges as
" well as suitors."—I may say here, every lord who had two or
more free tenants had a right to hold a Court.—" Lastly, on
" failure of the tenant's heirs, his lord had the right to have the
" lands again as his escheat. That is, as falling into the lord
" who, or whose predecessors, had granted the fee, now brought
" to an end for want of heirs. The tenant's heirs might fall,

"either from natural causes, or by reason of his or their attainder,
"or corruption of the blood so as to lose its inheritable quality.
"Escheat upon attainder was, however, subject to the right of
"the Crown to hold for a year and a day, and to waste the
"attainted person's lands, a right usually compounded for. And
"the lands of one attainted for high treason were forfeited
"absolutely to the Crown, and did not escheat to the lord of the
"fee." In all other cases the escheat was to the immediate lord of the vassal. That was the state of things when the Feudal System was established in this country, but it did not seem to meet the wants and requirements of civilization. As men progressed, and, bit by bit, the military service was commuted for a payment of money, and most of the other rights of the lord over the vassal were used for the purpose of extorting or exacting money from the tenant. And, ultimately, all tenants became, and were made by Act of Parliament, tenants in free socage. Knight's service was done away with in all these tenures, and the heavier part of their burdens was got rid of. In order that you may understand what was done, you ought to know what a tenant in free socage was, because, at this day, all owners of land in fee are tenants in free socage, whether he holds land, a house, or other building. What, then, is a tenant in free socage? When the country was parcelled out by the Norman conqueror and his successors on the throne, manors were created. In those manors there sprung up a class of tenants called free socagers. They were not tenants by knight service, but by fixed service. They had to render certain services to their lord, either the payment of a fixed amount of rent, or certain agricultural services, that is, to do certain work on the property of the lord for so many days in the year and so on. These were fixed services, and the free socager was liable originally to certain aids and reliefs, but he was free from those dreadful exactions which the lord could exact from a tenant by knight service, such as wardship and marriage. There were no rights of that kind to the lord over his vassal if his tenant was what was called a free socager. These free socagers grew in number. It was a very pleasant sort of tenancy. They paid very little rent, and had very great liberties, and they had the protection of the law. The lords, on the other hand, with respect to their tenants who were not free socagers, used their powers in a most—I will not say brutal fashion—but a most unreasonable way. And the result of it was, that when

the Rebellion came, the Parliament of the day put an end to them all on the 24 February 1645. But, of course, what that Parliament did ceased to have any effect when Charles II came to the throne, but the people were so determined to get rid of this Feudal System in its worst aspects, that the first Parliament of Charles II in the year 1660 passed an Act of Parliament to the like effect, and I want to draw your attention to that, for it will show you exactly what our tenures are now. The Act of Parliament is the XII of Charles II, chap. xxiv, that is dating his reign from the death of his father—but the first year he was actually on the throne was the year 1660. Its enacting part is substantially this—"All tenures of any honours, manors, lands, "tenements, or hereditaments, or any estate or any inheritance at "the common law, held either of the king or of any other person "or persons, bodies politic or corporate, were thereby turned into "free and common socage to all intents and purposes from the "said twenty-fourth day of February 1645, and shall be so "construed, adjudged and deemed to be from the said twenty-"fourth day of February 1645, and for ever thereafter turned "into free and common socage. And the same were for ever "hereafter to stand and be discharged of all tenure by homage, "escuage, voyages royal and charges for the same, wardships "incident to tenure by knight's service, and values and forfeiture "of marriage and all other charges incident to tenure by knight "service, and of and from aids for marrying"—that is, to provide a portion for the eldest daughter of the lord when about to be married—"and aids for knighting the lord's eldest son— "and all conveyances of any manors, lands, tenements, and "hereditaments, made after the 24th day of February, were to "be expounded to be of such effect as if the same manors, lands, "tenements, and hereditaments had been then held, and continued "to be holden, in free and common socage." That, gentlemen, is the law of the land to this day. I think you will now fully understand why it was necessary—all landowners, as we say now, being tenants in free socage—that you should know something of the Feudal System. A tenant in free socage at the present time is bound to take an oath of fealty. It is never exacted from him. If his land is subject to a quit-rent, he is still bound to pay that quit-rent, because the statute of Charles II does not abolish fealty or a quit-rent, which may still be an incident of an estate in free socage. And if there were any other incidents to such an estate not abolished, he is bound by them. For instance, if there is such an incident as that the tenant should pay a relief upon his succeeding to the estate upon the death of his ancestor, that is still payable. It is still payable on some estates in England. I think it is generally, if not always, I am not quite sure, one year's rent. So you see a tenant by free socage is a pretty free person. As to the lord's rights, he has the right to that fealty, worth nothing, and he has the right to the quit-rent, which is generally extremely small, because the value of money has so much increased, and the quit-rent is sometimes never exacted or asked for, and is often not paid. But there is something still left which is occasionally of value, it is the right of escheat, which is, as I told you a few minutes ago, the right of the lord to the estate if the tenant dies without heirs. Now that a man can dispose of his property by will, one seldom hears of an escheat; but if the tenant of an estate in fee now dies without heirs, and without having disposed of his estate in his lifetime, or by will, the land then goes to his lord. Sometimes it goes to the lord of the manor, but, as I said just now, generally to the Crown, because it is very difficult nowadays to produce sufficient evidence that a freehold tenement is part of a manor, and held of anyone but the Queen. I do not know what the value of the escheats in recent years has been, but formerly they were considerable. But ever since a man has had the power, as I said just now, of disposing of his property by will, it is entirely his own fault if he allows his estate, when he can have no heir, to fall in to the Crown. And as people get better educated, and know more of the law, that happens more and more seldom. But a man in that unfortunate position in life ought to know the law. Well, gentlemen, having said so much as to the relation of the tenant or owner of land in fee simple to his lord, I think you will understand what it now is. Let us now consider what are his powers over his estate. At first, as I have already said, there was a personal relation between the lord and the tenant, which could not be determined without the consent of both of them. By the statute "Quia emptores", to which I have drawn your attention, the tenant was enabled to dispose of his estate by sale, but that Act did not enable him to dispose of it by will. But, by degrees, the lawyers invented a mode of disposing of estates by will. They invented a system of conveyances to trustees to the use of such persons as the tenant in fee simple should appoint by will, and in that way they kept the estate in the hands of the persons to whom the tenant himself wished it to go. But, in the reign of Henry VIII, that device was summarily put an end to by a statute, to which I shall have to refer, I am afraid more than once, further on. That was simply a device, a lawyer's device, to enable a man to do indirectly what he could not otherwise do directly. That was stopped by a statute, passed in the 27th year of the reign of Henry VIII, called the Statute of Uses; but, strange enough, five years afterwards, by statutes passed in the 32nd and 34th years of the reign of Henry VIII, tenants who held their lands in free socage were empowered to dispose of the whole of their estates—but tenants by knight service were only empowered to dispose of two-thirds of their estates. You will bear in mind the distinction there drawn between a tenant by knight service and a tenant by free socage. A free socager is allowed to dispose of the whole or any part of his estate, as he pleases, by will. Then comes the statute of Charles II, to which I have drawn your attention, which makes all tenants by knight service tenants by free socage, and by virtue of that Act all persons holding land, having become tenants by free socage, get the right to dispose of the whole of their property by will. I think you could not understand that unless you knew how it came to be the law. Then in the year 1837, by the present Wills Act, it was enacted that everybody might dispose of the whole of his property of whatever nature, kind or description, by will. Thus, you see what the position of a tenant or owner of land in fee simple is at the present time; he can now dispose of his estate in his lifetime or by his will, speaking generally, in any way he pleases. The only thing, so far as I know, as a lawyer, that he cannot do is, that he cannot grant his estate in fee to another person to be held of himself but only to hold it of the lord of whom he held it, who is generally the Queen. That, to the mind of a layman, is as near absolute ownership as anything can be. It is not, however, absolute ownership, because the lord still has rights in respect of the estate. If the tenant dies without heirs and without having disposed of his estate in his lifetime, or by will, it becomes the lord's estate. It is not like the ownership of goods. A man may be the absolute owner of goods, he does not hold them of any lord or other person, he can not only do what he likes with them, but the right of his legal representatives to them at his death is not defeated in any case by his dying without heirs. I said at the beginning of my lecture that the form of our Law of Real Property depends upon its history, and that you cannot understand what it is at the present day, without having an intelligent knowledge of the way in which it came to be the law; and I have now dealt substantially with the history of the law with regard to an estate in fee simple, but I must pray of you to be good enough to fill up the gaps I have left as you think fit. I am not here to dictate to you what you should do, but if you have the time, and the desire, I shall be glad if you will fill them up by reading the first 80 to 100 pages of Joshua Williams' book.

THE LAW OF REAL PROPERTY IN ENGLAND.

SECOND LECTURE.

[Delivered 28 January 1897.]

IN my first lecture I explained to you the Feudal System of tenures established in England under the Norman kings and their successors, and I also gave you so much of the history of those tenures down to the present time as I thought it was necessary that you should know before you could understand what is now the law as to estates in land. For the sake of simplicity we examined particularly the tenure of an estate in fee simple, and we saw what I desired particularly to impress upon you, that no man is in law the absolute owner of lands, and that he can only hold an estate in them either of the Crown or of some other lord, who in his place holds of the Crown. Though, in modern times, as I showed you, the incidents which mark the relation of lord and tenant of a fee rarely occur in practice, and are really very insignificant, and the burthen on the tenant has been reduced, the rights of the lord diminished, and the profit which the lord can derive from his position at the present time is extremely small, and is substantially reduced to the possibility of what I explained to you was called an escheat, that is, the right of the lord to succeed to the estate in case the tenant dies intestate, that is without having disposed of the estate by his will, and also without heirs. Having dealt generally with an estate in fee simple, I ought to tell you, for you ought to know, that an estate in fee simple is not the only estate in land which is known to the law. There are also other estates in land, and having dealt with the largest estate in land known to the law, an estate in fee simple, I propose this evening, if time permits, to deal more particularly with other estates in land. I explained to you on the last occasion what an estate in fee simple was, but before I deal with the other estates I should like to recall to your minds what really an estate in fee simple is. You will find a very concise statement in the book to which I referred you, Mr. Joshua Williams on the Real Property Law, p. 64. " It is an estate given to a man and his heirs simply and without " restriction, and inheritable, therefore, by his blood relations, " collateral as well as lineal, according to the legal rules of the " descent of a fee. Such an estate is, as we have seen, the most " absolute property which a subject can have in land." Now, the other estates which a man can have in land are called either freehold estates or estates less than freehold. An estate in fee simple is a freehold estate. The other freehold estates are—and you will find them stated on p. 62 of Williams' book in these words: " Freehold estates are either estates of inheritance, which " are in fee simple (inheritable by heirs generally), or in fee tail " (inheritable only by heirs of the donor's body), or else estates " not of inheritance "—it ought to be donee's body—" or else " estates not of inheritance, but for some definite period of " uncertain duration, as where land is given to one to hold for his " life, or the life of another, or until some particular event shall " happen. Estates less than freehold arise where one gives land " to another to hold for a certain period or term, or at the donor's " will only, or where one occupies another's land on sufferance." So that you will see freehold estates are tenancies in fee simple, tenancies in tail, and tenancies for life, speaking generally, and that any estate less than a tenancy for life is not a freehold estate. For instance, a tenancy for a term of years—it does not matter how long the term is, the term may be seven, fourteen, or twenty-one years, it may be a building lease for ninety-nine years, it may be a mining lease for a thousand years, it may be a term created under a settlement for the purpose of raising portions for younger children of even two thousand years. With all those terms of years, lawyers and persons who deal with land are in modern times perfectly conversant. They are not freehold estates, and the person in possession for any term of years is not a freeholder; he may be a leaseholder, or he may not. For instance, if you grant your land to a man to hold it as long as you think fit to let him, that is a tenancy at will; if a man gets into possession of your land and you do not turn him out, he is called a tenant at sufferance. All those are estates in land, but those persons are not necessarily leaseholders. The word freehold is so often used with respect to estates in land, that I think you ought to get that into your minds very early, because freeholds are generally considered very much more valuable than leaseholds, but it does not always follow, because a freehold estate may be worth little if it is subject to a long lease, unless it is a lease at a rack rent, when the annual value of the property is payable under the lease. Now, gentlemen, those being the estates which can be held in land, let us deal particularly, having already dealt with an estate in fee simple, with what is called an estate in tail. You will remember that an estate in fee simple is an estate granted to a man and his heirs, that means that it goes to his heir whether the heir is his issue (that is, a descendant of his), or it is some other person, either a collateral relation or even an ancestor, so long as he has an heir that estate continues whether he has descendants or not. On the other hand, a tenancy in tail, or fee tail—sometimes one expression is used and sometimes the other—is a grant to a man and the heirs of his body. You will notice the distinction between the two grants, the grants to the heirs generally and a grant to a man and the heirs of his body. That estate would continue if left alone, that is to say, if left to itself and nothing were done, only so long as the person to whom it was granted had some lineal descendant who could be his heir when he died. When the time arrived that there was no such lineal descendant that estate reverted or went back to the grantor and his heirs, and there was a determination of the estate in fee tail. Now fee tails were either general or special. For instance, a grant in fee tail might be granted to a man and his heirs by a particular wife. Only heirs begotten of that particular wife could take. Those estates were originally common, but such estates are not generally granted in these days; they have gone out of fashion and you very seldom hear of them. The ordinary grant is a grant in fee tail generally. Now fee tails general may be granted either to the heirs generally or to the heirs male or to the heirs female of the grantee's body. If the grant is general, then the heir, whether a man or woman, can take. If the grant is to the heirs male of a man's body, then only an heir male could take; and in the same way, if the grant is to a man and his heirs female, an heir female only could take the estate. And, as the case may be, upon the failure of such heir, the estate reverts to the original grantor of the fee tail. Now, when those estates were first granted the intention no doubt of the lord granting them was that the estate, on the happening of the event, such as I have mentioned, of a failure either of the heir male or the heir female, should go back to the grantor. But every device was used by lawyers, and many of those devices were sanctioned by the judges in order to defeat the lord of his right to the estate upon the failure of the issue, and the result was that grants of that kind were construed to be grants conditional upon the birth of some person who could take as heir, and then upon the birth, say, of a son of the grantee in tail male, or of a daughter in case of a grantee in tail female, the grantee could put an end to the reversion of the grantor and dispose of the estate and bar the lord of all his rights in the property. Then, gentlemen, that being so, to put it quite shortly, the lord having been defrauded of his rights by these devices, a very important statute was passed which made another epoch in the law of this country, and it is a statute I think you ought to read. It is rather a long one, it is not like the short one to which I drew your attention on the last occasion; it is called the Statute *De donis conditionibus*, that is, concerning conditional gifts. All these fee tails were called conditional gifts, and were construed by lawyers and, with the assistance of the judges, were held to be conditional upon the birth of someone who could take. Then this statute, commonly called *De donis conditionibus*, was passed in the year 1285. It is the Statute of Westminster II, and it was passed in the thirteenth year of Edward I, and is in force to this day in terms. Now the effect of that statute—I cannot read it to you because time does not permit; it is too long, and you must take the effect from me—now the effect of that statute was to restore to the lord the rights which he intended to reserve to himself when these conditional estates, or estates in fee tail, were granted, and give effect to the original intention of the parties, the grantor and the grantee, when these estates were first conferred. But again, the lawyers, with the assistance of the judges, set to work, and they again succeeded in defeating, to a considerable extent, the lord. They invented a solemn piece of jugglery, which was known as a common recovery. I doubt whether I could, in under an hour or two, explain to you satisfactorily that piece of solemn jugglery, and I shall not attempt it. It is not necessary, as you do not intend to be lawyers, that you should understand anything about it except this—you should know that the result of it was to give the tenant the power to, what was called "Bar the entail." A collusive or sham action was brought against the tenant in possession of the estate, and the tenant in possession of the estate, in collusion with a nominal person by whom the estate was presumed to have been granted, consented that judgment should go against him. That was recorded in the Courts, and that was considered by the Court to be conclusive upon all parties as to the right to the estate. That is, shortly, what the solemn jugglery was, and in that way the lord's rights were defeated and the person who recovered the land held to be entitled to hold the land free from the lord's rights. And that mode of barring an estate tail existed in this country up to the year 1833, when an Act of Parliament was passed absolutely abolishing the fines that I mentioned to you in my last lecture, and the common recoveries which I have just mentioned to you, and so put an end to all those farces which were played by lawyers with the object of defeating the lord of his estate, and it was enacted that a person in possession—you will bear in mind that I told you the collusive action was always brought against the person in possession of the estate, who must have been a party to the action—that a person in possession of an estate in tail could simply by a deed enrolled in the Court of Chancery bar the reversion, and so put an end to the estate in tail. If he was not in possession, and there was a person who was called the tenant for life in actual possession of the freehold, then that person had to concur in barring the entail and depriving the lord of his rights in the reversion. And in that simple way now all these tenancies in tail can be barred except in one case, and that the statute does not provide for, and I do not think a tenant now in that particular case can bar the entail, and that is when a man is in possession of an estate in fee tail. "After possibility of issue extinct", that is, suppose a man is entitled to an estate, or in possession of an estate in fee tail limited to him and the heirs of his body by a particular woman, then on the death of that woman without having had any child, there is no possibility of issue which can take the estate, and in that particular case the entail cannot be barred. In every other case, speaking generally, as one must always do in speaking of matters of law, an estate tail can be barred by consent of the persons who are entitled under the Act of Parliament to protect, as it is said, the entail, or by the consent of the tenant for life in actual possession of the estate, that is, in receipt of the rents and profits, he need not be actually living upon the property, but he must be in possession of the rent and profits, which is possession in the eye of the law. In that simple way at this present time these estates in tail can be barred, and that is the present law upon the subject. But, if the estate tail is not barred in the lifetime of a tenant in tail, and he should happen to die without an heir, and without having done anything to alter the estate, then that estate still goes to the lord. You could not have understood that, gentlemen, unless I had explained to you the elements of the Feudal System. It is important for you never to forget in studying the law of real property in England that in theory a person is nothing more nor less than a tenant of his estate of some lord, however great that estate may be, even a fee simple. Now, gentlemen, the next estate we have to deal with is an estate not of inheritance, but it is yet a freehold, that is, a tenancy for life. A tenancy for life is a grant of an estate to a man either for his own life, or for the life of someone else. In the first case he is called the tenant for life; in the second case he is called the tenant *pour autre vie;* that means for another person's life,—both these estates are freehold. For instance, if a man is in possession of an estate for another man's life, and he dies during that other man's life, that estate goes to his heirs during the life of the man during whose life he holds the estate. If a man holds for his own life and he dies, there is an end of his estate. Having dealt quite generally with the several estates which are known to the law, I do not think I can do better than deal more particularly with an estate for life. You will see that when the estate was granted, it was granted to a man for his own life. He could not do as he liked with it; he had no interest in it beyond his own life. If he granted a lease of it, say, for 10, 14, 21 years, or for any term, and he happened to die, that lease came to an end, because after his death his interest in the property came to an end, and no man could then grant to another a greater interest in land than he had himself, therefore the lease came to an end. For instance, he could not cut timber; he could not open mines; in fact, he could only use the estate and have what was called the usufruct of it. If mines had been opened by his predecessor in title and they had been worked, he could also go on working them, but he could not open fresh mines. His estate, or rather his powers over his estate were limited very much indeed. That was thought to be a very disadvantageous state of things for the country at

large, and a very important Act of Parliament was passed, to which, in your practice, I have no doubt your attention will often be directed, and I will direct your attention to it now. I have said an Act of Parliament, but there are really two, the "Settled Land Acts" of 1882 and 1890. I shall only trouble you now with the first Act, the Act of 1882. Those being the limited powers of a tenant for life, this Act of Parliament was passed substantially to give tenants for life very extensive powers over the land—to give them power to make grants which their own estates were not sufficient to authorize; but it was provided that the advantages, or the pecuniary returns from the exercise of those powers should be treated as capital, the money being invested and the income paid to the tenant for life, and the capital to the persons interested in the estate after his death. That was the general scheme of the Act, and I want now to draw your attention to the third section of that Act, and you will see how very extensive the powers given to a tenant for life are:
" A tenant for life may sell the settled land, or any part thereof,
" or any easement, right, or privilege of any kind over or in
" relation to the same"—so that he may sell it right out-and-out; and, secondly, "Where the settlement comprises a manor, he
" may sell the seigniory of any freehold land within the manor,
" or the freehold and inheritance of any copyhold or customary
" land, parcel of the manor, with or without any exception
" or reservation of all or any mines or minerals, or of any
" rights or powers relative to mining purposes, so as in every
" such case to effect an enfranchisement"; and, thirdly, "He may
" make an exchange of settled land, or any part thereof, for other
" land, including an exchange in consideration of money paid for
" equality of exchange"; and, fourthly, where the settlement comprises an undivided share in land, or, under the settlement, the settled land has come to be held in undivided shares, " may
" concur in making partition of the entirety, including a partition
" in consideration of money paid for equality of partition." There are certain restrictions upon the exercise of those powers; but, to put it quite shortly, as long as the tenant for life acts honestly in the interests of all persons who are concerned in his acts, he can do pretty well as he pleases with that estate. But I will just give you a few specimens of the restrictions imposed upon the tenant for life. "Every sale shall be made at the best price that can reasonably be obtained"; that means, he shall not give the estate away. " Every exchange, and every partition, shall be made for

"the best consideration in land, or in land and money, that can
"reasonably be obtained. A sale may be made in one lot or in
"several lots, and either by auction or by private contract", and
so on. Then he has also this very extensive power of leasing given
to him by the Act. "A tenant for life may lease the settled land,
"or any part thereof, or any easement, right or privilege of any
"kind over or in relation to the same, for any purpose whatever,
"whether involving waste or not, for any term not exceeding, in
"case of a building lease, 99 years; in case of a mining lease,
"60 years; in case of any other lease, 21 years." Then there
are similar provisions with respect to leasing, insuring that the
tenant for life shall act honestly towards all parties interested in
the estate. However land may be tied up, the tenant for life has
those powers. And the Statute also provides that he shall not
contract himself out of those powers, that whatever he does those
powers shall remain his. He cannot get rid of his powers. If
he sells his interest as tenant for life in the property, he still
retains the powers of a tenant for life. I will draw your attention
to the section in which that is enacted. It is the 51st, and you
will see how general it is. "If, in a settlement, will, assurance,
"or other instrument executed, made before or after, or partly
"before and partly after, the commencement of this Act, a
"provision is inserted purporting or attempting, by way of
"direction, declaration or otherwise, to forbid a tenant for life to
"exercise any power under this Act, or attempting, or tending,
"or intended by a limitation, gift or disposition over of settled
"land, or by a limitation, gift, or disposition of other real or any
"personal property, or by the imposition of any condition, or by
"forfeiture, or in any other manner whatever to prohibit or
"prevent him from exercising, or to induce him to abstain from
"exercising, or to put him into a position inconsistent with his
"exercising any power under this Act, that provision, as far as it
"purports, or attempts, or tends, or is intended to have, or would
"or might have, the operation aforesaid shall be deemed to be
"void." So that you see the legislature has done all that it
possibly could, in the widest possible terms, to prevent the tenant
for life being restrained from exercising or bargaining away his
right to exercise the powers given to him by that Act. It also
goes on to say this: "For the purposes of this section, an estate
"or interest limited to continue so long only as a person abstains
"from exercising any power, shall be and take effect as an estate
"or interest to continue for the period for which he would

"continue if that person were to abstain from exercising the "power discharged from liability to determination or cesser by "or on his exercising the same." The effect of that is this, that you cannot grant an estate to a man for his life until he exercises the power, because that limitation is for him, and he holds the estate for his life and has the right to execute the powers given to him by that Act. And the result of the Settled Land Acts is practically to free the land of this country, for they enable it to be dealt with substantially in any way in which any tenant for life of land, having regard to the interest of other persons in that land, would, as an honest man, wish to deal with it. You will understand, gentlemen, those are only general words. In any particular case I think it would be as well to consult a lawyer; but you may take that as a general proposition, subject to legal qualifications and modifications. In addressing men of business, it is impossible to be as accurate and as precise as one would have to be in arguing a case in Court, or writing an opinion upon a legal question submitted to one; but you may take it generally from me that that is substantially the effect of those Acts. And in many cases where the tenant for life has not power to do a thing by himself, the Court has the power upon application. So that now, really, landed property in this country is freed from all those ancient fetters to which it was subject under the Feudal System. Well, gentlemen, in considering these estates, I have over and over again used the word "heirs." Most people think that a man can make an heir. In law he cannot. We often say that a rich man has made Tom Jones, or William Brown, or Henry Robinson his heir. He cannot do it. No man, to begin with, can be the heir of a living person. The law declares who shall be a person's heir if he die intestate. The heir, then, is the person declared by the law to be entitled to succeed to his estate if the tenant of the estate dies without having disposed of it, if he had the power to dispose of it. The heir to every person is declared, as I said, by the law, and you will find who is a person's heir from reading a Statute too long for me now to draw your attention to. It is the Inheritance Act of 1833, and from that Act you will gather who is appointed by law the heir of a person. I said just now that many persons think a man can make an heir, but he cannot in law do so. The heir is the person appointed by law. In the words of lawyers, "*Nemo est heres viventis*", that is, no man is the heir of a living person. The heir only comes into existence, and can only be known upon the death of a person. I will give you an instance. We often speak of the eldest son of a nobleman, or other gentleman, titled or not, who is the owner of an estate. We speak of his eldest son as his heir. In law, gentlemen, that person is not his heir, because, as I have said just now, no one can be an heir to another as long as that other lives—he is really the "heir apparent." That means this, that he is the person who would, according to law, be the heir to that person if that person died *instanter*, at this moment. He is only the heir apparent. If on the other hand he is not the person who would be his heir directly, such as an eldest son would be on the death of his father, if he survived his father, but some collateral relation, whose position, whose right to succeed to that man's estate on his death would depend upon his having no son, we call that person the presumptive heir. For instance, if a man has a nephew and no son, that nephew is called a presumptive heir. It means this, that if the owner of the estate died without a son being born to him before his death, that nephew would succeed to the estate. That is, he is presumed to be the heir unless someone nearer in blood to the owner of the estate comes into existence before his death. The Prince of Wales is spoken of commonly as the heir to the throne of England. He is not in law. Popularly you may speak of him as the heir, but in law he is not. The heir, as I say, can only be determined upon the death of the person to whom he succeeds. That can only be determined upon the death of the Queen. But he is the heir apparent, and you will always hear him spoken of by lawyers as the heir apparent, not as the heir. Again, immediately before the death of William IV, Queen Victoria was the heir presumptive, because she would succeed to the throne if William IV should not have a son, but if William IV had had a son before he died, or within the period of gestation afterwards, that son would have been the heir, and Queen Victoria was in law only the heir-presumptive to the throne, she was not the heir. It was only on the death of William IV that Queen Victoria was his heir; and it is only on the death of Queen Victoria herself that the Prince of Wales will, if he lives, be her heir. It is necessary you should understand that, because it leads to a great deal of confusion. In consequence of the great powers of disposition which men have acquired over their estates, it is very seldom now that estates do descend to the heir. The property in large estates is nearly always settled. If it is not settled, a man generally makes a will, and he generally consults a lawyer, and he ought always to do so, I think, if he does make a will. If he does not, he generally makes a mess of it; he does what he does not want to do, he commits sins of omission and commission without end, and provides work for the lawyers. Now, I have explained to you who the heir is. Do not forget he is the person appointed by law to succeed to an estate in the case of an intestacy. There is one other matter about which there is considerable confusion. Having told you that the heir is the person fixed by law, I ought to tell you that under that Act of Parliament the eldest son of a man is his heir, if he has an eldest son, and he has the right, in the case I put just now of intestacy to succeed to that ancestor's estate. That is what is called, what you have often heard of and read of, I have no doubt, the law of primogeniture, the right of the eldest son to succeed to his father's estate, that is, all estates. The father can deprive him of that right by making a will. Of course, if the estate is limited to a man and his heirs in tail, then the father alone, if he is only tenant for life, cannot deprive the son of the remainder; but the son and the father together can bar the estate and do as they please with it. So that the persons in existence, provided they are of full age, that is of capacity, not lunatics or under any other disability, can deal with the estate as they please, and there would be no heir to take it if they dispose of it either by will or otherwise. That is the whole law of primogeniture about which you hear so much in this country. But the consequence of that being the law of the land in this country is, that most of the large estates in this country, especially estates held by those who hold titles, are what is called brought into settlement, that is, the persons interested, and the interest they are to take in these estates, are determined by a settlement. They are settled generally upon a man for his life, and then on his eldest son or the first-born son, because there may not be a son born at the time it is made. The father, or the prospective father, takes an estate for life, the prospective son or the future son when he comes into existence takes an estate in tail; but when the son comes of age, the father still living, he may, by executing a deed such as I have mentioned just now, bar that entail; and it is often done. When an estate gets into difficulties, and estates very often get into difficulties, because under these settlements there is generally a power to raise money as portions for younger children, and the ancestors may have charged these estates with so many portions that there is very little left, and the best thing for all parties to do is to sell the estate, or to go to some insurance office—perhaps they have been paying five percent for their money—go to some insurance company to get rid of the incumbrances. No insurance company will take the estate unless they can get the fee simple in a transaction of that kind. Then the entail is barred in the way I have mentioned, and when it is barred, absolutely barred, it is conveyed to the insurance company by way of mortgage to secure the money they lend. And in that way, having freedom to deal with the estate, they pay off the incumbrances, and whatever is left belongs to the persons interested in the estate, the father, and the son, in any way they think fit. That is the present condition of affairs in this country. Now, I have told you that most statements about real property law require some modification or qualification. I told you on the last occasion, because I did not want to embarrass you with details, that a man who was the owner of an estate in fee simple could do what he liked with it. That, of course, was only a general expression. Now, I want to tell you what he cannot do. I did tell you that he could not grant his estate to another to hold of him in fees; but he cannot grant an estate to a person who is the unborn child of an unborn person. You cannot grant an estate beyond lives in being and 21 years afterwards. That is the policy of our law to prevent estates being indefinitely tied up. You cannot grant an estate to A, and if A has a son who is not then in existence called B, and after him to his son not then born, who may hereafter come into existence called C; you cannot do more than grant an estate to A and his son after him if he is not born. All estates, as lawyers say, must vest, must necessarily vest within the existence of lives in being or 21 years afterwards. If an estate is granted, as lawyers say, limited beyond that period, the limitation is absolutely void, and the preceding estates take effect; but the estates limited beyond prescribed periods do not take effect, they are void, and that is what is called the doctrine of perpetuity. Now, that doctrine was to prevent estates being tied up for an unconscionable period, or for a very awkward period. That was the policy of our law, I believe it is said to be the common law of the land, at least it was so propounded by the judges. The judges are supposed to have had the common law of the land in their breasts, and they gave it out as they thought fit. Nobody knew the law until declared by the judges, and it was only after a long series of cases that anyone could know what the Common Law with regard to estates in land really was; and the doctrine of perpetuity was not declared by any statute, but it was declared by the judges to be the Common Law of the land, and that is still the Common Law of the land with regard to estates in land. I hope I have made that perfectly clear to you. It is an important matter. Many people do not know it, they attempt to tie up their property, they attempt to do so, either from pride or some other reason of family they want to tie up their property, but beyond the term I have mentioned it is impossible for them to do so. I shall leave to a subsequent lecture the question of estates which are not freeholds. Those are leaseholds, speaking generally, because they stand upon quite a different footing to freehold estates, and I think I can best deal with them entirely separately, and not mix them up with what are called freehold estates. But so far, even with regard to freehold estates, I have only dealt with them from the point of view of legal estates. But there are other estates known to the law called " equitable estates in land ", and I intend, if I have the time, to draw your attention shortly, to tell you shortly, what an equitable estate in land is. It is rather technical, but I must ask you to follow me step by step. The owner of land, to speak generally, often wanted to defeat the right of his lord in that land under the Feudal System, and he, to do that, resorted, again with the assistance of the lawyers, to certain devices to prevent those lands going to the lord under that system. For instance, the land was conveyed to persons, say three or four or five, that is to say, the feudal estate, or as it is now called the legal estate or the legal property in that estate was conveyed to these persons, who were afterwards called trustees, upon a secret understanding that they should hold the estate and deal with it as the person to whom it really belonged should direct, and in that way the person who owned the estate was able to deal with them secretly. Having no legal rights in that land, having passed from himself, having given over to those persons all legal property he had in the land—the feudal freehold —he had at law no right to that land, and there was no means at first of compelling the persons to whom the land was conveyed upon that secret understanding to obey the directions or to carry out the intention of the person who granted the land. But, in time, so many persons to whom land was conveyed upon a secret understanding of that kind, denied the secret understanding and tried to keep the land for themselves, that petitions were presented to the King, and the King handed them over to the Lord

Chancellor, and the Lord Chancellor examined these petitions and made enquiries as to the truth of the statements in them, and as he was the keeper of the King's conscience he made an order that the persons who held those lands should do as they ought to do with them. That is the origin of an equitable estate. This went on for some time, until the lords were absolutely deprived in substance of their rights. The lands were held by people who had no real interest in them for the use of somebody else who had, and the Statute of Uses was passed in the reign of Henry VIII to put an end to that system of things. Now this Statute is another landmark in the history of our law, and it is really so interesting that I must ask you to let me read it in the text. The main object of the Statute was to put an end to these secret uses, as they were called, uses, confidences, or trusts, that was a conveyance of land to A for the use of somebody else in confidence or trust. Uses, confidences, or trusts mean exactly the same thing, that is to say, one man was to be the legal owner of the estate, and another person was to have the enjoyment of it, that is, to take the rents and profits, and the recital in this Act, or the preamble, is very interesting, and it shows you what happened. It is the Statute of Henry VIII, passed in the 27th year of his reign, Ch. X, and it is commonly called by lawyers the Statute of Uses, and, as I have said, the object of that Statute was to put an end to these transfers or conveyances of estates to mere nominees for the benefit of somebody else, and it did so effectually at the time, as I shall tell you presently, but this is the preamble:

" Where by the common laws of this realm lands, tenements,
" and hereditaments be not devisable by testament, nor ought to
" be transferred from one to another but by solemn livery and
" seisin matter of record writing sufficient made *bond fide* without
" covin or fraud, yet nevertheless divers and sundry imaginations,
" subtle inventions and practices have been used whereby the
" hereditaments of this realm have been conveyed from one to
" another by fraudulent feoffments, fines, recoveries, and other
" assurances craftily made to secret uses, intents and also by
" wills and testaments, sometimes made by *nude parolx* and
" words, sometimes by signs and tokens, and sometimes by
" writing, and for the most part made by such persons as be
" visited with sickness, in their extreme agonies and pains, and
" at such times as they have scantly had any good memory or

" remembrance, at which times they being provoked by greedy
" and covetous persons lying in wait about them, do many times
" dispose indiscreetly and unadvisedly their lands and inheritance,
" by reason whereof and by occasion of which fraudulent
" feoffments, fines, recoveries, and other like assurances to uses,
" confidences, and trusts divers and many heirs have been
" unjustly and at sundry times disinherited, the lords have
" lost their wards, marriages, reliefs, harriots, escheats, aids
" *pur fair fitz chevalier et pur file marier*", and so on.

And by this Statute it was enacted, to put it shortly, that where one person had the seisin and possession of land to the use of another, such other person who had the use should be deemed to have the seisin and possession, or, in other words, the legal estate in the land. That is the effect of it. It provided that the person who holds the estate nominally shall lose his estate, and that the feudal estate, the freehold or legal estate, shall vest in the person who had the use and was really entitled to it. This was a deathblow to persons conveying their estates upon trusts and uses for a time, but for a time only. Before the Statute, when lands were granted to one person either upon a secret or expressed trust—to the "use" it was called—of another person, the legal estate was in the first person and the use was in the second, and the effect of the Statute was to take the legal estate out of the first person and put it into, to speak colloquially, the second person who had the use. In this way the Statute got rid altogether of the first person. Well, that did not meet the wants and requirements of the owners of real estate. They were back in their old position, their lords for a time got their rights, and everything was restored to the pre-existing state of things, and I think that lasted for something like a century. But a way was found out of that position of things. It was held by the Courts of Common Law that there could not be a use upon a use. That meant this: that if land were granted to A to the use of B to the use of C, the legal estate went to B and nothing went to C. That was what the judges held, that the Statute only got rid of the first use and vested the estate in the person who had the first use, and that the person who had the second use took nothing. Well, then there was another chance for the Lord Chancellor and the Court of Chancery. They held that they would still, as keepers of the King's conscience, enforce against those persons who got the first use the rights of the persons who were intended to take the benefits and the estate under the second use. And all those estates taken in that way are really equitable estates, because the legal estate under the Statute vested in the person who had the first use and the Court of Chancery recognized that fact. It said, " Yes, you are the legal owner "—to use a colloquial term—" you " are the legal owner of the estate, but you hold it for the use of " somebody else. We recognize the effect of the Statute because it " puts the legal estate in you, but you still hold the estate for " somebody else, and we will enforce that use." In short, when a person was entitled in that way to the rents and profits of land, but had not the legal estate in it, the Court of Chancery enforced his right, and made the person who had the legal estate nothing more nor less than a trustee for the person who was entitled under the use, the second use, in equity to the estate. When that was clearly established, everybody almost made use of the power given to them, and the estates, which we call equitable estates, became very common. You will now understand, I hope, the difference between an equitable estate and a legal estate. Both kinds of estates still exist. You must not think that because in the year 1875, under the Judicature Act, law and equity were said to be fused, that law was swept away and only equity remained. It is still as necessary for you to know what a legal estate is as it was before, and I will tell you why, and I want to impress it upon you so that you may take the trouble to read more than I am able to tell you in the course of a lecture about the law of real property, and it is this: If the owner of an equitable estate deals with it, the purchaser takes the rights which he had; if, on the other hand, the owner of the legal estate deals with it, a person who purchases from him without notice either actual or constructive that he is a mere trustee or a person who holds for the use of another, he acquires a good title to the estate, but if the purchaser has such notice, he does not take any real interest in the property, because the Court under those circumstances says that the conscience of the purchaser is affected, that he has bought an estate of A which he knows A holds for the use of or in trust for somebody else, and has no right in equity to the property. Therefore, it is always necessary in dealing with property to have regard not only to the legal estate in it, but to any equitable estate or interest in it which may affect the purchaser. You may take it shortly that the legal estate in land is in the person who has, in law, the seisin or possession of that estate, whereas an equitable estate is one to which a person is entitled who has not the legal estate and whose rights formerly could only be enforced in a Court of Equity, but will now be enforced in the Supreme Court and recognized in all the divisions of that Court.

THE
LAW OF REAL PROPERTY IN ENGLAND.

THIRD LECTURE.

[*Delivered 9 February 1897.*]

WHEN treating in my last lecture of freehold estates in land, I explained to you that when an estate tail is not an estate in possession, but is preceded by a life interest to be enjoyed by some other person prior to the possession of the lands by the tenant in tail, that it was necessary for both the tenant in tail and the tenant for life to concur in barring the entail so as to convert it into an estate in fee simple, thus barring not only the issue of the tenant in tail, but the remainders expectant upon the determination of the estate in tail. But as far as I remember, I think I omitted to tell you that the tenant in tail, without the concurrence of the tenant for life, could, by a deed enrolled in Chancery, bar his own issue, leaving, of course, the remainders to take effect, or the reversion, or whatever it was, to come into effect upon the failure of his issue. And I want to refer you to a statement of the consequences of such a limited bar, which you will find in Joshua Williams on page 101. "If he"—that is the tenant for life—"should refuse to consent, " the tenant in tail may still bar his own issue, as he might have " done before the Act, by levying a fine, but he cannot bar " estates in remainder or reversion. The consequence of such a " limited bar is, that the tenant acquires a disposable estate in " the land for so long as he has any issue in descent living and " no longer; that is, so long as the estate tail would have lasted

" had no bar been placed on it." That is called a base fee; that is, a fee which exists as a fee so long as the tenant in tail has issue. The moment his issue fails, then the remainders come in; that is called a base fee. It is an estate which probably in your career you will very often come across, because eldest sons who are tenants in tail of estates very often wish to raise money, and they wish to do so without their father knowing anything about it, and sometimes it is advisable they should have that money—I won't say it always is, but sometimes it is advisable—and you may be asked to advise whether or not money can be raised upon such an estate. If you do not know what such an estate is, you are not qualified to say what can be done with it. That is why I call your particular attention to that estate. So far, I have dealt only with freeholds granted to one person. I have now to draw your attention to estates granted to more than one person, or in which more than one person is interested. They are known to the law as tenancies in common and joint tenancies. I will deal first with the joint tenancy. A joint tenancy is a gift of land to two or more persons, who take that land as one single owner for the purposes of the estate there considered. The two persons are considered as one with reference to that estate. Of course, between themselves they have separate rights, but so far as the lord of the estate is concerned, so far as their interest in the estate is concerned, they are regarded as one. Those rights are equal in every respect, it not being possible for one of them to have a greater interest than the other in the subject of the tenancy. That is the nature of a joint tenancy, and it is distinguished by unity of possession, unity of interest, unity of title, and unity of the time of the commencement of such title. You will see that all those four characteristics flow from or come out of the proposition that joint tenants are to be regarded as one single owner. Now, a joint tenancy can be created in any estate in land. I do not propose to deal with the peculiarities of a tenancy in tail; it will be sufficient for my purpose to show you exactly what a joint tenancy is of an estate in fee simple. That is, an estate which is created every day; it is the estate which is granted to trustees of marriage settlements and other trustees for the purposes of the settlement, or for any other purpose of an analagous character. It is an estate granted, say, to A, B, and C, and their heirs—three will be quite enough—and during the continuance of that estate those three persons are entitled to that estate equally. If one of them dies without the joint tenancy

having been severed, the two survivors take that estate jointly and equally. If the second one dies, then the longest liver of them, the third, takes the estate entirely, there being no one in existence to share with him, because the heirs of the person who died first take no estate, nor do the heirs of the person who died secondly take any interest in the estate; but the whole estate then is vested in the third, and when he dies his heir will take entirely, exclusively of the heirs of the other two persons who died first. So that you will see there is a right of survivorship, which is an incident of a joint tenancy. The estate continues in those who live during their lives and in the last liver during his life, and it goes to his heir after his death. That is the nature of a joint tenancy. And I should like to read to you, having made that preliminary explanation of it, a more accurate statement, from Joshua Williams upon the subject. You will find it at pages 134 and 135. "An estate in fee simple may also be given
" to two or more persons as joint tenants. The unity of this
" kind of tenure is remarkably shown by the words which are
" made use of to create a joint tenancy in fee simple. The lands
" intended to be given to joint tenants in fee simple are limited
" to them and their heirs, or to them, their heirs and assigns,
" although the heirs of one of them only will succeed to the
" inheritance, provided the joint tenancy be allowed to continue:
" thus, if lands be given to A, B, and C, and their heirs, A, B,
" and C will together be regarded as one person; and, when they
" are all dead, but not before, the lands will descend to the heirs
" of the artificial person (so to speak) named in the gift. The
" survivor of the three, who together compose the tenant, will,
" after the decease of his companions, become entitled to the
" whole lands. While they all lived, each had the whole; when
" any die, the survivor or survivors can have no more. The heir
" of the survivor is, therefore, the person who alone will be
" entitled to inherit, to the entire exclusion of the heirs of those
" who may have previously died. A joint tenancy in fee simple
" is far more usual than a joint tenancy for life or in tail. Its
" principal use in practice is for the purpose of vesting estates in
" trustees, who, as we shall see, are persons entrusted with the
" legal ownership of lands for the benefit of others, such persons
" are invariably made joint tenants. On the decease of one of
" them the whole estate then vests at once in the survivors, or
" survivor of them, without devolving on the heir-at-law of the
" deceased trustee, and without being affected by any disposition

" which he may have made by his will; for joint tenants are
" incapable of devising their respective shares by will; they are
" not regarded as having any separate interests, except as between
" or amongst themselves, whilst two or more of them are living.
" Trustees, therefore, whose only interest is that of the persons
" for whom they hold in trust, are properly made joint tenants.
" As a rule the survivor of several joint tenants in fee simple may
" devise the land as well as allow it to descend to his heir. But
" if such survivor be a trustee of the land on his death in the
" year 1881, his estate will vest in his personal representatives
" notwithstanding any testamentary disposition he may make."
Previously to the year 1881, if a sole trustee died possessed
of an estate in land, that estate descended to his heir if
he died without a will. If he made a will, he generally devised
that estate to certain persons, but there was very often an
omission to do that, and it was sometimes difficult for persons
interested to find the heir, at least it cost money to do so,
and the object of the Statute was to get over that difficulty
by making the estate descend or go to—it does not really
descend, but it devolves upon—the executors, or the personal
representatives who are easily found. Whether they are executors
or administrators, they can be discovered almost directly. And
in 1881 the law was altered in that respect so far as regards
joint tenancies held by trustees. Of course, where joint tenants
are trustees their powers are limited by the trusts imposed upon
them by the instrument appointing them and vesting the estate
in them. Joint tenants, however, are not always trustees. For
instance, an estate may be given to A and B and their heirs for
their own use, and they would then be beneficially interested in
that estate. The incidents which I have mentioned would follow
that gift, except that the estate would not pass to the executors
of the survivor; it would go, as it did before that Act of 1881, to
his heir. Yet, it is a very inconvenient state of things for two
persons to hold one estate; it is much better that each of them
should hold a share of it. And very early in the history of our
Law a writ of Partition was granted by the Court, and now every
joint tenant has the right to have the estate divided, he may say
to the other joint tenant or tenants, you shall have your equal
share, and I will have mine. During his life he can do that; he
can go to the Court of Chancery and have a partition by the
Court; or he can go now to the Board of Agriculture, a Board
which has succeeded the Enclosure Commissioners, who formerly

had the power; but the present Board of Agriculture, a recent institution, now has the power to grant and effect a partition of the estate, so that if A, B and C are interested as joint tenants, one-third of the estate may be apportioned to A, one third to B, and one third to C. Of course, being entitled to the whole estate, they may by agreement effect the same thing themselves; but if they cannot agree, they must go to the Court, or the Board of Agriculture, to effect a partition, and from the time when the partition is made, whether by agreement or by the order of the Court, or by the Board of Agriculture, each of those tenants has a separate part of that estate as his own, and he is possessed of that estate, that portion of the estate for all the estate he had in the whole of it before the partition, whatever that was, whether it was an estate in fee, or an estate of any other kind. But that must be done in the lifetime of the joint tenant; for he cannot do it by his will. If two persons have an estate of that kind—they are really one person in law—they must divide the estate during their lifetime, they cannot do it by will; because, as I explained to you, upon the death of one of them the whole of the estate remains entirely in the one who survives —by the right of survivorship. Now, that is joint tenancy, and I think I have said enough about it to enable you to understand both its character and the object of it. The other estate, where more than one person may be interested in the lands, is known as a tenancy in common. A tenancy in common exists where more than one person is interested in the estate, and their interests are not the same necessarily, but they have distinct and several titles to their shares, and the only thing in common between a tenancy in common and a joint tenancy, is unity of possession. Each joint tenant, as I explained to you, is in possession of the whole estate, and so with regard to a tenant in common, he is also in possession. He does not hold any part of the land for himself, or else he would have a several estate in that part, but he has an undivided share, as it is called, in the whole. Now, the shares in which joint tenants are interested are always equal, but the shares which tenants in common hold are not necessarily equal; they may be, they very often are, but not necessarily. One may have a half, another may have a third, another a fourth, and so on until you get the whole of the estate divided amongst them. And each one of those tenants in common can deal with his undivided share either in his lifetime or by his will. There is no right of survivorship. Each is possessed of his share for himself entirely, and he can do as he pleases with it; he also has the right, if he wishes, to have the estate divided. If two or more persons are interested, any of them can obtain an actual partition of the estate by the Court of Chancery or by the Board of Agriculture, just in the same way as joint tenants can get their estate divided, only, of course, it would then be divided according to their interests, whatever they may be, and not necessarily equally, as it would be in the case of a joint tenancy. To put it technically, tenants in common hold in severalty. You will have observed, I have no doubt, that up to this time I have spoken mainly of freehold estates in land of which the tenant has the *possession*. All those estates are called in law corporeal hereditaments, because the owner's right is accompanied with the possession of a tangible thing, such as land, a house, or, for instance, this Hall. But there are other estates and interests in land which are not corporeal, and they are called incorporeal, because the owner of them has not the possession of the thing; he has an estate or interest in the land, but he has not the feudal possession of it. And I think I have impressed upon you, at least I have tried to do so, the theory of our law with regard to the feudal possession of an estate. I explained to you in my first lecture that when the feudal system was established in this country, it created a relation between the lord and the tenant, and the tenant had the feudal possession; but other persons may be interested, or have estates in land, who have not the feudal possession, and not having the feudal possession, their interests or estates are called incorporeal hereditaments. The laws with respect to descent and powers of alienation are practically the same with regard to incorporeal hereditaments as they are with regard to corporeal. There was a difference originally in the way in which they were conveyed from one person to another, and that arose from the very nature of the thing. If a man was in feudal possession of an estate, he could convey that estate by putting another person into actual possession of it in a formal way, and giving it to him with certain formal words of limitation, and there was no necessity, originally, for a deed to effect a transfer of the estate. But when a person was interested in land, and he had not the feudal possession of it, he could not transfer his interest in the land in that way, because he was not in possession, and the right which he had, an incorporeal hereditament, was always conveyed by a deed; and lawyers very often did, and, I think, still do, draw a difference between corporeal and incorporeal hereditaments, by saying that incorporeal hereditaments lie in grant, whereas corporeal hereditaments lie in delivery, that is, delivery of possession; but it is not very material for you to consider that now, because, by Act of Parliament, all grants of land must now be by deed, with an exception that I ought to mention. It is this. There is a custom in Kent with regard to the tenure of land; it is called Tenure in Gavelkind. There an infant can pass his estate in land by actual delivery of possession, with proper words of limitation, to anybody. But with that exception, I think—and there may be some places in Yorkshire, Durham, and a few isolated places in the country, where a custom of that kind still exists; but, apart from those special exceptions, which I need hardly, perhaps, have troubled you with, you may take it that all grants of estates, whether corporeal or incorporeal hereditaments, must now be by deed.

Let us consider first what is called a reversion, which is, of a mixed character, because it is corporeal at one time, and incorporeal at another. It arises in this way. We will take the simplest case—a tenancy in fee simple. A man is a tenant of an estate in fee simple, and he grants out of that estate some lesser estate, or any number of lesser estates short of granting away the whole of the fee simple. Take the case of his granting an estate only for life to a man. It is clear that he has not parted with the whole of his estate in the land, because, being a tenancy in fee simple, it is larger than a tenancy for life, and there is something left; what he has not granted remains in him; and, taking the simple case I have put of a tenant in fee simple granting an estate for life, upon the death of the tenant for life the estate comes back to him in its entirety, or, as lawyers say, reverts, and that is a reversion; that is the simplest instance of a reversion. It may occur where a tenant in fee has granted a tenancy in tail, or any number of estates tenancies for years, and so on, but still leaving something in himself. When all those estates are exhausted, the estate will come back to him in fee simple, and that is called a reversion. Now, that arises in the case of a man making a grant of less than his whole estate, and what is left in him is called his reversion. It is an implication of law that what he has not parted with he still retains. When the tenant in fee grants an estate for life to one man, and the rest of his estate—that is a tenancy in fee, subject to that life estate—to another, he has passed from himself all his interest in that estate, he has no reversion. The tenant for life is in possession, and the person who is entitled to the estate subject to that tenancy for life is said to have an estate in remainder. It would have been if it had remained in the grantor an estate in reversion, but when it goes to another person it is called a remainder. That is the chief distinction between a reversion and a remainder; and for business purposes I do not know that there is any real difference. One has, in studying law, always to bear in mind that although things are substantially the same, they are very often theoretically very different, but for the purposes of your work in life, I do not know that you will have any occasion to draw any distinction between a reversion and a remainder. Now, a remainder may be of two kinds: it may be a vested remainder, which I will explain, or it may be a contingent remainder, which I will also explain. You will find the definition of a vested remainder at page 351 of Joshua Williams, and before I read to you his definition I will explain in my own words what it is. It is an estate which is ready to come into possession immediately upon the determination of the previous estates to which it is a remainder, and that is why it is called vested. The moment the prior estate—for instance, the case of the tenancy for life that I mentioned just now—the moment that determines by the death of the tenant for life, the remainder, such as I mentioned just now, is ready to come into possession at once. The moment the tenant for life dies, there is somebody ready to come in, and when that is the case it is called a vested remainder. I do not think I can do better, gentlemen, than read to you what Joshua Williams says about that. You will find it at page 318. " A remainder chiefly differs from a reversion in this: that " between the owner of the particular estate and the owner of the " remainder, called a remainder man, no tenure exists." I want to explain that to you. In the case I put, the very simple case of a tenant in fee, granting an estate for life to A, and granting the whole of the fee to B subject to the tenancy for life, he has parted with his whole estate. The tenant for life does not stand in the relation of tenant to him, nor does the tenant in fee simple. Each of them holds his estate of the chief lord from whom the grantor held the whole estate before he divided it in the way I have mentioned. " They both derive their estates from the same " source, the grant of the owner in fee simple; and one of them " has no more right to be lord than the other. But as all estates " must be holden of some person,—in the case of a grant of a

" particular estate with a remainder in fee simple—the particular
" tenant and the remainderman both hold their estates of the same
" chief lord as their grantor held before." I must ask you to forgive
me now for having given you so much of the Feudal System. You
could not possibly understand that unless you knew what the
Feudal System was. "It consequently follows that no rent
" service is incident to a remainder, and it usually is to a
" reversion; for rent service is an incident of tenure, and in this
" case no tenure exists. The other point of difference between a
" reversion and a remainder we have already noticed, namely, that
" a reversion arises necessarily from the grant of the particular
" estate, being simply that part of the estate of the grantor
" which remains undisposed of, but a remainder is always itself
" created by an express grant." "Thus, a grant may be made at
" once to fifty different people separately for their lives. In
" such case the grantee for life, who is first to have the
" possession, is the particular tenant to whom, on a feoffment,
" seisin would be delivered, and all the rest are remaindermen;
" whilst the reversion in fee simple, expectant on the decease
" of them all, remains with the grantor. The second grantee
" for life has a remainder expectant on the decease of the
" first, and will be entitled to possession on the determination of
" the estate of the first, either by his decease, or in case of his
" forfeiture, or otherwise. The third grantee must wait till the
" estate both of the first and second shall have determined; and
" so of the rest. The mode in which such a set of estates would
" be marked out is as follows:—To A for his life, and after his
" decease to B for his life, and after his decease to C for his life,
" and so on This method of limitation is quite sufficient for the
" purpose, but it by no means expresses all that is meant. The
" estates of B and C and the rest are intended to be as immediately
" and effectually vested in them as the estate of A; so that if A"
—that is the first man—" were to forfeit his estate, B would
" have an immediate right to the possession; and so again C
" would have a right to enter, whenever the estates both of A
" and B might determine. But, owing to the necessary infirmity
" of language all this cannot be expressed in the limitations
" of every ordinary deed. The words 'and after his decease'
" are, therefore, considered a sufficient expression of an intention
" to confer a vested remainder after an estate for life. In the
" case we have selected of numerous estates, everyone given only
" for the life of each grantee, it is manifest that very many of the

"grantees can derive no benefit; and should the first grantee
"survive all the others, and not forfeit his estate, not one of
"them can take anything. Nevertheless, each one of these grantees
"has an estate for life in remainder, immediately vested in him"
—that is, gentlemen, because he is there ready to take the
estate immediately upon the estate given to the man in front
of him coming to an end, that is why it is called a vested
remainder—" and each of these remainders is capable of being
"transferred, both at law and in equity, by a deed of grant, in
"the same manner as a reversion. In the same way a grant
"may be made of a term of years, to one person, an estate
"for life to another, an estate in tail to a third, and last of
"all, an estate in fee simple to a fourth; and these grantees
"may be entitled to possession in any prescribed order, except
"as to the grantee of the estate in fee simple, who must
"necessarily come last."—The reason of that is when a man
has granted the fee simple he can grant no more, there is no
virtue left in him, and he cannot confer it upon anybody else—
"for his estate, if not literally interminable, yet carries with it an
"interminable power of alienation, which would keep all the
"other grantees for ever out of possession. But the estate tail
"may come first into possession, then the estate for life, and then
"the term of years; or the order may be reversed, and the term
"of years come first, then the estate for life, then the estate tail,
"and lastly the estate in fee simple, which, as we have said,
"must wait for possession till all the others shall have been
"determined. When a remainder comes after an estate tail it is
"liable to be barred by the tenant in tail, as we have already seen.
"This risk it must run. But, if any estate, be it ever so small,
"is always ready, from its commencement to its end, to come
"into possession the moment the prior estates, be they what they
"may, happen to determine, it is then a vested remainder, and
"recognized in law as an estate grantable by deed." I want
to read that definition again to you. "If any estate, be it
"ever so small, is always ready, from its commencement to its
"end, to come into possession the moment the prior estates,
"be they what they may, happen to determine, it is then a vested
"remainder." If that state of things does not exist, it may be
something else, but it is not a vested remainder; it may be a
contingent remainder, or it may be something else, but that is the
definition of a vested remainder. "It would be an estate in
"possession, were it not that other estates have a prior claim; and

"their priority alone postpones, or perhaps may entirely prevent, possession being taken by the remainderman. The gift is immediate; but the enjoyment must necessarily depend on the determination of the estates of those who have a prior right to the possession." I think, gentlemen, that is sufficient to give you a perfectly clear idea of what a vested remainder is. It is a future estate in that sense that it is ready to come into possession the moment the prior estate is determined. Upon this head there is a rule of law with which you must be acquainted, and that is called the rule in Shelley's case, and the rule in Shelley's case is this: "That where an estate, a freehold, is granted to a man, and other estates to other people, and ultimately an estate in fee is given to him, he takes the estate in fee subject to those intermediate estates." That is putting it very generally, and not very accurately, and I should like to read to you, from Williams, an accurate expression of the law upon the subject; it is not very long. "In all the cases which we have as yet considered, each of the remainders has belonged to a different person. No one person has had more than one estate. A, B, and C may each have had estates for life; or the one may have had a term of years, the other an estate for life, and the last a remainder in tail or in fee simple. But no one of them has as yet had more than one estate. It is possible, however, that one person may have, under certain circumstances, more than one estate in the same land at the same time—one of his estates being in possession, and the other in remainder, or perhaps all of them being remainders. The limitation of a remainder in tail, or in fee simple, to a person who has already an estate of freehold as for life, is governed by a rule of law known by the name of the rule in Shelley's case, so called from a celebrated case in Lord Coke's time, in which the subject was much discussed, although the rule itself is of very ancient date. As this rule is generally supposed to be highly technical, and founded on principles not easily to be perceived, it may be well to proceed gradually in the attempt to explain it." I do not think, gentlemen, I ought to weary you by reading the explanation of it, but you will find the explanation of it in the next few pages in Joshua Williams. And the result of the rule is that, where an estate for life is granted to a man, and also another estate in fee or fee tail is granted to him, the two estates coalesce and become one, subject to any intermediate interest or estates that are created. Now with regard to a contingent remainder, it is one which may not come into possession upon the determination of the prior estate, and that is why it is called a contingent remainder. It is a future estate in land, existing no doubt, but it may or may not come into immediate possession. It may not be in such a state, as the lawyers say, to come into possession immediately upon the determination of the prior estate, and therefore it is called a contingent remainder. Now, those estates were originally illegal, the Common Law would not recognize them; but the Courts at last, I think in the time of Henry VI or VII, recognized such estates and gave effect to them, and from that time down to the present they have been recognized by the law with all the usual consequences of such recognition, but they were liable always to be defeated. I should like to give you an accurate definition after the general exposition of what a contingent remainder is from Williams. You will find it at page 335. " Let us now obtain " an accurate notion of what a contingent remainder is, and " afterwards consider the rules which are required to be observed " in its creation. We have already said that a contingent " remainder is a future estate. As distinguished from an " executory interest, to be hereafter spoken of, it is a future " estate which waits for and depends on the determination of " the estates which precede it." In that respect it is like a vested remainder. " But, as distinguished from a vested " remainder, it is an estate in remainder which is not ready, from " its commencement to its end, to come into possession at any " moment when the prior estates may happen to determine. For " if any contingent remainder should at any time become thus " ready to come into immediate possession whenever the prior " estates may determine, it will then be contingent no longer, " but will at once become a vested remainder. For example "— now the example will help you to understand what a contingent remainder is; I ask you to follow it rather carefully, gentlemen,— " for example, suppose that a gift be made to A, a bachelor, " for his life "—the point there is that A is a bachelor—" and " after the determination of that estate, by forfeiture or otherwise " in his lifetime, to B and his heirs during the life of A, and after " the decease of A to the eldest son of A and the heirs of the " body of such son." You see A is a bachelor, and therefore he has not a son at the time of the grant. " And in that case we " have two remainders, one of which is vested and the other " contingent. The estate of B is vested." You will remember that it was a grant to A for his life, and subject to that to B on the determination of A's estate during A's lifetime. Now that is a wretchedly small estate, but still it is an estate, and it is a vested estate, because B can take that estate the moment A forfeits his, either by treason or anything else which led to forfeiture in early times, and therefore it was called a vested remainder, but the estate of the son, if there was no son, did not exist, and if A died without a son, would never come into existence at all. I will read to you how Joshua Williams puts that. " Here we have two remainders, one of which is vested and the " other contingent. The estate of B is vested. Why? Because, " though it be but a small estate, yet it is ready from the first, " and so long as it lasts continues ready, to come into possession " whenever A's estate may happen to determine. There may be " very little doubt but that A will commit no forfeiture, but will " hold the estate as long as he lives, but if his estate should " determine the moment after the grant, or at any time whilst B's " estate lasts, there is B quite ready to take possession. B's " estate, therefore, is vested. But the estate tail to the eldest " son of A "—the bachelor—" is plainly contingent. For A, " being a bachelor, has no son, and if he should die without one " the estate tail in remainder will not be ready to come into " possession immediately on the determination of the particular " estates of A and B; indeed, in this case, there will be no estate " tail at all. But if A should marry and have a son, the estate " tail will at once become a vested remainder; for, so long as it " lasts, that is, so long as the son or any of the son's issue may " live, the estate tail is ready to come into immediate possession " whenever the prior estates may determine, whether by A's " death or by B's forfeiture, supposing him to have got possession. " It will be observed that here there is an estate which, at the " time of the grant, is future in interest as well as in possession, " and till the son is born, or rather till he comes of age, the " lands are tied up and placed beyond the power of complete " alienation. This example of a contingent remainder is here " given as by far the most usual, being that which occurs " every day in the settlement of landed estates." I do not know, gentlemen, whether you are familiar with the ordinary settlement in this country of large landed properties, but taken quite shortly it is this: It is to ensure the estate being enjoyed by the father during his lifetime, and after his death by his eldest son. That is, substantially, what it is, and that is effected in this way: by granting to the father or trustees for the father the life estate, with the remainder for the son. Now, when that settlement is made there is no son in existence, but if one is born and attains the age of 21 years, then they are free to do what they please with the estate, as I told you in my last lecture, but until that son is born and attains the age of 21, the estate is tied up.

"Of the rules required for the creation of a contingent " remainder the first and principal is that the seisin, or feudal " possession, must never be without an owner." As I cannot again too strongly impress that upon you, I will read it again. " Of the rules required for the creation of a contingent remainder, " the first and principal is that the seisin, or feudal possession, " must never be without an owner, and this rule is sometimes " expressed as follows, that every contingent remainder of an " estate of freehold must have a particular estate of freehold to " support it. The ancient law regarded the feudal possession of " lands as a matter the transfer of which ought to be notorious; " and it accordingly forbade the conveyance of any estate of " freehold by any other means than an immediate delivery " of the seisin, accompanied by words, either written or openly " spoken, by which the owner of the feudal possession might at " any time thereafter be known to all the neighbourhood. If, on " the occasion of any feoffment, such feudal possession was not at " once parted with, it remained for ever with the grantor. Thus, " a feoffment or any other conveyance of a freehold made to-day " to A, to hold from to-morrow, would be absolutely void, as " involving a contradiction." And that is still our law. I will read it again. I know how difficult it is to grasp these propositions myself, and therefore I am sure you will forgive me for reading them again to you. "Thus, a feoffment or any other " conveyance of a freehold made to-day to A, to hold from " to-morrow, would be absolutely void as involving a contra- " diction." That is, the feudal possession would be without an owner for the day if it were not void, and there would be nobody in feudal possession. "For if A is not to have the seisin till " to-morrow, it must not be given him till then. So, if on any " conveyance the feudal possession were given to accompany any " estate or estates less than an estate in fee simple, the moment " such estates, or the last of them, determined, such feudal " possession would again revert to the grantor." That is, suppose the contingency did not happen upon which a contingent remainder was to become a vested one, the estate would go back to the grantor and the remainder would fail. "Accordingly, "suppose a feoffment to be made to A for his life and after his "decease and one day to B and his heirs. Here, the moment "that A's estate determines by his death, the feudal possession "which is not to belong to B till one day afterwards reverts to "the feoffor, and cannot be taken out of him without a new "feoffment." So that the ultimate estate would be lost and would go to the grantor. "The consequence is that the gift of "the future estate intended to be made to B is absolutely void. "Had it been held good, the feudal possession would have been "for one day without any owner; or, in other words, there would "have been a so-called remainder of an estate of freehold without "a particular estate of freehold to support it. Let us now take "the case we have before referred to, of an estate to A, a "bachelor, for his life, and after his decease to his eldest son in "tail." That is the ordinary limitation in a marriage settlement at the present day. "In this case it is evident that the moment "A's estate determines by his death, his son, if living, must "necessarily be ready at once to take the feudal possession, "irrespective of his estate tail. The only case in which the "feudal possession could, under such a limitation, ever be "without an owner at the time of A's decease would be that of "the mother being then *enceinte* of the son. In such a case, the "feudal possession would be evidently without an owner until "the birth of the son." And that was considered a very hard case indeed, because if the son was not born in A's life the estate would go back again to the grantor, and when the son was born, a few months afterwards, he would lose the estate. "In such "case the feudal possession would be evidently without an owner "until the birth of the son"—because the son had not been born, and the estate would go back to the grantor—"and such "posthumous son would accordingly lose his estate were it not "for a special provision which had been made in his favour. In "the reign of William III an Act of Parliament was passed to "enable posthumous children to take estates as if born in their "father's lifetime. And the law now considers every child "*en ventre sa mere* as actually born, for the purpose of "taking any benefit to which, if born, it would be entitled. "As a corollary to the rule above laid down arises another "proposition, frequently itself laid down as a distinct rule, "namely, that every contingent remainder must vest, or become

"an actual estate, during the continuance of the particular
"estate which supports it, or *eo instanti*,"—that is, at the very
moment—"that such particular estate determines; otherwise
"such contingent remainder will fail altogether, and can never
"become an actual estate at all. Thus, suppose lands to be
"given to A for his life, and after his decease to such son of A
"as shall first attain the age of 24 years." The grant is to A
for his life, and after his death to such son of A as shall first
attain the age of 24 years—24 is the point of this example.
"As a contingent remainder, the estate to the son is well created;
"for the feudal seisin is not necessarily left without an owner
"after A's decease."—Because he may leave a son 24 years of
age, and then the son would take; but suppose he left a son
21 years of age, he is not to take the estate till he is 24 years of
age. So for three years there would be no one to take feudal
possession of the estate, and that remainder would lapse, and the
estate would become the grantor's estate again, because there was
no one to take feudal possession of the estate immediately upon
A's death. "If, therefore, A should, at his decease, have a son
"who should then be 24 years of age or more, such son will at once
"take the feudal possession by reason of the estate in remainder
"which vested in him the moment he attained that age. In this
"case, the contingent remainder has vested during the continuance
"of the particular estate,"—and has become a vested remainder.
"But if there should be no son, or if the son should not have
"attained the prescribed age at his father's death, the remainder
"will fail altogether. For the feudal possession will then,
"immediately on the father's decease, revert, for want of another
"owner, to the person who made the gift in right of his reversion.
"And, having once reverted, it cannot now belong to the son
"without the grant to him of some fresh estate by means of some
"other conveyance." Well, that was not intended, and an Act
was passed in 1877—you see how recent it is—to cure that to a
certain extent. The Act of 1877, however, now saves from the
operation of this rule every contingent remainder which has been
created by an instrument executed, or by a will re-published on
or after the 2nd of August 1877, and which would have been
valid if originally created as a shifting use or executory devise.
Now, that is perfectly unintelligible to you yet, and I cannot
make it intelligible to you in a few words. But it means, if it
had been created as a shifting use or executory devise, which I
shall hereafter explain to you as well as I can, the remainder

shall not lapse. "For such contingent remainder shall be capable of taking effect notwithstanding the particular estate determining before the contingent remainder vests." I will now read to you from Joshua Williams, p. 344: "One of the most remarkable incidents—as I pointed out to you—of a contingent remainder, was its liability to destruction by the sudden determination of the particular estate upon which it depended,"—because if it was not then ready to come into possession it lapsed altogether. "This liability was removed by the Real Property Act of 1845: it was in effect no more than a strict application of the general rule, required to be observed in the creation of contingent remainders, that the freehold must never be left without an owner. For if, after the determination of the particular estate, the contingent remainder might still, at some future time, have become a vested estate, the freehold would, until such time, have remained undisposed of, contrary to the principles of the law before explained. Thus, suppose lands to have been given to A, a bachelor, for his life, and after his decease to his eldest son and the heirs of his body, and, in default of such issue, to B and his heirs."— That is creating a tenancy in tail, and the remainder over to B and his heirs.—"In this case, A would have had a vested estate for his life in possession. There would have been a contingent remainder in tail to his eldest son, which would have become a vested estate tail in such son the moment he was born, or, rather, begotten; and B would have had a vested estate in fee simple in remainder. Now, suppose that, *before A had any son,* the particular estate for life belonging to A, which supported the contingent remainder to his eldest son, should suddenly have determined during A's life, B's estate would then have become an estate in fee simple in possession. There must be some owner of the freehold; and B, being next entitled, would have taken possession. When his estate once became an estate in possession, the prior remainder to the eldest son of A was for ever excluded. For, by the terms of the gift, if the estate of the eldest son was to come into possession at all, it must have come in before the estate of B. A forfeiture by A of his life estate, before the birth of a son, would, therefore, at once have destroyed the contingent remainder by letting into possession the subsequent estate of B." That was our law. Again, on page 346: "It is a rule of law, that 'whenever a greater 'estate and a less coincide and meet in one and the same

"'person, without any intermediate estate, the less is immediately
"'annihilated: or, in the law phrase, is said to be merged, that
"'is, sunk or drowned in the greater.' From the operation of
"this rule, an estate tail is preserved by the effect of the Statute
"*De donis*. The Real Property Act of 1845 altered the law in
"all these cases, for, whilst the principles of law on which they
"proceeded have not been expressly abolished, it is, nevertheless,
"enacted that a contingent remainder shall be, and if created
"before the passing of the Act shall be deemed to have been,
"capable of taking effect notwithstanding the determination by
"forfeiture, surrender, or merger of any preceding estate of
"freehold, in the same manner in all respects as if such deter-
"mination had not happened. This Act, it will be observed,
"applies only to the three cases of forfeiture, surrender, or
"merger of the particular estate. If, at the time when the
"particular estate would naturally have expired, the contingent
"remainder be not ready to come into immediate possession, it
"will still fail as before, except in the cases provided by the Act
"of 1877,"—to which I have drawn your attention—"and which
"enacted that if the contingent remainder had been created as
"a shifting use or an executory devise, and could have taken
"effect as such, then it cannot fail." That is our law, gentlemen.
It is in a most unsatisfactory state, it is hardly intelligible, it is
extremely difficult to make it intelligible, but it is necessary that
you should know something about it. I have done my best to
make the law intelligible by keeping as closely as I can to the
simplest cases that occur in ordinary life. Well, gentlemen, I
think I have exhausted your patience with a very dry part of
Real Property Law, and I thank you very much for the attention
with which you have listened to me. But if you really care to
master it, you will have to read Joshua Williams most carefully.
I can only give you a mere outline of it, and I hope I have made
it as intelligible as the nature of the subject permits a mere
outline to be.

THE

LAW OF REAL PROPERTY IN ENGLAND.

FOURTH LECTURE.

[*Delivered 23 February 1897.*]

WHEN treating in my last lecture of the very difficult subject of remainders, I explained to you that a contingent remainder is a future estate which waits for and depends upon the determination of a prior estate or prior estates, but, as distinct from a vested remainder, was not ready at any moment from its commencement to come in possession at the very moment when the prior estates should happen to determine, and that, in consequence of the doctrine of the Common Law that the feudal possession could never be vacant, if the prior estate happened to determine before a contingent remainder was ready to come into possession, the contingent remainder failed. I incidentally drew your attention to an Act of Parliament passed in the year 1877, which saved certain contingent remainders from the operation of that general rule as to failure, but I mentioned that the Act in effect saved from the operation of the rule only such contingent remainders as would, if created on or after the 2nd August, 1877, be valid, if they were originally created as a shifting use or an executory devise, and I told you at the time that it was absolutely necessary for you, before you could understand the operation of that statute, to know what shifting uses and executory devises were, and I propose to-day to begin by explaining to you as far as I can what a shifting use and an executory devise is. It is absolutely necessary for you to understand them; not merely to grasp the operation of the statute, but that you may be able to understand the very simplest marriage settlement of real estate at the present day; and, speaking generally, almost every other conveyance requires, I will not say a complete knowledge, but a general knowledge, of what a shifting use or an executory devise is. Now, shifting uses and executory devises are generally coupled together as executory interests. An executory interest may be a shifting use, or it may be an executory devise. In the one case it is created by deed, and in the other case it is created by will. That is why it is called, I suppose, an executory devise. You will find this subject treated of in Joshua Williams, beginning at page 351 in the last edition. And he first points out, as I wish to point out to you, that an executory interest is in its nature indestructible. It does not depend in any way like a contingent remainder upon its coming into effect by way of possession immediately after the determination of any previous estate, and in that respect it differs materially and fundamentally from a contingent remainder. Executory interests may now be created in two ways—under the Statute of Uses and by Will. I have referred in one of my previous lectures to the Statute of Uses, and I explained it to you pretty fully, so it will not be necessary for me to go into it at any great length to-day, but as some of you may be here to-night, who were not here on that occasion, I will just state to you shortly what the Statute of Uses did. Before the Statute of Uses passed, the Court of Chancery was in the habit of giving effect to uses declared which were unknown to the Common Law; for instance, when an estate was conveyed to A and his heirs to the use of B and his heirs, the Common Law disregarded the use, but the Court of Chancery held that the use, which is another word for trust and confidence, operated upon a man's conscience, and was binding upon him, and consequently that the first man who held the estate at law should hold it in equity for the benefit of the second man. And the object of the Statute of Uses was to put an end to that state of things, and the way it was done was this: The Statute declared that whoever had the use of land should have the legal seisin, and so got rid of the use by vesting the feudal seisin in the person who had the use—in the case I have put, the estate passes under the Statute to B, and A takes nothing. Well, that put an end to all uses for a time, as Courts of Law having then to deal with persons who had not only a use but at the same time a legal seisin, adopted the previous doctrine of the Court of

Chancery and gave effect to uses. You will find that clearly stated in Joshua Williams, at page 350, and I should like to read it to you : " Executory interests created under the Statute of Uses " are called springing or shifting uses. We have seen that " previous to the passing of this Statute of Uses the use of land " was under the sole jurisdiction of the Court of Chancery ; as " trusts were afterwards. In the exercise of this jurisdiction it " would seem that the Court of Chancery, rather than disappoint " the intentions of parties, gave validity to such interests of a " future or executory nature, as were occasionally created in the " disposition of the use. For instance, if a feoffment (or " conveyance of land) had been made to A and his heirs to the " use of B and his heirs from to-morrow " (that, you will remember, I told you would be void at Common Law, because the feudal seisin would be vacant from now until to-morrow), " the " Court would, it seems, have enforced the use in favour of B "— that is, the man who was to take from to-morrow—" notwith- " standing that by the rules of the law the estate of B would " have been void. Here we have an instance of an executory " interest in the shape of a springing use, giving to B a future " estate arising on the morrow of its own strength, depending " upon no prior estate, and, therefore, not liable to be destroyed " by its prop falling. When the Statute of Uses was passed, the " jurisdiction of the Court of Chancery over uses was at once " annihilated. The uses in becoming by virtue of the Statute " estates by law, brought with them into the Courts of Law many " of the attributes which they had before possessed whilst subjects " of the Court of Chancery. Amongst others which remained " untouched was this capability of being disposed of in such a " way as to create executory interests. The legal seisin or " possession of lands became then for the first time disposable, " without the observance of the formalities previously required," —such as delivery of actual possession—" and amongst the " dispositions allowed were these executory interests in which the " legal seisin is shifted about from one person to another at the " mercy of the springing uses to which the seisin has been " indissolubly united by the Act of Parliament "—that is the Statute of Uses. " Accordingly, it now happens that by means " of uses the legal seisin or possession of lands may be shifted " from one person to another in an endless variety of ways." He gives presently an instance which I shall ask you to pay attention to carefully, because if you understand the example I think you will understand the history of shifting uses. "We have seen," he says, "that a conveyance to B and his heirs to hold from "to-morrow, is absolutely void, but by means of shifting "uses the desired result can be obtained, for the estate may "be conveyed to A and his heirs to the use of the conveying "party and his heirs until to-morrow. A very common instance "of such a shifting use occurs in an ordinary marriage "settlement of land. Supposing A be the settlor"—he may be the father, or he may be the husband—the intended husband—or the settlor may be the intending wife, or any other person,— "supposing A to be the settlor, the lands are then conveyed by "him by settlement executed a day or two before marriage." He conveys the land to the trustees, say B and C, and their heirs to the use of A—that is the settlor—and his heirs until the intended marriage is solemnized, so that he has the use, he has the fee simple—if it is a fee simple estate he is dealing with—until the marriage. Up to that time he has really parted with nothing. If the marriage does not take place he remains just as he was—"until the intended marriage shall be solemnized, and "from and immediately after the solemnization thereof the uses "agreed upon." The uses are different in different marriage settlements, but it depends very often whether the property comes from the husband's side or the wife's side of the family. The uses are different in these cases from one another. They are not always the same. Let us take an ordinary case of a gentleman getting married, and the father making a settlement of the family estate upon marriage. In that case the ordinary uses are from and after the solemnization of the marriage—"to the use of B, the intended husband, and his assigns for his life." And the result of that is, that the moment the marriage takes place the use springs up and takes effect, and the married man takes that estate for life. And so on after his death, the limitation may be to use of the wife for life, and any other use that the parties agree upon. What I want you to note is that B and C, to whom the estate is conveyed—the trustees, really—take nothing, permanently at all events. Here B and C take no permanent estate at all, as we have already seen. That is, the Statute operates and the use goes to D, the husband—puts the legal estate in him at once, directly the event happens upon which his estate springs into use. "A continues as he was"—that is the settlor—"a "tenant in fee simple until the marriage, and if the marriage "should never happen, his estate in fee simple will continue in

" him untouched. But the moment the marriage takes place
" without any further thought or care to the parties, the seisin or
" possession of the land shifts away from A to vest in D, the
" intended husband, for his life according to the disposition made
" in the settlement. After the execution of the settlement until
" the marriage takes place, the interest of all parties, except the
" settlor" (because he retains the fee simple) "is future and
" contingent also on the event of the marriage, but the life estate
" of D, the intended husband, is not of a kind called a contingent
" remainder, for the estate which precedes it, namely, that of A,
" is an estate in fee simple, the settlor still retains the estate in
" fee simple until the marriage." And there can be no limitation
of any estate, as I have mentioned to you before, after a fee
simple, because that is the greatest estate known to the law—
there is nothing left. "After which no remainder can be limited.
The use of D"—that is the husband—"for his life springs up
" on the marriage taking place, and puts an end at once and for
" ever to the estate which belonged to A, the settlor, in fee
" simple." Here, then, is the destruction of one estate—the
settlor's, that is—and the substitution of another—that is D's
estate—for life. The possession of A is wrested from him by the
use to D—because under the Statute of Uses, having the use he
has the legal seisin—" instead of D's estate waiting until A's
" possession is over, as it must have done had it merely been a
" remainder. Another instance of the application of a shifting
" use occurs in those cases in which it is wished that any person
" who shall become entitled under the settlement shall take the
" name and arms of the settlor." I will not trouble you with
that now; it is a matter which is too much one of detail to go
into now. If you have really grasped that particular example,
you will know what a shifting use is. It is an excellent example
—it is an everyday matter which comes before, not only lawyers,
but men of the world who have to do with marriage or marriage
settlements. There is, however, another convenient and useful
application of springing uses to which I ought to draw your
attention, because it is also very common. It is in creating
powers. Joshua Williams—you will find it at page 356—treats
of the matter in this way, and he puts it very shortly and
concisely. I cannot put it more shortly; I have tried to, but I
cannot; therefore, I will read this page to you. "One of the
" most convenient and useful applications of springing uses
" occurs in the case of powers, which are methods of causing a

"use, with its accompanying estate, to spring up at the will of
"another person." And if you will follow the example you will
understand what that means. "Thus, lands may be conveyed to
"A and his heirs to such uses as B shall, by deed or by his will,
"appoint, and in default of, or until any such appointment to
"the use of C and his heirs, or to any other uses." Now you
will notice there that there is a conveyance to A and his heirs to
such uses as B shall appoint, and until B appoints the use the
estate is to go to C and his heirs, so that at any moment B,
by exercising his power of appointment, can destroy the estate of
the third man, C. "This use will accordingly confer vested
"estates on C, or the parties having them, subject to be
"divested or destroyed at any time by B exercising his power of
"appointment. Here B, though not the owner of the property,
"has yet the power at any time at once to dispose of it by
"executing a deed, and if he should please to appoint it to the
"use of himself and his heirs, he is at perfect liberty to do so, or
"by virtue of his power he may dispose of it by his will." That
is where the power given is to be executed by deed or by will.
But, of course, if the power given to him is only to be executed by
deed, he cannot execute it by will, but only by deed. And
similarly if the power given to him is only to be executed by will,
he cannot execute it by deed. A familiar instance of that is
where a lady has property and it is wished that she should not,
during her lifetime, execute the power of appointment given to
her. If she has power to appoint by deed or will under marital
influence, she might exercise it at any time in her husband's
favour, when the object in giving her the power was that she
should be free from such influence, and therefore a wife's power
of appointment under her marriage settlement is given to her
sometimes so that she can only execute it by will.

"A general power of appointment is evidently a privilege of
"great value; it is nearly as good as ownership, and has,
"accordingly, been made to share the liability of ownership."
For instance, if you have a general power of appointment and
become bankrupt, the trustee in bankruptcy may exercise that
power for you and sell the estate. If B dies without having
executed that power, then the estate goes to C, because, if you
remember, the estate is given to A and his heirs to such uses as
B should, by will, appoint, and in default of or until any such
appointment, to the use of C and his heirs. In the case of a
power of appointment being exercised, the case is put an end to,

and another estate takes its place under the power, and that is, really, what a shifting use, in substance, is. So far with regard to shifting uses created by deed. But executory interests may also be created by will, and you will find that dealt with at page 372 of Joshua Williams. He there says: "Before the " passing of the Statute of Uses, wills were employed only in the " devising of uses under the direction of the Court of Chancery, " except in some few cities and boroughs where the legal estate " in lands might be devised by special custom. In giving effect " to these customary devises, the Courts, in very early times, " showed great indulgence to testators; and perhaps the first " instance of an executory interest occurred in directions given " by testators that their executors should sell their tenements. " Such directions were allowed by law in customary devises"— that is, where there was such a custom in a city or borough— " and in such cases it is evident that the sale by executors " operated as the execution of a power to dispose of that in " which they themselves had no kind of ownership." Because, as you know, gentlemen, executors do not take real estate under a will; as executors, they only take personal property,—" for " executors, as such, have nothing to do with freeholds. Here, " therefore, was a future estate or executory trust created. The " fee simple was shifted away from the heir of the testator "— that is, when the executor sold the property under the will— " the fee simple was shifted away from the heir of the testator, to " whom it had descended, and became vested in the purchaser on " the event of the sale of the tenement to him. The Court of " Chancery, also, in permitting the devise of the *use* of such " lands as were not in themselves devisible, allowed of the " creation of executory interests by will, as well as in transactions " between living persons. And, in particular, directions given " by persons having others seised of lands to their use, that such " lands should be sold by their executors, were not only per- " mitted by the Court of Chancery, but were also recognized by " the legislature. For, by a statute of Henry VIII, previous to " the Statute of Uses, it is provided that in such cases where " part of the executors refuse to take administration of the will, " and the residue accept the charge of the will, then all bargains " and sales of lands to be sold by the executors made by him or " them only of the said executors that doth accept the charge of " the will, shall be as effectual as if all the residue of the executors " so refusing adjoined with him or them in the making of the "bargain and sale." This was a recognition by the legislature of the practice by the Court of Chancery to enforce the intention of the testator as expressed in his will, when he said that his executors were to sell his estate and dispose of the proceeds as he directed by his will. "But, as we have seen, the passing of the "Statute of Uses abolished for a time all wills of uses, until the "Statute of Wills restored them." That, I mentioned to you, was passed shortly afterwards, in 32 Henry VIII. "When wills "were restored, the uses of which they had been accustomed to "dispose, had all been turned into estates at law, and such estates "then generally came, for the first time, within the operation "of testamentary instruments. Under these circumstances, the "Courts of Law, in interpreting wills, adopted the same lenient "construction which had formerly been employed by themselves "in the interpretation of customary devises, and also by the "Court of Chancery in the construction of the devises of the "ancient use. The Statute which, in the case of wills and uses, "had given validity to sales made by executors accepting charge "of a will, was extended in its construction to directions now "authorized to be made for the sale, by the executors, of the "*legal estate*, and also to cases where the legal estate was devised "to the executors to be sold. Future estates at law were also "allowed to be created by will, and were invested with the same "important attribute of indestructibility which belongs to all "executory interests. These future estates were called executory "devises, and in some respects they appear to have been "more favourably interpreted than shifting uses contained "in deeds, though, generally speaking, their attributes are the "same." You see, gentlemen, a shifting use was created by a deed—an executory is created by a will. There is no substantial difference between the two, and they only take different names on account of their different origins; but unless you knew what the origin of each was, you would not understand either. Joshua Williams, on page 175, gives a very good example, and one of the great advantages of Joshua Williams is, that he does not rest contented with general propositions and statements of law, but he gives you examples, which a diligent and careful student can understand, and which throw a very great light indeed upon the general propositions which he enunciates. Here is the example which he gives in this particular case: "Take a "common instance; a man may, by his will, devise lands to his "son A, an infant,"—that is, under 21 years of age—it may be

a baby—" and his heirs; but in case A should die under the age
" of 21 years, then to B and his heirs. In this case, A has an
" estate in fee simple in possession"—that is, the infant, you
know—the baby takes under that will an estate in fee simple in
possession, subject to an executory interest in favour of B,
because, if you will remember, the devise was that if A, the
infant, died under 21, the estate should go to B—the child takes
the estate in fee simple at the death of the testator, subject to the
executory interest in favour of B. " If A "—that is, the baby—
" should not die under age, his estate in fee simple will continue
" in him unimpaired, but if he should die under that age nothing
" can prevent the estate of B from immediately arising and
" coming into possession, and displacing for ever the estate of A
" and his heirs." That is, the baby in this case takes a fee
simple, subject to his losing it if he dies under 21, and then
immediately upon his death B takes the fee simple. " Precisely
" the same effect might have been produced by a conveyance to
" uses. A conveyance to C and his heirs for the use of A and
" his heirs, but in case A should die under age, then to the use
" of B and his heirs, would have effected the same result." In
one case it is done by will—there is an executory devise—if the
testator had done it by deed in his life it would have been called
a shifting use. Not so, however, the direct conveyance independently of the Statute of Uses. "The conveyance directly to
" A and his heirs would vest in him the fee simple, after which
" no limitation could follow. In such a case, therefore, a
" direction that if A should die under age the land should belong
" to B and his heirs would follow the period on the legal seisin,
" and the estate in fee simple to A would, in the case of his
" decease under age, still descend, without any interruption, to
" his heirs-at-law. A good illustration of the difference between
" a contingent remainder and an executory devise, occurs in the
" case of a devise of lands by will to A for life, with remainder in
" fee to such son of B as shall first attain the age of 21 years "—
that is a common devise.—" In this case, the limitation to the son
" of B is either a contingent remainder or an executory devise,
" according as A, the tenant for life, may, or may not, survive
" the testator. If A should survive the testator, there will be
" an estate of freehold subsisting in the premises for the deter-
" mination of which the limitation to the son of B must wait
" before it can take effect and pass." This limitation is, therefore,
a remainder, and as it remains upon the contingency of B having

a son who may attain 21 years of age, it is a contingent remainder, but if A should die in the lifetime of the testator the will would start on the testator's death with the simple limitation to such son of B as shall first attain the age of 21 years. This limitation is not to wait for the determination of any prior estate at freehold, but it arises of itself, in the event of a son of B attaining the age of 21 years, and it displaces, when it takes effect, the estate in fee simple, which, not being otherwise disposed of, descends immediately on the death of the testator to his heir-at-law. It is, therefore, in this case, not a contingent remainder, but an executory devise. Here comes in the importance of that Act of '77, to which I have drawn your attention more than once—at the last lecture, and at the very beginning of my lecture to-day. Under the law as it stood, before the Act of '77 amended the law as to contingent remainders, if A survived the testator before any son of B attained 21, the limitation failed for want of an estate of freehold to support it, whereas, if A died in the lifetime of the testator, it was not liable to any failure. It was to remedy the hardship occasioned by the failure of such a limitation as this, when it occurred in the shape of a contingent remainder, that the Act above mentioned was framed. With regard to executory interests, I need not trouble you with more of the history of them, and I will only add that they can be disposed of by deed like any other interest in land. Having explained to you what shifting uses and executory devises are—how they arise and how they work in the simple cases that Mr. Joshua Williams puts—it is necessary that I should draw your attention to the law of Perpetuities, because at present, except for a casual reference to it in a previous lecture, I have not drawn your attention to it. But it is a very important branch of the law, and I think this is the time that you will best be able to understand what that law is. It is not statute law, it is judge-made law, and, to put it colloquially, it is this—"that you cannot tie an estate up for a longer period than an existing life and 21 years afterwards." Sometimes it is said perfectly truly, that you cannot give an estate to the child of an unborn person. But it comes back to the general proposition, colloquially stated, that you cannot tie an estate up for more than the existence of lives in being at the time it is attempted to tie it up and 21 years afterwards, or the possible addition of a few months for the period of gestation, when the gestation really exists. The way that came about is stated in Joshua Williams, at page 379, to be this: "The

" limitation of estates to arise at a future time by way of shifting
" use or executory devise must conform to the requirements of the
" Rule known as the Rule against perpetuities, or else it will be
" void for remoteness"—that is the legal term—"void for
" remoteness." This rule is founded upon a general principle of
policy guiding the judges, that all contrivances shall be void which
tend to create a perpetuity, or to place the property for ever out
of the reach of the exercise of the power of alienation. " This
" principle appears to have been first applied after it had become
" well settled that an estate tail might be barred by a common
" recovery as a reason for holding that any contrivance to restrain
" a tenant in tail from suffering a recovery shall be of no effect."
If you will remember, I told you a common recovery was a sham
action or solemn piece of jugglery, by which a tenant in tail was
enabled to disentail an estate. " When the law came to recognize
" as valid the limitation of estates in remainder to unborn
" children, and further to admit the creation of future estates by
" way of shifting use and executory devise, it was seen that such
" devises, unless restrained within due bounds, might pave the
" way to perpetual settlements of land, and the same principle of
" policy was again invoked. In the case of future estates to arise
" by way of shifting use and executory devise, these due bounds
" were gradually settled by successive decisions" I
need not take you through the history of it, but I will come to
the end and tell you what was finally done. " Finally it was
" settled that the time allowed after the duration of existing lives
" should be a term of 21 years independently of the minority of
" any person, whether entitled or not, with a possible addition of
" the period of gestation, but only where the gestation actually
" exists." That is the law of the land at the present day. It
has been restricted in one respect by the Conveyancing Act of
1882, but I will draw your attention to that in a minute. " The
" rule so settled is generally what is called the rule against
" perpetuities, and it will be convenient so to refer to it. It
" requires every future estate limited to arise by way of a shifting
" use or executory devise, to be such as must necessarily arise
" within the compass of existing lives and 21 years afterwards,
" with the possible addition of the period of gestation in case of
" some person entitled being a posthumous child. But if no lives
" are fixed on, then the term of 21 years only is allowed." Now
the next point is a very important point. " Every executory
" estate which might in any event—not merely an event which

e

" happens, but which might in any event—transgress the limits " so fixed, will from its commencement be absolutely void." I wish you to bear that in mind. " For instance, a gift by way of " shifting use or executory devise to the first son of A, a bachelor, " who shall attain the age of 24 years, is void for remoteness. For " if A were to die, leaving a son a few months old, the estate of the " son would arise under such a gift at a time exceeding a period " of 21 years from the expiration of the life of A, which, in this " case is the life fixed upon. But a gift of the first son of A " who shall attain the age of 21 years "—you will mark the difference between 21 and 24—" would be valid as necessarily falling within the allowed period "—because the son must be born, except in the case of a posthumous child, within the life of the father, and therefore must attain 21 years within that period after the death of the father. Therefore, that is a good limitation —it is not rendered void for remoteness. And that is a very, very ordinary limitation. "When a gift is infected with the vice of " possibly exceeding the prescribed limit, it is at once and " altogether void, both at law and in equity, and even if in its " actual event it should fall greatly within such limit, yet it is " still as absolutely void as if the event had occurred which " would have taken it beyond the boundary." In the first case I put, it is perfectly immaterial whether the child is, in fact, 24 or more at the death of his father, because the original limitation was void for remoteness on the ground that it might possibly exceed the period allowed. " If, however, the executory limitation " —this is the exception. I think I have told you more than once that there is hardly a general proposition of real property law which has not some exception. Now this is the exception, and it is founded on good sense. " If, however, the executory limitation " should be in defeasance of, or immediately preceded by, an " estate tail, then as the estate tail, and all subsequent estates, " may be barred by the tenant in tail, the remoteness of the " event on which the executory limitation is to arise, will not " affect its validity "—Because the tenant in tail, if he gets in possession, being entitled to bar all remainders, can deal with the estate, and it is not tied up. That is why the law has grafted that exception upon the general rule. That was the law until 1882, but there have been a very great many changes in the last fifteen or twenty years, and a very great change in very many respects has been made by the Statute which is known as the Conveyancing Act of 1882. It is an Act which some time or other you will probably have to consult, but at the present moment I shall only draw your attention to one section of it, and that only where executory limitations contained in instruments come into operation after 1882, so that all other deeds, wills and instruments are governed by the laws which existed before 1882. By section 10 of "The Conveyancing Act 1882 ", it is enacted that " where there is a person entitled to land for an estate in fee, or " for a term of years absolute or determinable on life or for term " of life with an executory limitation over on default or failure of " all or any of his issue, whether within or at any specified period " of time or not, that executory limitation shall be or become void " and incapable of taking effect if, and as soon as, there is living " any issue who has attained the age of 21 years, of the class on " default or failure whereof the limitation over was to take effect." That is, the moment the son attains 21 years, any limitation in that particular case beyond that period, would be incapable of taking effect, so that it cuts it down in that particular direction. So much, gentlemen, for the doctrine of perpetuities. Now I have dealt, practically I hope, but not as sufficiently as I should have liked, with freehold estates. There are other estates known to the law as copyholds, and I will put before you, shortly, the law of Copyholds. As for details, you must work them up for yourselves; I cannot undertake to supply you with details. I can only give you the general outline of the law, and ask you to fill in the details by your own studies. Copyholds arose in the following manner. Some time after the Norman conquest—one or two centuries, perhaps—England was parcelled out into Agricultural Estates; that was when the Feudal System was completely established. It took some years, or, perhaps, one, two, or three centuries, to completely establish that system; but when the system was established, the land in England was parcelled out into, what I have called, Agricultural Estates. Some of those estates were large, some small, some neither large nor small, of all sizes and all values, and very nearly of all descriptions, except that they were land they were all alike in that respect. These agricultural estates were called manors, and they were held either directly or indirectly of the King by persons who, in those days, were called great men—we now always speak of them, and, I think, they were very early spoken of, as Lords of the Manor—but they held those manors of the King, either directly or indirectly, and, as I explained to you with respect to the creation of freehold estates, the Lord of the

Manor granted certain parcels of the land in his Manor to freehold tenants for freehold estates. Now, I told you that the smallest freehold estate known to the law was an estate for life. The holders of those estates were called the freehold tenants of the manor; but, having done that, there remained to the lord, say, the castle in which he lived, or his residence—mansion house, as we call it now—and certain lands about that mansion, which he had not disposed of or granted away to freehold tenants upon freehold tenures. And in every manor, besides the freehold tenants, there existed a class of inhabitants called villeins— "villein" is not spelled with an "a", it is spelled with an "e", v-i-l-l-e-i-n—they were the inhabitants of the manor who were not freehold tenants, and they were, for the most part, tied to the land. By that, I mean this: they could not move from one manor to another; they had no power of leaving one district and going to another; they were tied to the land; there they were, and they had to live there, and the lord, on the other hand, wanted the land which he retained cultivated, his woods cut, and other services of a like nature, and these villani, or villeins, were persons who, in consideration of their rendering such services, were put, by the lord, into actual possession, but had not the feudal seisin, or legal possession, of lands in the manor, which they might cultivate for themselves, and thereby live; and that is the origin of copyholds. These villeins held their lands at the will of the lord, and to this day, in strict legal terms, every copyholder holds his land at the will of the lord. But, in the course of time, such tenants acquired rights by custom, so that now, if one were to speak absolutely correctly, one would describe a copyholder as a man who holds lands in a manor of the lord of that manor at the will of the lord, according to the custom of the manor. Mr. Kenelm Edward Digby, who is now Permanent Under-Secretary at the Home Office, delivered a course of lectures on Real Property Law, which he published under the title of "An Introduction to the Law of Real Property," and as to Copyhold Tenures, at page 213, he says this: "It has been already seen that at the time of Domesday"—that was towards the end of the reign of William the Conqueror—"besides the "freemen there was commonly a large class of persons of an "inferior status, residing within the limits of the manor, and "bound, as a general rule, to render services upon the domain "lands of the lord."—I ought to have mentioned to you that the lands which the lord held in his own hands, and did not grant

away, were called his domain.—" The various names which
" prevailed at the time of Domesday, and earlier, cease to be
" recognized, and we hear only of villeins. These were either
" villeins *regardant* "—that is a Norman-French word meaning
attached to the land—" in which case the right to the services of
" the villein passed with every alienation of the land ; or villeins
" in gross, attached to the person of the lord, the right to their
" services being saleable by deed."—It seems rather strange to
speak of men being in gross; it is a legal term, the meaning of
which is, that they were not attached to the land.—" It is with
" the former class that the history of the law of land is mainly
" concerned."—That is, the villeins who were tied to the land,
like paupers now are to the parish in which they have a settlement, and to which they are said to belong. " Where a villein
" was attached to the land, it followed, as a matter of course,
" that he had a permanent habitation, and the means of
" supporting himself and his family by the occupation of a plot
" of ground. This must have been the practice long before the
" Conquest." I won't trouble you with anything before the
Conquest, it is quite enough to trouble you with things since the
Conquest. The tenant in villenage had no legal protection; the
only protection he had was where the lord entered into a
covenant with him, and that was a personal covenant. Apart
from that, he had only the actual occupation. The lord retained
the feudal possession. No feudal rights passed to the tenant by
his being let into the occupation for the purpose of tillage of any
plot of land. He was very little better than a slave. The lord
had not the right of life and death, or rights of that kind, over
him, but he was practically at the mercy of the will of his lord,
who could, at any moment, turn him out. Mr. Kenelm Digby
says this: " The lawyers described the position of the tenant in
" villenage by the expression that he held his land at the will of
" the lord. But, as a matter of fact, the customs and practices
" which prevailed in the various manors tended to protect and
" perpetuate the interests of this class of tenants. Custom fixed
" the rights of the lord, the amount of service to be rendered to
" him, the heriots "—that is, what the lord was entitled to take
—" upon the death of the tenant "—generally the best beast
of the tenant—" the fine on the admittance of a new tenant,
" the mode of succession and devolution of the lands to the
" tenant's eldest or youngest sons, or to all the sons alike, and
" so forth. These customs, though the institutions of the

"country afforded no means of enforcing them as against the
"landlord by judicial action"—because, I told you, the law gave
the villein no protection—"were deeply rooted in the habits of
"the people, and in all probability the lord who ventured to set
"them aside, and deprive the villein of his customary rights,
"must have been exceptionally grasping and defiant of public
"opinion." That was his position. "It appears that the tenants
"in villenage were present at the manorial Courts, not on a level
"with the freeholders or free-suitors to the Court"—who were
the judges, by whose voice all matters were decided—"but in an
"inferior position. The customary heir would appear at the
"Court"—that is, where a custom had sprung up that the
heir of the copyhold tenant should succeed him—"and humbly
"request admittance to the land of his deceased father on
"payment of the customary dues; the tenant who had sold his
"holding in villenage would appear and surrender his land to
"the lord or his steward, and the purchaser would request
"admittance." And so it is to this day. If a copyholder now
sells his lands, he executes a deed, in which he covenants to
surrender them to the lord of the manor, to the use of the
purchaser, and the purchaser has to be admitted tenant of the
manor, and the deed is registered in the Court Rolls. "These,
"and similar transactions are recorded on the Rolls of the Court.
"The Rolls of the Court, therefore, contain the evidence of the
"customs of the manor"—because everything is entered in the
Court Rolls—"the authorized copy of the entry on the Rolls of
"the Court delivered to the tenant is his muniment of title, and
"gives him his name of 'copyholder'"—and that is how you
get the word "copyholder", because the document of title by
which he holds is a copy of the Court Roll. "Gradually the
"interest of the copyholder came to be recognized by the regular
"tribunals. The great step seems to have been the recognition
"of the right of the tenant in villenage to maintain an action of
"trespass against his lord"—that is, if the lord turned him out
contrary to the custom of the manor, the tenant acquired a right
to bring an action against his lord.—"Thus, incidentally and
"gradually, the Courts of Common Law came to recognize and
"enforce the customs which had grown up in different manors.
"For example, the custom of allowing the eldest son to succeed
"his father in his holding, of admitting to the holding the
"person to whom the previous owner had sold his rights. As
"the character of the rights depended upon the customs proved

"to prevail in the different manors, the rights of copyholders "varied accordingly." You must always bear that in mind, gentlemen; there is no general custom applicable to all manors. When you are dealing with copyhold property you must ascertain what the custom of the particular manor is in which the land with which you are dealing lies. "We find various customs, as "to the rules of descent, duration of interest, modes of alienation, "extent of power of user and otherwise prevailing in different "manors, the customs of each manor constituting the law "prevailing therein. Except where altered by special custom, "copyholds, as to duration of interest, time of enjoyment, mode "of descent, joint tenancy, and tenants in common, in general "resemble freehold interests." That is a very short statement of the tenure of copyholds; but the rights of the lord against a copyhold tenant are very much more extensive than his rights against a freehold tenant. I explained to you that the freehold tenants were practically free, but the copyhold tenants, even to this day, are not; but they can now enfranchise their copyholds against the will of the lord under certain Acts of Parliament. Until enfranchisement the tenant is not in feudal possession of the land, for, although a copyhold tenant may have an estate in his copyhold analagous to that of a tenant in fee simple, he holds at the will of the lord according to the custom of the manor, and the feudal seisin is in the lord. The result of that is this, that the lord has all his rights, except such rights as the tenant gets under the custom of the manor. For instance, the lord has a right to all mines and minerals under the land, but, strange to say, he has not the right to dig a pit or sink a shaft on the tenant's lands to get them, and the only way he can get them is by working underground. I happen, as trustee, to be at the present moment one of the lords of a manor in Yorkshire. Happily for us, a noble lord, our next door neighbour, has spent a large sum of money in sinking pits or shafts on his own land, by means of which the coal under the manor can be got. The rights of the lord of that manor were thought nothing of, not many years ago, but they are now valuable. The lord not only retains the right to the mines and minerals which are under the surface, but he also has a right to the timber growing on the land. But again, he cannot go on to the land to cut the timber without the tenant's leave. Therefore, a lord who wants to cut his own timber on his tenant's land, has to come to terms with his tenant before he can cut it and carry it away. The consequence, gentlemen, is, throughout England, that when you see any large tract of land with very few trees upon it, you may safely assume, if trees would grow upon it, that it is copyhold property. You do not see on copyhold property any of the beautiful trees in the hedgerows, which add so much to the charm of England, because if the tenant planted them they would not belong to him, and the lord has not the right to plant them. As the land gets enfranchised, so, by degrees, trees are planted, and the land looks happier. That is, shortly, gentlemen, the history of a copyhold.

THE LAW OF REAL PROPERTY IN ENGLAND.

FIFTH LECTURE.

[Delivered 9 March 1897.]

IN my previous lectures I explained to you, as far as the time at my disposal permitted, the nature and incidents of what are called freehold estates. You will remember they are, estates in fee simple, in fee tail, and estates for life. There are other estates and interests in land generally comprised under the term of leaseholds, and I propose this evening to tell you as much as I can about the nature and incidents of a leasehold estate in land. But before doing so I want to explain to you the meaning of the words " real property." I have not done so hitherto because I thought it would be more convenient to do so when I had explained to you generally the character of freehold estates. The term real property, strictly, is confined to those freehold estates in land of which I have hitherto spoken to you. I believe, or at least it is said, that those estates were called freehold because the smallest estate amongst them —an estate for life—was the smallest estate which a freeman would accept. And, I have impressed you, I hope, fully, with the importance, at least in law, of what is called feudal possession, and I have explained to you that the feudal possession of those estates was in the freeholder. I have now to explain to you how those estates came to be called real property. Our Courts of Law for a long time only recognized the feudal possession of land, and if a person who was entitled to anyone of those freehold estates was dispossessed of his lands, our Courts would issue a writ in an action by him to recover possession of the lands to which he was entitled. Those actions were called, by lawyers, real actions; they were actions brought by persons entitled to the feudal possession to recover, by the assistance of Courts of Law, the feudal possession of which they had been deprived by trespassers or wrong-doers, who had turned them out of possession. But the Courts of Law would not grant a writ in an action, or, as lawyers say, an action would not lie, by any person who had any lesser estate or interest in land to recover possession. That was the state of the law originally, and it continued for several centuries, down to the reign, I think, of Edward IV. That being the state of things, there were persons who were in actual possession of lands who had not the feudal possession of which I have spoken. Tenants to whom the land was let by the freeholder for the purpose of cultivating the land, and for other purposes, but chiefly for agricultural purposes upon certain terms. These tenants were allowed to occupy the land to till it, and to get the fruits of the cultivation of the land upon the terms of their paying the freeholder a certain sum per annum, which was called a rent; and upon such other terms as might be agreed upon, but they were regarded as holding possession of the lands on behalf of the freeholders. A person who held lands in that way had no right to recover possession, or, which is substantially the same thing, there were no means by which he could recover possession, if he was turned out wrongfully. You will find on pages 17 and 18 of Williams, a very short account of that state of things: "Tenant for a term of years was regarded " in early law as holding possession on behalf of the free- " holder as his bailiff, and was never allowed to use the " freeholder's remedies for dispossession"—I have told you what those remedies were, real actions—" Originally he had no remedies in case of his ejectment "—ejectment means being turned out—" unless he held under a covenant with his landlord "—A covenant is a stipulation in a deed on which an action can be brought by either party for the breach of it—" If so, he might have an action of covenant against his " landlord, in case he had been ejected by the landlord himself, " or anyone claiming the land by superior title; and might " recover, in the former case, possession of his holding for the

" rest of his term, if unexpired, but otherwise damages only.
" But afterwards special actions were given to a tenant for
" years against any person who had wrongfully ousted him or
" acquired possession of his land from a wrongful ejector.
" And though at first it was doubted whether these actions
" enabled him to recover anything but damages, in the reign
" of Edward IV. it was established that he should therein
" recover possession of his holding as well." Now, a person who held an estate for a term of years, or any less estate than a freehold, having no right to institute a real action to recover his property, lawyers did not call his estate real estate, but only those freehold estates of which I have spoken to you, and to this day, strictly, those are the only estates which come within the meaning of the term; in other words, real estate was so called because the action by which the right to it was enforced was called a real action, and in time the word realty came to be used to denote the freehold. And the expressions real and personal property, with which we are so familiar now, whether we are lawyers or whether we are men of business, did not come into common use until the time of Charles II., but the expression "real estate" was known to lawyers long before, and those words, as I have told you, comprise only freehold estates. A term of years, therefore, is not real estate, it is what lawyers call a chattel real; that is to say, it is a chattel or personal property which concerns the realty. Not being real estate and not being exactly a chattel, lawyers have termed it a chattel real, but it is personal property, and it differs in many important respects from real estate. I explained to you a tenancy in fee simple. If a man died without having disposed of an estate in fee simple in his lifetime, or by his will, his heir became entitled to it. But, on the other hand, if a man is possessed of a term of years, and he dies without having disposed of it in his lifetime, the term does not go to his heir, but it goes to his executor or administrator, because it is part of his personalty. And now you will understand the use of that word hereditaments that is so often used, and that I have so often used in explaining these matters to you. Real estates are called hereditaments, because they go to the heir. A term of years is called personal property, because it goes to the personal representatives, the executors or the administrators. And that is, substantially, the distinction

between real property and personal property, and therefore, although to-day I am going to treat, as far as the time at my disposal permits, of leaseholds, you must bear in mind they are not strictly part of the subject upon which I was asked to lecture to you—the Law of Real Property—but they are closely connected with it. Before considering the interest of a person who holds an estate in land for a term of years, a leaseholder, let us consider what other tenancies there are. There are not many. A tenancy at will arises when the owner of the freehold, or other person entitled to land, lets it to another to hold it at the will of the lessor or person letting. The lessee, or person who takes the lands, is called a tenant at will; he may be turned out at any time by his landlord, and the tenant may leave when he pleases. If he is turned out by his landlord, the tenant has the right to reap what he has sown, or, as it is expressed in law, take the "emblements"; which in some parts of the country are called "away going crops." Then there is another tenancy, which is of a still more precarious character, without any rights at all, and that is a tenancy by sufferance. If a person rightly gets into possession of land, and his interest comes to an end, and he does not go out, he is said to be a tenant by sufferance. The next tenancy with which we have to deal is a tenancy from year to year. When land is let to a person to hold from year to year, both landlord and tenant are entitled to notice before the tenancy can be determined by the other of them. By the Common Law at least half-a-year's notice must be given, but, by Statute, in the case of agricultural holdings, one year's notice is required. It is the common agricultural tenancy in many parts of the country, and the Statute to which I have referred is "The Agricultural Holdings' Act, 1883." This Act, and the Amending Acts, affect the rights of landlord and tenants of agricultural or pastoral land in several important respects, besides the length of the notice required to be given to determine the tenancy. A tenancy from year to year, therefore, can only be determined by either half-a-year's notice, or a year's notice, as the case may be, and such notice must be given the required time, before the expiration of the current year, ending at the same time that the tenancy commenced. For instance, if the tenancy commenced on the 25th March, neither party can determine the tenancy, except by a notice which would expire on the 25th March in some subsequent year. That is the nature of a tenancy from year to year, and it is a very common one. Of course, there are other tenancies, but they are analagous. We have quarterly tenancies, and even weekly ones; but I will not trouble you with them, because you are not likely to have to deal with them, in the course of your practice, and they are not matters of any serious importance in dealing with estates. To return to the consideration of a term for a number of years. There are two classes of terms of years. Joshua Williams, you will find, at page 469, describes them in this way :—" Terms of "years may be practically considered as of two kinds: first, " those which are created by ordinary leases, which are subject " to a yearly rent, which seldom exceed ninety-nine years, and " in respect of which so large a number of the occupiers of "lands and houses are entitled to their occupation ; and "secondly, those which are created by settlements, wills, or " mortgage deeds, in respect of which no rent is usually "reserved, which are frequently for 1,000 years or " more, which are often vested in trustees, and the object of " which is usually to secure the payment of money by the " owner of the land. But, although terms of years of different "lengths are thus created for different purposes, it must not, " therefore, be supposed that a long term of years is an " interest of a different nature from a short one. On the " contrary, all terms of years, of whatever length, possess " precisely the same attributes in the eye of the law." I will give you an instance: suppose there is an old gentleman 90 years of age, and he is tenant for life of an estate, he has in law a larger estate than any person who is only a termor, as the phrase is, say for 1,000 years. If the old gentleman were to buy the term, the term would, according to the Common Law, be merged in the larger estate; the 1,000 years would be gone, and the old gentleman would still be tenant for life, he would be nothing more. When he died, his estate, being one for life, would be determined. That is an illustration of the doctrine of our law—that a freehold estate is larger than a term of years, however long the term may be. Now, as to granting one of these leases for years. There are several statutory provisions with which you ought to be acquainted. You may grant a lease from year to year by word of mouth. I explained to you what a tenancy from year to year was, and that it could be determined only by notice on one side or the other; but you may grant a lease of that kind, notwithstanding the possibility of its continuing for any number of years, by word of mouth. And you can also grant a lease for term of years by word of mouth, if the term does not exceed three years from the making of it, and if the rent reserved amount to two-thirds, at least, of the full improved value of the land. The Statute of Frauds, passed in the reign of Charles II., required all other leases to be put in writing, and signed by the parties making the same, or their agents thereunto lawfully authorized by writing. Then, in the seventh and eighth years of the Queen, an Act was passed called the Real Property Act of 1845, which effected a great many changes in our law, and amongst other things, it enacted that every lease that was required to be in writing should be void at law unless made by deed; and therefore, now, a lease for more than three years is invalid at law unless granted by deed. But, on the other hand, if there is an agreement in writing which the Courts can construe as an agreement to grant a lease, they will compel the parties to execute a lease upon the terms of the writing. But, to make a lease valid under the statute, it must be by deed if it is for a term which exceeds three years, or if it is for less than three years, and the rent is less than two-thirds of the full improved value. There are no formal words required in granting a lease, but one of the ordinary words used,—in these days when lawyers are not paid according to the number of words they use in a document, they are becoming reasonable in the number of words they use—is the word "demise", and if you "demise" lands for a thousand years to A.B., that is all that is necessary. The words commonly used are "demise, lease, and to farm let"; but it is quite sufficient to use the one word "demise" in the deed. A lease must have two incidents; it must have a definite time for its commencement, and a definite time for its termination; it must be a lease as we say in law for a term certain. If no time is mentioned for the commencement of a term in the deed granting it, it is presumed in law to commence from the day of the execution of the deed, and to continue till the day specified in the deed for its termination, and it is this fixed period for its coming to an end which distinguishes a term from an estate of freehold. A term also differs from an estate of freehold, for it may commence at any future period.

For instance, a lease, made to-day for a term of years, to commence on the 25 December next, would be good. A lessee, however, does not become complete tenant until he actually enters into possession, and in the meantime has no estate, but only a right to have the land for any term that is granted him, a right which is called in law an *interesse termini*. As Williams put it: "Before entry, he has no "estate, but only a right to have the lands for the term by "force of the lease, called in law an *interesse termini*." But a lease may be made under the Statute of Uses, to which that observation would not apply. That is a technical matter, and I do not think it necessary for me to go into it now. Then he goes on to say this: "The circumstance, that a lease for years "was anciently nothing more than a mere contract, explains a "curious point of law relating to the creation of leases for "years, which does not hold with respect to the creation of any "greater interest in land. If a man should, by indenture"—that is a deed—"lease lands, in which he has no legal "interest, for a term of years, both lessor and lessee will be "*estopped* during the term,"—that is to say, precluded, "from "denying the validity of the lease. But the law goes "further, and holds that if the lessor should, at any time "during the lease, acquire the lands he had so let, the lease, "which before operated only by estoppel, shall now take effect "out of the newly-acquired estate of the lessor, and shall "become for all purposes a regular estate for a term of years. "If, however, the lessor has, at the time of making the lease, "any interest in the lands he lets, such interest only will pass." For instance, suppose I had an interest in this hall for five years, and I granted a lease for 99 years, I should be purporting to grant a great deal more than I had a right to do, but still I had some interest, an interest for five years, and that would pass—"and the lease will have no further effect "by way of estoppel, though the interest purported to be "granted be really greater than the lessor had at the time "power to grant. Thus, if A, a lessee for the life of B, makes "a lease for years by indenture, and afterwards purchases the "reversion in fee, and then B dies, A may at law avoid his "own lease, though several of the years expressed in the lease "may be still to come; for as A had an interest in the lands "for the life of B, a term of years determinable on B's life "passed to the lessee. But if, in such a case, the lease was "made for valuable consideration, equity would oblige the "lessor to make good the term out of the interest he had "acquired." So that in the case of my having an interest for five years and purchasing the freehold of this hall, after having granted a lease of it for 99 years, equity would compel me to grant a good lease for the whole term, 99 years, which I professed to grant previously. The rights of a leaseholder with regard to his term are pretty complete; subject, of course, to any stipulation in the lease to the contrary, to which I shall draw your particular attention presently, he can dispose of it in any way he pleases. For instance, if he has a lease for 99 years, he can grant, or assign, that is convey, all his interest to some other person for all the residue still to come of the term. That is called an assignment. By parting with all his interest, he does not get rid of all his liabilities, as I shall show you presently. Then, again, if he holds a lease for 99 years, 90 years of which are unexpired, he may grant a lease for 7, 14, or 21 years, or for any period less than 90 years, and he can deal with his interest generally as he pleases, subject, as I have said just now, to any stipulation to the contrary in the lease itself. You will, however, often find in a lease, a covenant by the lessee that he will not assign it without the consent of the lessor; and a provision that if he does, the lessor shall be entitled to re-enter and determine the lease. Under those circumstances he cannot assign without obtaining the consent of the lessor, or at least, if he does, the assignee is liable to be ejected or turned out by the lessor. Such a stipulation sometimes, especially with reference to such properties as public-houses, goes further, and is to the effect that the lessee shall not assign, underlet or part with the possession of the premises let without the consent of the landlord. For this and other reasons whenever you are dealing with leasehold property, it is essential that you should see the lease. Now, with regard to other matters. A lease, as I have said, of the first kind, is generally a lease at a yearly rent. In all well-drawn leases there is a covenant by the lessee with his lessor that he will pay the rent either half-yearly, or quarterly, or at some other periods. Notwithstanding that the lessee disposes of all his interest in the property, he remains liable on that covenant, and he cannot get rid of his liability to his landlord on that covenant. For instance, if you take a lease for 99 years and covenant with your landlord that you will pay the rent, you cannot get rid of that liability; if you die, it continues a liability on the part of your executors or administrators, and so on until the lease is at an end. Of course, in practice, it is sometimes extremely difficult to find out who are the personal representatives of the lessee after a considerable period, but if the lessor can find them, and they are worth powder and shot, he can sue them upon the covenant. The lessor is not bound to go to the person in actual possession and make him pay, but he can go at once to the lessee, or his personal representatives, and make him or them pay. Now, that being so, whenever a lessee sells his property out-and-out—by that I mean all his interest in the term of years—to another person, that other person is bound to indemnify him against that payment of rent. So that if the original lessee is called upon by the original lessor or the reversioner to pay the rent, he can come upon the purchaser, or his personal representatives, to indemnify him as against the claim of the landlord, and so with all other similar covenants. Generally, besides the covenant to pay the rent, there is the covenant by the lessee with the lessor to keep the property in repair. That, again, is a covenant upon which the lessee is liable during the whole of the term. The lessee, notwithstanding that he has disposed of the property absolutely, that is to say, all his interest in it, still remains liable, although he has a remedy against the person to whom he has sold the property. On the other hand, the landlord can, if he thinks fit—where the whole interest of the lessee in the property has been disposed of by the tenant—proceed against the assignee for any breach of covenant committed while he is assignee. The landlord may sue either the original lessee or the assignee of the lease. In nine cases out of ten a landlord sues the assignee of the term; but if he cannot recover from him he can sue the original lessee, and that right on the part of the landlord continues however many assignments there may have been. On the other hand, the assignee is liable to the landlord only for breaches of covenant committed during the time that he is the assignee of the term, for the assignee, unlike the original lessee, can get rid of his liability, because his liability arises from the privity of estate which exists between him and the landlord, and this only continues so long as he is assignee, and directly he parts with the whole of his interest in the estate and ceases to be the assignee, he ceases to be liable for any subsequent breach of covenant. So that the only person who can not get rid of his liability under the lease, is the person to whom it is originally granted; any other person to whom the whole term is assigned is only liable so long as he holds the term, and no longer, and he can get rid of his liability by selling or otherwise disposing of the property. Now, with regard to an under-lease the liabilities are entirely different. An under-lease is a lease for a term of years or period less than the original term. For instance, to take the case I put just now of a lease for 99 years, of which 90 years are now unexpired, if the lessee grants a lease for 80 years to some other person, that person is not an assignee of the term. You see, there are ten years still remaining in the lessee; he only parts with his interest for 80 years. When a conveyance of that kind is made, that is called an under-lease, and that does not create, as lawyers say, any privity of estate between the under-lessee and the landlord, and the landlord has no rights whatever against the under-lessee personally. The only person who can sue the under-lessee upon the under-lease is the lessee who granted it to him for the 80 years, or the person in whom the reversion expectant on the determination of that term is vested. The landlord has nothing to do with the under-lessee, and has no right against him, and the under-lessee has no obligations to the landlord so far as the terms of the lease are concerned; in fact, he is the tenant of the lessee, not the tenant of the original grantor of the lease. It is important that you remember that, because I daresay, in after life, you will be called upon to advise as to lending money upon leasehold property. Leasehold property is now of very great value, especially in a city like London, or a place like the Metropolis. I cannot tell you what the value of leasehold property in the Metropolis is, but it is many, many millions. And when you are called upon to advise as to advancing money on leasehold property, you ought to bear in mind that you do not want to incur any liability, or those whom you are advising do not want to incur any liability, to the freeholder or reversioner, and, therefore, if you are going to advance money upon the security of a 99 years' lease, and there are 90 years unexpired, you will not take an assignment of that lease, that is, for the whole 90 years, because that will create privity of estate between the lender and the landlord, and entitle the landlord to sue him for any breach of the covenant in it. And the way that is got over is very simple indeed; an under-lease is taken from the person who wants to borrow the money, the lessee, for 99 years, less three days or ten days, and those ten days being still in the lessee, prevent privity of estate being created between the person who advances the money and the landlord. There is very often in a security of that kind a stipulation that the lessee shall hold those three or ten days, or whatever other short period it may be, as trustee for the lender, and dispose of those ten days in any way he may direct. So that in effect and in substance the lender gets the full benefit of the lessee's interest in the whole term without coming under any obligation to the landlord. If the property is allowed to go to rack and ruin the lender is not liable. Of course it is to his interest that the rent should be duly paid, and the property should be kept in repair, for otherwise the lease might be forfeited by the landlord.

There are two classes of covenants in a lease; those which do and those which do not run with the land, and to determine to which class any particular covenant belongs is a rather difficult branch of law. Covenants which run with the land are covenants which relate to the land in such a way that their benefit or burthen is capable of running with it. The rights and obligations under such covenants are transmissible on the one hand to the owner of the reversion, that is the landlord's interest in the property; and on the other hand to the assignee of the term, that is the lessee's interest in the property; but other covenants, those that do not relate to the land; for instance, a covenant to do something on some other land than that demised by the lease, would not run with the land. But if you want to know whether a particular covenant does or does not run with the land, I can only tell you you must look up the authorities. There is, at this very time, a case in the Privy Council, which has been argued for two days, involving the question whether a covenant to lay down a field of two acres in grass runs with the land, and the Privy Council has taken time to consider. But you ought to know that some covenants run with the land, and others do not. All the ordinary covenants, such as you generally find in a lease, do run with the land; but there are many covenants put into leases, in special cases, which do not run with the land, and, therefore, in a particular case you will do well to consult a solicitor.

In order to secure the performance of the obligations of the lessee to the lessor, there is contained in every well-drawn lease what is called a proviso for re-entry, that is, a stipulation in the lease that if the rent is not duly paid according to the terms of the lease, or, as it is often put, is not paid within twenty-one days after it becomes due, or if there be any other breach of covenant on the part of the lessee, the lessor may re-enter and take possession of the premises and put an end to the lease. Originally, full effect was given to such a proviso of re-entry. If a tenant committed a breach of covenant, however trivial or inadvertent, the landlord had the right at Common Law to bring an action of ejectment, and upon proof of the breach, he obtained judgment entitling him to possession of the property, however much it had improved in value. This right was one which might be, and was, used as an instrument of oppression. The Court of Chancery, in the course of time, upon the principle that the proviso, so far as it related to non-payment of the rent, was only a security for the payment of it, granted relief against a forfeiture for a breach of covenant to pay the rent upon the tenant paying the rent and all costs. And a Court of Equity was empowered, by Statute 22 & 23 Vict., c. 35, s. 4, to relieve against a forfeiture for breach of a covenant to insure, committed through accident, or mistake, or otherwise, without fraud or gross negligence. And under the Common Law Procedure Acts of 1852 and 1860, the Common Law Courts acquired powers similar to those of a Court of Equity to relieve against forfeitures for non-payment of rent and not insuring. Then we come to a very important Statute indeed, "The Conveyancing and Law of Property Act, 1881", the 14th section of which effected a revolution with regard to the proviso of re-entry. This section provides that (1) "A right of re-entry or forfeiture
" under any proviso or stipulation in a lease, for a breach of
" any covenant or condition in the lease, shall not be enforce-
" able by action, or otherwise, unless and until the lessor
" serves on the lessee a notice specifying the particular breach
" complained of, and, if the breach is capable of remedy,
" requiring the lessee to remedy the breach, and in any case
" requiring the lessee to make compensation in money for the
" breach, and the lessee fails within a reasonable time there-

" after to remedy the breach, if it is capable of remedy, and
" to make reasonable compensation in money to the satisfaction
" of the lessor for the breach."

(2) " Where a lessor is proceeding, by action or otherwise,
" to enforce such a right of re-entry or forfeiture, the lessee
" may, in the lessor's action, if any, or in any action brought
" by himself, apply to the Court for relief; and the Court may
" grant or refuse relief, as the Court, having regard to the
" proceedings and conduct of the parties under the foregoing
" provisions of this section, and to all the other circumstances,
" thinks fit; and in case of relief may grant it on such terms,
" if any, as to costs, expenses, damages, compensation, penalty,
" or otherwise, including the granting of an injunction to
" restrain any like breach in the future, as the Court, in the
" circumstances of each case, thinks fit."

(6) " This section does not extend—

(i) " To a covenant or condition against the assigning,
" underletting, parting with the possession, or
" disposing of the land leased; or to a condition for
" forfeiture on the bankruptcy of the lessee, or on the
" taking in execution of the lessee's interest; or

(ii) " In case of a mining lease, to a covenant or condition
" for allowing the lessor to have access to or inspect
" books, accounts, records, weighing machines or
" other things, or to enter or inspect the mine or the
" workings thereof."

The result of this legislation is, that a proviso of re-entry is now practically a security only for the performance by the lessee of his covenants. I daresay you are aware, gentlemen, that of recent years the policy of the Legislature has been, in certain cases, to prevent persons from contracting themselves out, as it is said, of the provisions of a Statute, and there is a provision, the 14th section of this Statute, that it shall apply to all leases, whether made before or after the commencement of the Act, and shall have effect notwithstanding any stipulation to the contrary. Any agreement by the parties to a lease that the provisions of the 14th section of "The Conveyancing and Law of Property Act, 1881", shall not apply to the lease, would be null and void. In other words, freedom of contract is restricted in that respect. I should here observe, that if relief from a forfeiture is not obtained before the landlord actually gets possession, either by entry or action, it cannot be granted under the Act afterwards. For instance, if the landlord brings an action and recovers possession in that action, the right to relief is gone, and the forfeiture is effectual, and the estate of the lessee, or the interest of the lessee, is at an end. And you will observe that the provisions of the 14th section apply to all leases whether made before or after the Act came into operation, but do not affect the law relating to re-entry, or forfeiture, or relief in case of non-payment of rent. That remains under the previous law under which a tenant could obtain relief against a forfeiture for non-payment of rent even after the lessor had obtained possession. Then there are some few exceptions to the operation to the Act—they are very few. The provisions of the 14th section of the Statute do not apply to a covenant or condition against the assigning, under-letting, parting with the possession, or disposing of the land leased. You should bear that in mind. If there is a covenant in the lease that the lessee will not assign, or under-let, or part with the possession of the demised premises, and does so, this Statute does not entitle him to relief from a forfeiture for so doing. Then there is another exception; in the case of a mining lease the Statute does not apply to a covenant or condition for allowing the lessor to have access to or inspect books, accounts, records, weighing machines, or other things, or to enter or inspect the mines or the workings thereof, and the provisions of the Statute did not affect a condition for forfeiture on the lessee's bankruptcy or on the taking in execution of his interest. This last exception is considerably qualified by "The Conveyancing and Law of Property Act, 1892", which provided that it should apply "only after one year from the date of the bankruptcy or "taking in execution, and provided the lessee's interest be "not sold within such one year." The effect of that is to prevent the landlord from deriving any benefit whatever from the lessee's bankruptcy, for if his interest is of any value, it will be sold by the trustee in bankruptcy. Before that Statute was passed, if a man became bankrupt the landlord, under a proviso of re-entry in the lease entitling him to re-enter on the bankruptcy of the lessee, had the right to re-enter, and, if he did, there was no right to relief against him, and the trustee for the creditors lost any benefit he might otherwise have derived from the lease. So the Legislature stepped in and enacted, that for one year after bankruptcy or execution the lessor should not exercise his right to re-enter, and then only if, in the meantime, the trustee in bankruptcy or the sheriff has not sold the interest of the bankrupt or the execution debtor, as the case may be. I have shown you what a very great inroad has been made upon the common law rights of landlords under their leases, and one cannot be sure that they will not be further restricted or otherwise affected by legislation. Now, with regard to that proviso of re-entry, whittled down as it is, you ought to know this, that at Common Law a proviso for re-entry was entire and indivisible. Upon this ground it was held that if the lessor once waived a breach of any covenant, he could not afterwards re-enter for a subsequent breach of the covenant under the proviso for re-entry. And upon the same ground it was held that the grantee of the reversion of part of the property comprised in the lease could not take advantage of the proviso for re-entry.

This is not now the law, for by Statute 23 and 24 Vic., c. 38, s. 6, it was provided that in future any actual waiver by the lessor in any particular instance of the benefit of any covenant or condition in any lease, should not be deemed of general waiver of the benefit of any such covenant or condition, unless an intention to that effect should appear. And by "The Conveyancing and Law of Property Act, 1881", section 12, it was provided that every condition or right of re-entry, and every other condition contained in a lease made after 1881, shall on the severance of the reversionary estate in the land leased be apportioned and remained annexed to the several parts of the reversionary estate so severed.

And by Sections 10 and 11 of the Act of 1881, it is provided that the benefit of the lessee's covenants and of every condition of re-entry and other conditions, and the obligations of the lessor's covenants, shall run with the reversion notwithstanding the severance of the reversionary estate.

It is now half-past six, gentlemen, and I have substantially got through the matter with which I propose to deal. There are some technicalities to which I have not referred, but I do not know that they are very material for your consideration. You should, however, know that a term can only be surrendered by deed, or by act and operation of law. I will give you an instance of a surrender by act and operation of law. If a tenant having a lease accepts a new lease from the reversioner for a term to begin at any time during the term granted by the first lease, his acceptance of the new lease operates as a surrender of the old lease by act and operation of law, because the tenant by accepting the new lease is estopped on precluding its validity, and it cannot be valid, the law says, that is a surrender by operation of law, unless the old lease is deemed to have been surrendered. And if a landlord accepts a new tenant and puts him in possession with the consent of the old tenant, that, too, is a surrender by operation of law of the old tenancy.

In conclusion, I would advise you to read the Conveyancing and Law of Property Acts of 1881 and 1882, from which you will learn a great deal about the law of Real Property, and also about the law with regard to leaseholds.

THE LAW OF REAL PROPERTY IN ENGLAND.

SIXTH LECTURE.

[*Delivered 23 March 1897.*]

WHAT I propose to consider with you this evening is a Mortgage on Land. A mortgage in its ordinary meaning is understood to be a conveyance of land, or any other property, for the purpose of securing the payment of money—generally, not always, borrowed money. Whatever may have been the original form of a mortgage of land in England, it, in the course of time, assumed a well-known form which is in use, substantially, without any very important variation, at the present day, and that form of mortgage has received interpretation both in Courts of Law and in Courts of Equity. And in consequence of the action of one Court not being the same as the other, law not being equity, and equity not being law, the position of parties to a mortgage at law and in equity are different. The ordinary form of mortgage is the conveyance of land from one person, called the mortgagor, to another person, called the mortgagee, for an estate in fee or other estate, upon the conditions that it shall be re-conveyed if the mortgage money is paid on a certain day. That is when A, the owner of an estate, mortgages it to B, he conveys the estate to B subject to the condition that if A pay the mortgage money to B on a certain day, B shall re-convey the estate to A; but at law A must tender the money on the specified day, because in the Common

Law Courts the tendency always was to hold persons to the strict terms of their bargains, and they held that if the money was not paid on that day, the condition was at an end; so that if A did not tender the mortgage money on the prescribed day he lost, at law, all right to have that property re-conveyed to him. A could not go the next day and say, "Here is your money B; re-transfer to me my estate", for at law B could say, "No, the day was fixed for you to pay the money, you "did not pay it on the day fixed, and I am not bound, "according to the strict terms of the mortgage, to re-convey "the property to you upon payment of the money after that "day." That was exactly the position at law of the mortgagor and the mortgagee with respect to the mortgaged property. But in the course of time, and no one seems to know exactly how it came about, or when it came about exactly, but it did come about, that a Court of Equity interfered and exercised its jurisdiction to relieve the mortgagor, from the consequences of his not having tendered the money on the prescribed day. And it was held in equity that the mortgagor was entitled, after the day fixed for the payment of the mortgage money, to have the mortgaged property re-conveyed to him upon his paying the mortgage money and interest, and all costs. Notwithstanding that he had lost his right, at law, to redeem the property, it was held that he had, in equity, the right so to do, and that was called his "equity of redemption." It is absolutely essential for you, gentlemen, to grasp those simple elements of the position of the mortgagor and the mortgagee, before you can in any way understand the real position of the parties. You will see that at law when the time had passed entitling the mortgagee to redeem at law the legal estate in the property vested for ever in the mortgagee, and the mortgagor had no right in respect of it, equity left the legal estate where it was, but declared that the mortgagor should have a right in Equity to compel the mortgagor to convey that estate to the mortgagee upon the payment of all that was due upon the security, the principal and interest, and what were called expenses, but which we now call costs. The result of that legal position was that the mortgagor had no legal rights after the prescribed day if he did not pay the money on the prescribed day, because the legal estate then became vested in the mortgagee. The mortgagee could, at law, turn him out of possession. If the mortgagee did not turn the mortgagor out of possession, the mortgagor remained in as a tenant on sufferance. You will remember I explained to you, quite shortly, the other day what a tenant on sufferance was. It was the smallest tenancy a man could have. When the mortgagee demanded possession and the mortgagor would not give it up, he might bring an action against the mortgagor to recover possession, and with that right equity has never interfered. So that at the present day the mortgagee can, at any moment, when the legal condition in the mortgage for the payment of money on the prescribed day has not been observed, turn out the mortgagor. It is not advisable for the mortgagee to do that unless he is absolutely forced to do so by circumstances, matters of business, which it is not necessary for me to enter into here, because equity makes a mortgagee who takes possession of mortgaged property strictly account for his dealings with the property; and the account required of a mortgagee in possession is so strict and so onerous, that generally it is found, as a matter of business, better for a mortgagee not to take actual possession of the property. He leaves the mortgagor, generally speaking, in possession of the property, and does not exercise the legal right which he has to turn him out. But still, that is his right. The mortgagee has the legal estate, he has the seisin, which I have explained to you before, and he can turn the mortgagor out if he thinks fit to do so; and equity, as I said, never interfered with that right. You will find in Joshua Williams, at page 510, a very clear and concise explanation of the Rights of a Mortgagor and a Mortgagee at Law and in equity, and I do not think I can do better than read it to you.

"For what is now called a mortgage of land, is the "conveyance thereof from one to another for an estate in fee, or "other estate, which is to be determined, or re-conveyed, on "condition of the payment of money by the former on a "certain day. And, at law, if the condition be broken by "non-payment of the money at the appointed time, the estate "of the person to whom the land was so conveyed, becomes "absolute, or discharged from the condition. So that, at law, "he will be entitled to hold the land, as his own, for all the "estate limited to him. For, in the Courts of Law, the parties "were held to the terms of their bargain, by which the land "was to be redeemed on a certain day, or, if not, to be for- "feited by the debtor. This strict construction of a mortgage

"appears to have prevailed for a long time. But, at length,
"a mortgagor who had failed to pay on the appointed day,
"obtained relief in the Court of Chancery against the for-
"feiture, which he had so incurred. It is not very clear when,
"or on what ground, this equitable jurisdiction was first
"exercised. But in the reign of Charles I. it was established
"as equity that a mortgagor should be allowed to redeem his
"estate after the legal day of payment had gone by; and the
"Court of Chancery, on application by the mortgagor, after
"the time fixed for redemption had elapsed, would decree
"that the mortgagee should, on re-payment of all that was
"due to him, re-convey the estate to the mortgagor.

"The main principles of equity, in respect of the redemp-
"tion of mortgages, were settled in the reign of Charles II.,
"about the time when modern equity began to take shape as
"a system of rules, resting upon principles evolved from
"precedent. The first principle established was that of the
"mortgagor's equity of redemption—that is, that the
"mortgagor, or anyone standing in his place, shall be admitted
"in equity to redeem a mortgage, after the day fixed by the
"contract for redemption is gone by, and the estate has
"become forfeited at law. It was further laid down as a
"general rule, subject to very few exceptions, that wherever
"a conveyance of an estate is originally intended as a security
"for money, whether this intention appear from the deed
"itself, or by any other instrument, or even by parol evidence,
"it is always considered in equity as a mortgage and redeem-
"able." I want to explain that to you by an example.
Suppose A conveys an estate absolutely to B, and there is
nothing whatever in the instrument to show that it is intended
to be a mortgage, or security for a debt, yet A can go into a
Court of Equity, in the face of such a deed as that, and show
that the real intention of the parties was to create a security
for a debt, and not to convey the property absolutely, and this
may be shown by some other writing, or, as Joshua Williams
says, by "parol evidence", that is, by word of mouth; and
upon being satisfied, by documentary or other evidence, that
such was the real intention of the parties, a Court of Equity
will give effect to it by holding that B is under an obligation
to re-convey the estate to A, from whom he received it, upon
payment of the money for which the estate was really held as
security. In short, equity looks at the real intention and

object of the parties, and not at the form of the deed in such a case as I have put to you,—" even though there is an " express agreement of the parties that it shall not be redeem- " able." That is, a Court of Equity, when the real transaction is, say, a loan of money upon the security of the conveyance of an estate, will not allow the mortgagee to say, " The " mortgagor agreed with me that he should not have the right " in equity to redeem the property upon payment of all that " was due to me." Equity does not listen to such an agree- ment as that, nor will it listen to an agreement " that the " right of redemption be confined to a particular time or to a " particular description of persons. In other words, it was " established that no agreement of the parties to a mortgage " that the mortgage should not be redeemable according to " the rules of equity, should have any effect in equity." Now you will understand a common phrase. "This principle is " shortly summed up in the phrase, ' once a mortgage, always " a mortgage.' Furthermore, it was held that, in equity, the " right of the mortgagee was to the money secured, and he " held the land only as security for his money." You see the importance of that rule of equity. The Courts of Equity did not regard the mortgagee—that is, the person who had lent the money—as the owner of the estate; they regarded him only as a person having a charge upon the estate. The Courts of Equity said the mortgagor in equity still remains the owner of the estate, but subject to the charge; and the result of that was that the equity of redemption was looked upon by Courts of Equity as an estate in land. I have explained to you that, when the condition was broken at law, the estate passed absolutely to the mortgagee, but equity said " No, that may be law, and we will recognize that, at law, the " mortgagee has the legal estate, but we will say in equity " that the mortgagor is really the owner of the estate, though " he has not got the legal estate, and we will treat the mort- " gagor's equity of redemption as an equitable estate in fee " simple, fee tail, or otherwise, as the case may be, subject " in equity to the same incidents as an estate of the same " description would be subject at law; we will allow him to " mortgage his property over again, we will recognize that the " first mortgagee has got the legal estate, but in equity we " will recognize the right of the mortgagor to deal with his " estate just as if he had not mortgaged it, but subject to the "charge already created by the first mortgage." It is important always to bear in mind that Courts of Equity recognize the legal estate, and how they recognize it, and especially when I come to show you what happens when a man has mortgaged his property more than once. The result was, that the legal estate in the property being in the mortgagee, on his death it passed to his heirs, devisees, or other persons who would take the legal estate if he were the real owner of the property, although in equity they will be trustees of the estate for the mortgagor. If it is an estate in fee simple, it goes to the heir if the mortgagee dies intestate, or if he has devised it by his will, it goes to the devisee under his will. That was the position of things until very recently, until the year 1881; and then an Act of Parliament, the Conveyancing and Real Property Amendment Act of 1881, was passed, enacting that on the death of a mortgagee of any freehold estate of inheritance, his estate, notwithstanding any testamentary disposition, should pass to the personal representatives of the mortgagee. So that, since that Act, instead of the legal estate passing to the heir or devisee of the mortgagee, it passes to his executors or administrators. The reason for that you will understand in a moment. In Equity, as I have told you, it was held that the mortgagee's right was only to payment of the money for the payment of which he held the estate as security, and the right to the money passed as personal estate to the executors of the mortgagee. And until that Act was passed the mortgaged estate passed to the heir of the mortgagee, and the right to the money secured by the mortgage passed to his executors or administrators—the personal representatives. This extremely inconvenient state of things was remedied by the Act, so that at the present time the mortgaged estate and the right to payment of the mortgage money pass to the same persons— the executor or administrators of the mortgagee. Joshua Williams goes on to say this: " Consequently, in equity the " mortgagor was regarded as the owner of the mortgaged " land, subject only to the mortgagee's charge, and the " mortgagor's equity of redemption was treated as an " equitable estate in the land of the same nature as other " equitable estates." That is shortly putting what I have endeavoured to explain to you at greater length. " These " principles of equity became so well settled and understood "that no substantial change was made in the usual form of "a mortgage." You will remember that I have explained to you that the usual form of a mortgage is a conveyance by A to B, with a proviso or condition that upon payment of the money on a certain day the mortgagee shall re-convey that property to the mortgagor. "And at the present day" —continuing Joshua Williams—"and at the present day, "when the repayment of a loan of money is to be secured by "a mortgage of land, the land is granted to the creditor in "fee simple"—to take the case of a mortgage in fee simple— "with a proviso for re-conveyance of the land to the debtor "in fee on payment of the principal sum with interest at a "specified rate on a certain day, usually six months after the "date of the mortgage deed." That is the simplest form of mortgage. You may vary that in any way you please, but substantially every mortgage is in that form; the estate is conveyed absolutely to the mortgagee in the event of the mortgagor not redeeming it on a certain day, six months, as Joshua Williams says, generally, but it may be any other time, it may be twelve months, there is nothing magical in the period. "By the same deed the mortgagor generally "enters into a personal covenant to pay principal and interest "on the day appointed for re-conveyance, and also to continue "to pay interest at the same rate in case of failure to redeem "at the appointed time." You see there is a covenant by the mortgagor to pay to the mortgagee the principal sum and interest, say for six months, and if he does not pay the principal on that day, after that day to go on paying interest at an agreed rate until actual payment. Some mortgages, unfortunately, through carelessness, are drawn without a covenant for the payment of interest afterwards. That leads to great difficulty. So that if ever you have to deal with mortgages, just see that the covenant expressly provides for the payment of interest at the agreed rate until payment of the principal, for if it does not, the mortgagee may be entitled only to interest in equity, which may be 4 per-cent, while the mortgage interest may be 6 per-cent—"Until the six months "are past, the mortgagor has a legal right to redeem the "land on the day named for repayment; but if he should "allow that day to pass without payment or tender of the "amount due, the mortgagee's estate will become absolute at "law, and the mortgagor will have no right to the land "save his equity of redemption. Mortgages are generally "employed as permanent investments of money, and there "is rarely any intention on either side that the loan should be "repaid in six months."—A very common clause in a mortgage is that the loan shall not be payable for two, three, four, five years, or any period the parties may agree upon. Persons investing money on mortgage do not want to be repaid in six months and have to look out for new investments. Their object generally is a permanent investment. By permanent, I do not mean for ever, but for a considerable period. "Nevertheless, so well understood is the construction "placed upon a mortgage in equity, so firmly established is "the mortgagor's right to redeem after the time fixed for "payment has gone by, that mortgage deeds are always "drawn in the form indicated. All that is expressed is "an immediate conveyance of the land to the mortgagee, "and the agreement for re-conveyance on payment six "months after; and the real intention of the parties is "left to be carried out by the operation of the rules "of equity." Let us now, gentlemen, consider what are the rights of the parties to a mortgage. In the first place let us consider the position of the mortgagor. As I have told you, he is at law in no better position than a tenant on sufferance—the mortgagee may turn him out at any moment. And one of the consequences of the legal estate passing from the mortgagor to the mortgagee absolutely when the condition for the re-payment of the money has been broken, was that the mortgagor could not afterwards grant any legal estate to anyone else. For instance, he could not lease the property, because he could not convey a term of years to any one. If the mortgagor did grant a lease, the mortgagee, notwithstanding the lease, might claim to be put in possession of the property, and it would be no answer for the lessee in possession to say "Oh, but I hold a lease from the mortgagor." The mortgagee would reply "He had no power to grant you that lease, you must go out." And that was the state of things, until an Act, which did a very great deal in the way of altering the rights of parties, was passed, the Conveyancing Act of 1881. Under that Act the mortgagor, while in possession, has power, by virtue of that Act, to make an agricultural or occupation lease for any term not exceeding 21 years, or a building lease for any term not exceeding 99 years upon the conditions defined in the Act. You see that power is given to the mortgagor so long as the mortgagee has not exercised his right to turn him out, so that if the mortgagor is in possession, he can grant these leases, but he could not grant them if he had been turned out by the mortgagee. If the mortgagee waits to take possession until the mortgagor has granted a lease of that kind, then he must take possession, or his right to possession would be subject to the right of a lessee to whom a lease had been granted under the provisions of that Act. Another consequence of the legal estate being in a mortgagee was that at law the mortgagor not having the legal estate could not maintain any action for any trespass or damage done to the property. It was not his at law. He could not bring an action of ejectment against a person to whom he had let the property; he could not do anything. He had always to bring his action in the name of the mortgagor in whom the legal estate was; but by the Judicature Act of 1873, it was enacted that where a mortgagor remained in possession he might maintain an action in his own name in respect of any trespass or wrong done to the property. The Judicature Act does not give any power of leasing, but it gives the mortgagor the right to bring actions, as if he were possessed of the legal estate, with regard to trespasses and injury done to property. For instance, if a tree was cut down by a wrong-doer the mortgagor formerly could not complain. Now he can; he can bring an action in his own name; formerly he had to obtain the leave of the mortgagee to bring an action in the name of the mortgagee, giving the mortgagee an indemnity against the costs of action. Now he can recover possession and maintain rights of possession against any person under that Act. One peculiarity of the mortgagor's position was, if a man had devised his mortgaged estate to any one, the debt that was charged on the mortgaged estate was payable out of his general assets, and the person to whom he had left the estate took the estate with the right to have the mortgaged debt paid out of the general assets of the estate. That was thought not really to be in accordance with the intention of most testators, and an Act was passed in 1854, commonly called Locke King's Act, which reversed the law in that respect, and said that unless there was something in the will to the contrary a person to whom an estate was devised, subject to a mortgage, should take that estate subject to the mortgage, and should not have the right to have the mortgage discharged out of the general assets of the testator. At the present time, if there be nothing in the will to the contrary, and the mortgaged estate is devised to anyone, or goes to an heir, he takes it subject to the mortgage, and has to pay the debt himself if he wishes to clear the estate; but that right, or that condition of things does not in any way affect the right of the mortgagee to have his money paid by the executors. Because, if you will remember, I have told you that in the form of mortgage in general use there was a covenant by the mortgagor to pay the mortgage money to the mortgagee, and when the mortgagor dies the obligation under the covenant passes to the mortgagor's executors or administrators. But if they are called upon to pay, and the heir or devisee does not pay and exonerate them, they would have a remedy against the heir or devisee in respect of the payment made by them under their obligation under the covenant. So far with regard to the mortgagor's position. I think I have stated all the principle matters with regard to him. Now let us see what the position of the mortgagee is. The mortgagee, I have already told you, is the owner of the legal estate, but let us consider what his rights are, bearing in mind that in equity he is regarded as a person who has only a charge upon the estate, which he may make available in certain ways. Now, the first thing a mortgagee may do, he may sue the mortgagor, or his personal representatives, upon the express covenant in the mortgage for the payment of the mortgage money and interest, or upon any other expressed covenant. The next thing he may do is, in legal language, to foreclose the mortgage. To understand what is meant by foreclosing, you will remember that the mortgagor has an equity of redemption, and you should know that the mortgagee may go to a Court of Equity and say " compel the mortgagor to pay " me what he owes me, or extinguish his equity of redemp- " tion "; and a mortgagee has the right under his mortgage, when default has been made in payment of mortgage-money, to go to a Court of Equity and say this, " Will you fix " a day for the payment of the money, and if the money is not " paid on that day, will you extinguish the right of the " mortgagor at any future time to redeem the property ? " And the Court will, in an action brought by the mortgagee

against the mortgagor, name a day for the payment of the money. It may be three months, I think it is usually six months, and then if the money is not paid on that day a decree will be made by the Court at the instance of the mortgagee foreclosing, as it is called, the equity of redemption; that is to say in effect declaring that from and after that day the property shall be absolutely, in equity as well as in law, the property of the mortgagee. That is called foreclosure, and that is a right incident to every mortgage. That can only be done by the Court; a mortgagee cannot do that himself, he must have a decree, and the law is quite shortly stated at page 520 of Joshua Williams. " To obtain foreclosure, it
" will be necessary for the mortgagee to take proceedings
" against the mortgagor in the Chancery Division of the High
" Court, claiming that an account may be taken of the
" principal and interest due to him, and that the mortgagor
" may be directed to pay the same with costs, by the day to be
" appointed by the Court, and that in default thereof he may
" be foreclosed his equity of redemption. A day is then fixed
" by the Court for payment; which day, however, may, on
" the application of the mortgagor, good reason being shown,
" be postponed for a time. Or, if the mortgagor should be
" ready to make repayment, before the cause is brought to
" a hearing, he may do so at any time previously, on making
" proper application to the Court, admitting the title of the
" mortgagee to the money and interest. If, however, on the
" day ultimately fixed by the Court, the money should not be
" forthcoming, an order will be made that the debtor do
" thenceforth stand absolutely foreclosed from all equity of
" redemption in the mortgaged premises. Such an order is
" considered to vest in the mortgagee for the first time the
" full beneficial title to the mortgaged land." That is, he becomes not only what the law said he was, the owner of the legal estate, but he was in equity entitled to the whole beneficial interest in that land upon that decree being made, and from that moment, and he will be entitled thereafter to keep and deal with it as his own. " The Court may now order
" a sale of the mortgaged property in foreclosure proceedings,
" instead of foreclosure." And it will generally do so, I may say, at the instance of the mortgagor, because they do not want to deprive him of his property if it is worth sufficient to pay the debt. On the other hand, they do not want to give

the mortgagee any profit from the transaction. All the mortgagee, in equity, is really entitled to, and regarded as entitled to, is the principal money and his interest and costs; as long as he gets that, the Court of Equity thinks he gets all he is entitled to. And I mentioned another right of the mortgagee, and I will refer to it again, that is the right of the mortgagee to take possession of the estate and receive the rents and profits; but, as I said just now, he will have to give a very strict account of what he receives and what he does with the property. Then there is another right which a mortgagee has. Before the Conveyancing Act of 1881, in every mortgage, speaking generally, there was inserted a power of sale. That is to say, the mortgagee, by the express terms of the deed, had a power to sell the mortgaged property for the estate conveyed to him upon default being made in payment of the principal or interest, and he might exercise that power of sale. And, as he had in him the legal estate, he could convey that to anyone, and if he sold the property, the person who bought the property acquired a good title to it, but the money received by the mortgagee in respect of the sale of the estate under the power remained subject to all the same trusts and equities as the estate did in his hands, and therefore if he sold for more than the principal, interest and costs, including the costs of sale, he would be a trustee of the surplus for the mortgagor and bound to hand it over to him. He could not make a profit out of the transaction; although he could give a title to the purchaser, he could not make a profit, and equity said, you shall hold the money on the same terms as you held the estate. Now it is not necessary to insert a power of sale in the mortgage, because under the Conveyancing Act every mortgage has incorporated in it, by virtue of the act, a power of sale in certain events, and the events provided are those people would wish it to provide for, and the result is that since the act, a mortgage is generally a shorter document that it was before. I should like to read to you the effect of the section in that Act of 1881, the Conveyancing Act. " By the latter Act, a mortgagee of any " property, under a mortgage made by deed after the year " 1881, has a power of sale, when the mortgage money has " become due, to the same extent as if the power had been " expressly conferred by the mortgage deed. But a mortgagee " shall not exercise this statutory power of sale unless and

" until notice requiring payment of the mortgage money has
" been served on the mortgagor, or one of several mortgagors,
" and default has been made in payment of the mortgage
" money, or part thereof, for three months after service of
" such notice; or some interest under the mortgage is in
" arrear and unpaid for two months after becoming due; or
" thirdly, there has been a breach of some provision contained
" in the mortgage deed, or in the Act and on the part of the
" mortgagor, or of some person concurring in making the
" mortgage, to be observed or performed, other than and
" besides a covenant for payment of the mortgage money or
" interest thereon." So that in any of those cases after
the lapse of the prescribed time under the statute, a mortgagee
may sell the mortgaged property for the estate only which
has been conveyed to him. "Power is expressly given by the
" Act to a mortgagee exercising his statutory power of sale
" to convey the property sold by deed for such estate and
" interest therein as is the subject of the mortgage, freed from
" all estates, interests and rights, to which the mortgage has
" priority." So that whatever the mortgagor may have done
subsequent to the mortgage, the purchaser of the estate from
the mortgagee under the power of sale is not affected. "The
" proper application of the purchase-money by the mortgagee
" is also provided for. Where a conveyance is made in
" professed exercise of the power of sale conferred by the Act,
" the title of the purchaser is not to be impeachable on the
" ground that no case had arisen to authorize the sales"; that
means this, the purchaser is not bound to see that the
conditions prescribed by the Act have happened, he takes a
a good title. "But any person damnified by an unauthorized,
" or improper, or irregular exercise of the power is to have
" his remedy in damages against the person exercising the
" power." If the mortgagee wrongfully exercises that power,
the exercise of the power stands, but if he has done so wrongfully he is liable to the mortgagor for any damages he may
have sustained by reason of the mortgagee having sold the
property improperly. "All these statutory provisions respect-
" ing a mortgagee's power of sale may be varied or extended,
" or entirely excluded by the terms of the mortgage deed.
" It is now usual in practice to rely upon the statutory
" power of sale instead of inserting express powers for the
" same purpose in mortgage deeds." I think I mentioned to

you on a previous occasion the great length to which our documents of title and deeds of all kinds was carried was due to this, that solicitors were paid by the length of the document, and they took care that they were not too short; but now a solicitor is paid by scale fee, and the result is nobody has any pecuniary interest in making a deed any longer than is necessary to carry out the object in view. Now there is another important right of a mortgagee, and that is to appoint a Receiver. If a mortgagee goes into possession himself, he has to account in the strict way I have mentioned, so that very very rarely, in practice, he goes into possession. But what he does is, he applies to the Court to appoint, or under the Statute appoints, a Receiver. "The same Conveyancing Act contains " provisions enabling a mortgagee under a mortgage made by " deed after 1881, in the absence of any stipulation to the " contrary, to appoint a Receiver of the income of mortgaged " property, but not before his statutory power of sale shall " become exercisable." That is to say, when a mortgagee has the right to sell the property, he may find that he cannot sell it, even for enough to cover the amount of the mortgage debt, but yet the property may be producing sufficient to keep down the interest on the mortgage, and perhaps leave something over, and in such a case the mortgagee may instead of selling appoint a Receiver of the rents and profits. In such cases, it is for the mortgagee to determine what he will do; what he should do is not a question of law, it is a matter of business. Will it be better to sell the property at a sacrifice now, or to hold on in the hope of better times when the property will sell for sufficient to pay the whole of the debt? When the mortgagee decides to hold on, the best course for him to adopt is to appoint a Receiver, and then the Receiver applies the income of the property in keeping down the interest on the mortgage. I cannot assist you in determining what in a particular case the mortgagee should do; all I can say is, all the circumstances should be taken into consideration. I am only here to explain the rights of mortgagees, and, as I have said, one of their rights is to have a Receiver appointed of the income, and then the Receiver has to account for that income to the persons interested. " A mortgagee in possession under " a mortgage made after 1881 is also empowered by the same " Act, in the absence of any stipulation to the contrary, to " grant the same leases as the mortgagor in possession." I told you that under the Act of 1881 the mortgagor, so long as he remains in possession, was entitled to grant leases under the Act, although he had no legal estate in the property. And this Act also empowers the mortgagee who has taken possession to grant such leases as the mortgagor himself, if he had remained in possession, might under the Acts have granted. If a mortgagee now takes possession he is not bound to keep it in his own hands; if it is a farm he is not bound to farm it; he may let it. "But, except under the " statutory or an express power of leasing, a mortgagee of " land is unable, before foreclosure, to make a lease, which " will be unconditionally binding on the mortgagor." That is stated very shortly there. But you should know why that is. The mortgagee cannot do anything that would deprive the mortgagor of his right of redemption, and if a mortgagee had power to grant leases he might grant a lease for a thousand years, and there would be a lessee in for a thousand years when the mortgagor came to redeem his property. Therefore the law does not allow him to do that; he must keep the equity of redemption free for the mortgagor. "If the " mortgagor wish to pay off the mortgage after the day fixed " for payment is passed, he must, as a rule, give to the " mortgagee six calendar months' previous notice in writing." That is an important matter. You must remember that; the mortgagor has not the right in equity to come at any moment and say: "There is your money, there is the interest up to to-day, re-convey to me my estate"; he must give six months' notice, or he can pay six months' interest. If he comes with all the money due for principal and interest and six months' interest in lieu of notice, he can then and there require the mortgagee to re-convey the property to him. So that if anybody comes to you to redeem a mortgage suddenly, and he says, "Here is your money, I want my deeds", you must say, "No, we must have notice." And then, very often, rather than wait the six months, the mortgagor will come to terms, and rightly come to terms, because it is generally inconvenient to the mortgagee to have a large sum of money put into his hands without previous notice, and have to find a new investment for it, especially in these days, when it is so difficult to find investments which will produce a moderate interest. " If the mortgagor wished " to pay off the mortgage after the day fixed for payment is

"passed, he must, as a rule, give to the mortgagee six
"calendar months' previous notice in writing of his intention
"to do so, and must punctually pay or tender the money at
"the expiration of the notice. For if the money should not
"be then ready to be paid, the mortgagee will be entitled to
"fresh notice, as it is considered reasonable that he should
"have time afforded him to look out for another investment."
This is the reason of the rule. "A mortgagor is, however,
"entitled, if he think fit, to pay the mortgagee six months'
"interest in advance in lieu of notice. When the mortgagor
"has duly paid or tendered the money due from him, either
"after proper notice, or with due interest in advance instead,
"he will be entitled to require the mortgagee to execute at
"his expense"—that is, the mortgagor's expense—"a re-con-
"veyance of the legal estate in the mortgaged land. And to
"enforce this right, or otherwise duly to enforce his equity of
"redemption, he may take proceedings for redemption in
"the Chancery Division against the mortgagee." That is,
suppose the mortgagee refuses to convey the property to the
mortgagor, he can bring an action in the Chancery Division
of the High Court to compel the mortgagee to re-convey to
him the legal estate, of course subject to the payment of what
is due on the mortgage; and even in these proceedings the
Court, instead of ordering redemption, may order a sale. I
won't trouble you, gentlemen, with the Statute of Limitations,
or its bearings upon the rights of mortgagor and mortgagee.
It is not a matter peculiar to mortgagor and mortgagee, and
I have not had time, in the course of my lectures, to explain
the Statute of Limitations. You may take it shortly, any
right to recover lands is lost after twelve years, so that if you
allow the mortgagor not to pay his principal money or any
interest on it for twelve years, if you let things slide for
twelve years, you lose all your rights, even your rights to sue
upon the covenant to pay. Therefore, as a matter of law as
well as a matter of business, it is just as well to keep your
mortgagor up to the mark, and do not let him run into your
debt too long, or if you do, get him to give you an
acknowledgment so as to take the case out of the Statute.
There are two matters with regard to mortgagees that are not
so important now as they were, but you must, I think, have a
sufficient knowledge of them, and they are what are called
"the doctrine of tacking" and "the doctrine of the

consolidation of securities," and having explained to you the difference between the position at law and in equity of the parties you will be able to understand now what is meant by "tacking." It is very shortly stated in Joshua Williams at page 533: "As we have seen," he says, "the " equity of redemption belonging to the mortgagor may again " be mortgaged by him; this may be either to the former " mortgagee by way of further charge, or to some other " person. In order to prevent frauds by clandestine " mortgages, it is provided by an Act of William and Mary " that a person twice mortgaging the same lands, without " discovering the former mortgage to the second mortgagee, " shall lose his equity of redemption." I may tell you, gentlemen, it is downright fraud for a man to mortgage his property to A and then to mortgage it again to B without telling B of the first mortgage. " Unfortunately, however, in " such cases the equity of redemption, after payment of both " mortgages, is generally worth nothing. And if the " mortgagor should again mortgage the lands to a third " person, the Act will not deprive such third mortgagee of his " right to redeem the two former mortgages. When lands " are mortgaged, as occasionally happens, to several persons, " each ignorant of the security granted to the other, questions " generally arise as to the priority of the various charges. " Such cases frequently illustrate the advantage of a legal " proprietary right, which avails against all the world, over an " equitable right which avails not against purchasers for value " without notice. Thus the claim of a mortgagee who has " obtained the legal estate, will take precedence over any " previous equitable charge, of which he had no notice, as " well as over subsequent charges." Take a common case. Suppose a man has deposited his deeds with a banker for an advance, and somehow or other the banker trusts him with those deeds, and he executes a legal mortgage of the property to which those deeds relate. That mortgagee having got the legal estate is regarded in equity as having a prior right to the banker, although the banker's equitable mortgage was prior in time. Thus the claim of a mortgagee who has obtained the legal estate will take precedence over any previous equitable charge of which he had no notice, for in equity notice affects the conscience, and in equity a man is not allowed to derive any benefit from doing what he knows to be

wrong, in short to keep an estate obtained by fraud. "And
" nothing short of connivance in fraud will deprive him of this
" advantage: though he may be postponed to a subsequent
" charge created with his authority, as where he gives up the
" title deeds that money may be raised on a deposit of them.
" So if a mortgagee having the legal estate makes a further
" advance without notice of an intermediate mortgage, he
" has a first charge on the lands for the whole amount of
" his advances, which must be satisfied before the second
" mortgagee can receive anything thereout." Let me
illustrate that to you. A, the owner of an estate, mortgages
it to B to secure a thousand pounds, and after that,
without telling the first mortgagee what he is doing, he
mortgages it to C, say for two thousand pounds, then he
goes to the first mortgagee and says, "I wish you would
let me have some more money," and he gets a further
advance. Then the first mortgagee, having got the legal
estate, and if he does not know of the second mortgage,
he can add that further advance on to the mortgage money
due to him, or payable to him, or secured to him by the first
mortgage, and in that way the second mortgagee might get
nothing, because when you add the further advance on to the
original advance, it may exceed or possibly amount, at all
events, to the full value of the estate, in which event the
second mortgagee would get nothing. "And if a third or
" subsequent mortgagee, who had no notice when he took his
" security of any but a first mortgage, can procure a transfer
" to himself of the first mortgagee's legal estate, he may
" tack, as it is said, his own mortgage to the first, and so
" postpone any intermediate incumbrancer." That is stated
very shortly, but if I give you an example you will understand
it at once. We will take the same case that I put just now,
with the exception of a further advance. We will take a
mortgage by the owner of property to A, then he obtains a
further advance from B upon the security of a second
mortgage, then he goes to C and obtains a third sum of
money from C, but without letting C know when C parts with
his money that there is a second mortgage on the estate; he
only discloses the first mortgage, that is generally known,
because when a man comes to borrow money you say to him
" where are your deeds?" "Well," he says, "I have
mortgaged my property already to A, he has the deeds."

You go to A's solicitor, who, we will suppose, knows nothing about the second mortgage, so that it is quite possible for a man to mortgage his estate a third time without disclosing the second mortgage. Well, if the third mortgagee has advanced his money in ignorance of the second mortgage, and after he has done so he discovers the second mortgage, he may go to the first mortgagee and say to him "I'll buy your mortgage, "you're on only for a thousand pounds, the estate is well "worth a thousand, here am I for ten thousand," or any number you like. He can go to the first mortgagee and say "I'll buy your mortgage if you will transfer it to me." If the first mortagee agrees to do so, and transfers his mortgage to the third mortgagee, the law says the third mortgagee may tack his mortgage on to the first, that is called the equitable doctrine of tacking. It is founded upon the principle that he has got the legal estate honestly. That is, when he advanced his money he did not know of the second mortgage, and his conscience is not affected by his having afterwards obtained that knowledge, and he may get the legal estate if he can ; and if he does he puts the first and the third mortgages together, and so squeezes out the middle man, and that is called tacking. It is one of the matters with regard to mortgages which is extremely important in practice, because it leads one to say this—one will very rarely have anything to do with a second mortgage—"If you cannot give me the legal estate, I won't have anything to do with you." Now, that is the doctrine of tacking, that whoever can get the legal estate honestly takes the precedence, or, as lawyers say, priority over an equitable mortgage of which he had no notice. Now, the doctrine of the consolidation of securities is this: It is a matter that you must really have in your minds in business; it is an important matter in business. There is one case in which the rules of equity singularly and, as Joshua Williams thought, unduly favoured the mortgagee, and it is this: "If one person should have mortgaged lands to another "for a sum of money, and subsequently have mortgaged other "lands to the same person for another sum of money, the "mortgagee was placed by the rules of equity in the same "favourable position as if the whole of the lands had been "mortgaged to him for the sum total of the money advanced." Now an example will show you what that means at once. A has an estate in Yorkshire called Whiteacre, and he has an estate in Middlesex called Blackacre. He first mortgages, say to an insurance company, his Yorkshire estate, and he then mortgages to the same insurance company his Middlesex estate. Equity says he shall not redeem either of those estates without redeeming both. That is the doctrine of the consolidation of securities. That is the simplest case I can put. " The mortgagor could not redeem either mortgage after it " has become absolute at law without also redeeming the " other; and the mortgagee might enforce the payment of " the whole of the principal and interest due to him on both " mortgages out of the lands comprised in either." You see why it is important. The lands in Middlesex may be insufficient to satisfy the mortgage debt on those lands, and in the case I put the insurance company can say, "There is this " Yorkshire estate, it is mortgaged to us for very much less " than the value of it, and if we sell the Yorkshire estate it " will be sufficient to pay the Yorkshire mortgage and the " Middlesex mortgage," and in equity they have the right to do so. " This rule, known as the doctrine of consolidation of " securities, was extended to the case of mortgages of different " lands made to different persons by the same mortgagor " becoming vested by transfer in the same mortgagee." That means this, gentlemen, in the case I put to you both mortgages were to the same insurance company. But suppose the Yorkshire mortgage was to X Insurance Company and the Middlesex mortgage was to Y Insurance Company, then the X Insurance Company might obtain a transfer of the mortgage from the Y Insurance Company, and then the X Insurance Company would have the right to consolidate just the same as if the X Insurance Company had originally been the mortgagee of both estates; so that the rule is that whether the mortgaged estates are vested in the same person originally or by transfer, the right to consolidate arises. " In " such a case it was held that the mortgagee, who had taken a " transfer of the different mortgages, might consolidate all his " securities as against the original mortgagor, or his assignee " of the equity of redemption of the whole of the lands." Even against his assignee. " But as against an assignee of the " equity of redemption of part only of the lands so mortgaged, " the mortgagee could not consolidate his securities unless he " should have acquired the right of consolidation previously " to the assignment of the equity of redemption. The right

" of consolidation arose at the time when two or more
" mortgages made by the same mortgagor, or any of his
" predecessors in title, became vested in the same mortgagee
" and absolute at law." Now comes the Statute, gentlemen,
to which I have so often called your attention as affecting the
rights of parties with respect to land—the Act of 1881—and
this is the effect of it : " The right of a mortgagee to
" consolidate his securities is now partially abolished by the
" Conveyancing Act of 1881, which enacts that a mortgagor
" seeking to redeem any one mortgage, shall, by virtue of this
" Act, be entitled to do so without paying any money due
" under any separate mortgage made by him "—that
apparently gets rid of the doctrine of the consolidation of
securities—" or by any person through whom he claims on
" property other than that comprised in the mortgage which
" he seeks to redeem. But this provision applies only if and
" as far as a contrary intention is not expressed in the
" mortgage deeds, or one of them; and only where the
" mortgages, or one of them, are or is made after the year
" 1881." So that the doctrine of consolidation of securities
remains to its fullest extent with regard to mortgages
before 1881, and if made after the Act there is anything in
either deed, either the mortgage of the Yorkshire estate or the
mortgage of the Middlesex estate, negativing the effect of the
statute, then that rule still applies. Therefore you never can
be safe unless you see both deeds. " The rules of equity as
" to consolidation of securities thus appear still to remain in
" force "—that is a very guarded expression—" in force in all
" cases in which the mortgages sought to be consolidated by a
" mortgagee were made before the year 1882, or in which one
" of the mortgages, though made after 1881, was created by
" a deed expressing an intention to exclude the application of
" the above enactment. A declaration of such an intention is
" not unfrequently inserted in mortgage deeds." So that you
must look out for it. " It follows, therefore, that no person can
safely lend money on a second mortgage." And if I have
done you gentlemen any good at all, and you have grasped
that, I shall be satisfied. "It follows, therefore, that no person
" can safely lend money on a second mortgage. For, in addition
" to the risks of some third mortgagee getting in and tacking
" the first mortgage,"—I have explained to you what tacking
is—" there is this further danger, that the first mortgagee may

"have previously acquired a right to consolidate with his
"security some other mortgage, by which property of the
"same mortgagor has been charged for more than its value,
"and may, by exercising this right, exclude the second
"mortgage." That is in the case I put of the Yorkshire
estate being more than sufficient to satisfy the Yorkshire debt,
and the Middlesex being less, the Yorkshire second mortgagee
would get nothing. "The purchaser of an equity of
"redemption is exposed to similar risks. Hence it follows
"that, in the words of an eminent judge, 'It is a very
"'dangerous thing at any time to buy equities of redemption,
"'or to deal with them at all.'"

THE LONDON DAILY STOCK

AND

SHARE LIST:

A COURSE OF LECTURES

BY

GEORGE CLARE.

DELIVERED AT THE

Institute of Actuaries, Staple Inn Hall,

During the Session 1897-98.

LONDON:
CHARLES AND EDWIN LAYTON,
56, FARRINGDON STREET, E.C.

1898.

PREFACE.

I gladly respond to the invitation to introduce these Lectures on Finance with a few Prefatory words.

The more modern history of Life Assurance administration (especially in view of the continued decline in the rate of interest) has conclusively shown that, in addition to a sound mathematical equipment for discharge of his technical duties, the Actuary must be equally competent as a practical Financier. A theoretical acquaintance with financial problems and their relations, such as can be obtained from the study of books, is not simply futile but delusive also, and, indeed, dangerous, when confronted with the actual treatment of monetary affairs. As in all other departments of practical labour, capacity and judgment can alone be adequately cultivated by means of direct experience and examination of the course of financial movements, with their uniformities and interactions. The essential distinction between Theory and Practice is especially manifest in work like ours. In the interpretation of Nature, a Theory deduced and generalized from actual observations and experiments may be entertained by a student as useful and valuable information quite independent of experiments of his own; but, in Practical work, theoretical principles must absolutely be combined with direct experimental knowledge in one and the same person. The *passive* sense of vision, to adopt an illustration, affords but an imperfect and fragmentary acquaintance with the properties of phenomena: the *active* muscular sense must be exercised in order to secure that complex and co-ordinated knowledge which expresses the nature of the objects examined.

And, similarly with all masses of social facts dependent upon the operation of the human Will and motives, it will be discovered that commercial arrangements exhibit no arbitrary character but involve processes and results of causal and approximately calculable nature. On this ground, the empirical generalizations thus deduced enter within the range of general Science.

It is obvious that, in the early stage of an Actuarial Student's progress, this direct and intimate method of study is not feasible; and the sole efficient mode of training is to induct him into the consideration of such problems by means of Lectures which embody the experience and discriminated learning of *practical experts*. Hence the origin of these Lectures as an implement of Instruction in extension of the original design contemplated by the Founders of the Institute of Actuaries.

But the student must carefully observe that these Lectures do not constitute a sufficient Corpus in themselves of information or enquiry; they are to be accepted as providing *hints* for personal study and investigation: they are intended to assist in the stimulation and direction of the student's own observing and reflecting powers, and will prove idle and useless, as an *Educative* instrument, unless the individual mental activity is called simultaneously into play. The student must apply their teaching to the direct examination and consideration by himself of the course of the Money Market as presented in the newspapers; the dissection of the accounts and financial records of Companies; and the ascertainment and analysis of the influences and factors which affect the monetary values (as the expression of Demand and Supply) of pecuniary Interests.

In connection with the subject, it is very important to become early acquainted, for the purpose of avoiding widespread misconceptions, with the genuine scope and necessarily restricted nature of Political Economy; and I venture, accordingly, to suggest to the student two very brief but luminous references, which may be readily grasped, and which will prove of helpful value in his enquiries,—namely, (i) "'The Postulates of English Political Economy", by Bagehot (Students' Edition), pp. 7, 8, 9, 21, and 32; and (ii) Volume I of Buckle's "History of Civilization in England" (New Edition), p. 249, and Volume III, pp. 305–309, and 314.

I venture, further, as the "conclusion of the whole matter", to emphasize the proposition that, in the complete government of Life Assurance business, every administrative and financial element of its working is related intimately to *Actuarial* knowledge and aptitude. Omitting the methods of Valuation and Distribution, which are, by universal admission, of an exclusively Actuarial character, I would add that every question of expenses; the discussion of every Investment of every description; and the consideration of the modes of extending business, are not simply dependent, as is too frequently assumed, upon native or acquired acumen and commercial shrewdness and foresight, but, by reason of their *financial* aspects, are essentially connected with sound and sagacious Actuarial learning, and—distinctly bearing, as they accordingly do, upon systems of *Valuation* and *Distribution*—demand the skill of the trained Actuary for their fitting adjustment to these large and vital departments of his work. In brief, the successful administration of a Life Office, even regarded solely from the administrative and financial points of view, requires, as the controlling and supervising force, a competent Actuarial Education.

T. E. YOUNG.

14th June, 1898.

LECTURES

ON THE

LONDON DAILY STOCK AND SHARE LIST.

BY

Mr. GEORGE CLARE.

1897–1898.

INDEX.

	PAGE
Actuary—	
equipment	iii
education	iv
sphere of action	v
Arbitrage operations	8, 11
Artizans' Dwellings Act	54
Bank Act, 1844	57
Bankers' investments	33
Bank of England—	
management of National Debt	41
capital stock	56
Government debt	56
effect of Bank Act, 1844	57
form of accounts	57
British Government securities, *see* National Debt.	
Capital, growth of	3
Colonial Stocks, transfer of	102
Consols, *see* National Debt.	
Corporation Stock, *see* Local Debt.	
Dividends, accrued	6, 11
Elementary Education Act	54
Enfaced Rupee paper	61
Exchequer and Audit Department Act, 1866	16, 42

	PAGE
Exchequer Bills and Bonds	19
External and Internal Loans	59
Foreign Exchanges—	
arbitrated par	9
conventional rates used on Stock Exchange	10
affected by arbitrage operations...	13
Foreign Government securities...	23
Foreign prices	8
French Rente	37
Funds—General, Aggregate, South Sea, Consolidated	25
"Goschens"	34
Income Tax	38
Indian Debt—	
rupee paper	7, 15, 59
expediency of borrowing in England or India...	62
borrowing powers of Indian Government	62
security for debt...	64
Interest—	
accrued	6, 11
rate affected by gold production	26
rate yielded by British Government securities	52
Lectures—	
object	iv
scope	1
Local Debt—	
borrowing powers of Local Bodies	54, 78
advances by Treasury	55
Local Loans Stock	54, 56
history and growth of debt	70
local authorities and areas	75
security for debt	77, 85
Local Loans Act, 1875 ...	77
Corporation Stocks	78, 85, 98
Local Government Board	79
redemption of debt	80
standing order of House of Commons ...	82
amount of debt	88
productive and unproductive outlay	89
Metropolitan Consolidated Stock	78, 93

Local Debt (continued)—
    stamp duty on transfers ... 95, 99
    transfer regulations ... 100
    inscribed and registered stocks ... 101
Local Government Board ... 79
Local Loans Fund ... 56
Local Loans Stock ... 54, 56
Metropolitan Consolidated Stock ... 78, 93
Municipal Corporations Act, 1882 ... 73
Municipal Reform Act, 1835 ... 72
National Debt—
    security for debt ... 15, 42
    history of debt ... 15
    deficiency loans ... 16
    funding system ... 17
    floating debt ... 19, 35
    funded debt ... 23, 35
    the Consolidated Fund ... 25
    items of funded debt ... 25
    conversion schemes of 1853 and 1884 ... 26
    Consols ... 29
    issue of Consols below par ... 30
    conversion scheme of 1888 ... 32
    saleability of Consols ... 33
    redemption of Consols ... 36
    taxability of debt ... 37, 60
    management of debt ... 41
    transfer regulations ... 42
    redemption of debt ... 43, 70
    price movements of Consols ... 50
    interest yield ... 52
    National Debt Act, 1870 ... 37, 101
Official List—
    history ... 1
    description of securities, not guaranteed ... 4
    admission of securities to List ... 4
    prices given in List ... 4
    prices "cum div." and "ex div." ... 6
    comparison with foreign prices ... 8

	PAGE
Official List (continued)—	
foreign currencies	10
Political Economy—	
scope	v
test of maxims	43
Poor-Rate Valuation	86
Public Health Acts	54, 74, 79
Public Works Loan Commissioners	55
Rupee paper, *see* Indian Debt.	
Settlements, on Stock Exchange	6
Sinking Funds, National Debt	45
Stamp Duty on Transfers	95, 99
Stock	84
Stock Exchange Securities—	
investigation of yield	3
valuation	5
Taxation—	
of national debts	37, 60
incidence of local taxation	83
Terminable Annuities	48
Town Councils	73
Treasury Bills	19
Trustee Securities	15, 67, 85
War—	
effect on capital	3
payment for	18
effect on National Debt	45, 49
effect on price of Consols	51
Wealth, growth of	2
Wetenhall	3

LONDON DAILY STOCK AND SHARE LIST.

FIRST LECTURE.

[*Delivered 13 December 1897.*]

GENTLEMEN, as you will see from the syllabus that has been circulated, I have undertaken to deliver a short course of lectures, with the object of introducing to you that somewhat formidable-looking document, the London Daily Stock and Share List, and also of making you acquainted, as far as time will permit, with some portion of its contents. But as I have not imposed this task upon myself with a view to converting you into either "bulls" or "bears", I shall avoid discussing the merits or the demerits of the securities enumerated in the List in their character of investments or of speculations, but shall confine myself to directing your attention to the nature and to the distinctive peculiarities of the classes into which they are grouped. I also purpose treating the subject historically, as I am convinced that in all cases it is far easier to comprehend and co-ordinate the inherent qualities of a security if we know something of its origin and of the early stages of its development.

The Official List, I may begin by informing you, claims to possess a very respectable antiquity. According to Lord Macaulay, the business of stock-jobbing first assumed importance a few years after the Revolution, from which period we, as a matter of fact, date the beginnings of our development into a nation of shopkeepers. Prior to the

Revolution there existed no stocks to deal in: which is a simple reason why the business was unknown. But about three years after the establishment of the Bank of England, the existence of a recognized market in securities was signalized by the appearance of a so-called "Course of Exchange", which came out twice a week, and which at the outset contained six securities only. This was in 1697, exactly 200 years ago, so that we may consider we are celebrating its bi-centenary here to-night. In 1797, a century later, the number of securities had grown to 20, but in 1897 it has increased to something like 3,000—and what is more, the number is being added to every month, at a rate which must bring despair to the soul of the publisher. What the List will be like in 1997, I dare not venture to prophecy, but it certainly looks as though long before then it will have to be published in sections. I may remark, in passing, that those who practised the business of stock-jobbing in early days, do not somehow appear to have gained the esteem of their contemporaries, for you will find if you refer to an original, or early, edition of Dr. Johnson's dictionary, that a stock-jobber is there defined (and this is not in jest, but in sober earnest) as "a low wretch, who gets money by buying and selling shares in the funds." Whether Dr. Johnson had ever been induced by by one of these "low wretches" to sell a "bear" of "shares in the funds", and got "cornered" over the operation, history does not tell us, but the definition is so spiteful that I "hae ma doots." To-day's List, then, contains the names and descriptions of upwards of 3,000 securities, practically the whole of which, with the exception of the first group "British Funds, &c.", have been called into existence since 1837. I know of no more striking proof of the enormous growth of our national wealth and resources during the 60 years of the Queen's reign. But without going back so far as that, let me take half the period. In the current volume of the Stock Exchange Official Intelligence, there is an article written by Sir Henry Burdett in which he points out the amazing fact that the total nominal value, so far as it can be ascertained, of the securities listed on the 1st of January 1867—only the other day, as it were—was £2,362,000,000, but that on the 1st of January 1897, the total nominal value was £6,065,000,000, so that in the last 30 years alone the British public have absorbed something like £4,000,000,000 of securities, and are still clamouring for more. At the present time our savings as a nation amount to about £200,000,000 a year—I should say considerably more rather than less, but that is a very safe estimate—and if we continue to grow rich at the same rate of progression, we shall require an outlet during the next 30 years for something like 6,000 to 8,000 million pounds of surplus capital. Well, I suppose some outlet will be found for it, as one always has been found, but on looking through the List, I must confess that I am quite unable to discover it. As to the first group, "British Funds, &c.", the National Debt is being fast paid off, while as regards municipalities and colonies, I think you will agree that they have already borrowed quite as much as appears justifiable. Foreign countries—the next head—have also had more of our money than is good either for them or for us. Our railway system, too, is practically complete; and so on throughout the list. Every channel, in fact, appears to be full to overflowing. It may be, however, that the development of electricity may in some way supply an opening, or it is also possible that a great war—*the* great war of the future—may swiftly sweep away the accumulations of a century of peace. Before concluding these prefatory remarks, it just occurs to me to say that if any of you wish to take up a congenial and original line of research—original, that is to say, as far as I know—I think I can suggest one. It would be very interesting, namely, to know the comparative yield during the last 30 years of each of the principal groups of securities. Suppose, for instance, a capitalist, on the 1st of January 1867, had invested a stated sum in Consols, would he have done better or worse to have spread his money over an assortment of English railway stocks? and in like manner, taking of course the dividends into account, what would the result have been if he had divided it amongst American Railway bonds or foreign stocks? You would, of course, have to allow for the losses caused by defaults and re-organizations, &c. I simply throw out the suggestion for what it may be worth;—the ground I am sure is fruitful, but whether the seed is worth growing is another matter. Turning now to the List we first notice that it is published by Mr. J. G. Wetenhall, and here I may remark, as a noteworthy circumstance, that the same name has been connected with the List for upwards of a century, at it is recorded in the archives of the Stock Exchange that in November 1787, Mr. E. Wetenhall was unanimously elected publisher by the members. That is followed by a notification that the List is published under the authority of the Committee of the Stock Exchange, and the superintendence of the Secretary of the Share and Loan department; but closely on the heels of this notification comes another that "the titles are taken from the securities as issued." I think there is more in this latter clause than meets the eye. You may take it for granted, I think, that although the List is under official supervision, yet the mere fact of a security being described in a certain manner is no guarantee whatever that it corresponds to such description. If, for instance, a stock or bond is described as "first mortgage", the buyer is not to assume without further enquiry, either that the mortgage actually is a first charge, or even that there exists any mortgage at all. The List, large as it is, does not claim to contain every share which is quoted on the Stock Exchange. Dealings take place every day in hundreds of shares which are not listed. Admission to the privilege of official quotation—for it is a privilege, and confers a certain status on an undertaking—depends to a certain extent (assuming that there exist no special grounds for exclusion) upon the importance of the concern, and this is gauged generally by its magnitude. Hence numbers of small companies have to be shut out, not because there is any question as to their *bonâ fides*, but simply because the inclusion of these small fry would render the List so bulky as to impair its utility. So far, however, as mining shares are concerned, there appears to exist some prejudice against them on the part of the Committee, as in no other way is it possible to explain the exclusion of so many well known concerns.

You will observe that the prices in the List are arranged in two columns, headed "Closing" and "Business done." Of these the "Closing quotations" are merely valuations and are not official in any sense whatever, which is a fact which I commend to your careful notice, because it is one as to which considerable misapprehension appears to prevail. The publisher of the List depends upon the dealers in the market to give him what they consider to be a fair estimate of the market value of the different stocks at the close of the day, but beyond the fact that the boards on which the clerk marks down the prices that have been supplied to him are hung up in the "House" for the inspection of members, no supervision whatever is exercised over these appraisements. In the case of securities that are currently dealt in, they afford, of course, a close and reliable indication of the value, but in regard to those in which transactions occur only rarely, the "Closing quotation" is frequently quite nominal and is only to be looked upon as an expert's opinion of the price at which business might perhaps be done. The closing quotation is useful, however, in one respect. If a broker on going into the market finds it impossible to deal at the quoted price, he can insist on having it altered to the limits at which he can deal. What is true of the closing quotation also applies to the well-known "tape" prices supplied by the Exchange Telegraph Company. These are likewise in no way official; but the dealer who supplies each particular price is held responsible for it, and if, when challenged by a broker, he refuses to deal, the quotation is not allowed to appear again. Under these circumstances you will easily understand that it is by no means a simple matter to assess the value of a parcel of stock, if required for probate or other purposes, and if this duty should ever devolve upon you, I can only advise you not to trust to the List quotation, but to call in the advice of a broker or other expert. The official part of the quotation is that which under the head "Business done" records the transactions that have actually taken place. When a broker concludes a bargain on the Stock Exchange, it is competent to him to have it "marked" if he so pleases. This is accomplished by passing a slip containing the necessary particulars to one of the clerks of the House, who officially registers the price by writing it on a certain board kept for that purpose, from whence it is copied down for publication in the List. The figures registered must be the actual market prices, and if any member considers the marking to be outside the current quotation, he may at once call the attention to it of two members of the Committee, who, if they find the objection justified, will order the marking to be expunged. By asking his broker to get a bargain marked, a buyer can, therefore, always satisfy himself that there has been no collusion between broker and jobber, and that the purchase or sale in which he is interested has been in all respects a genuine one. It is neither obligatory nor usual to give notice of every transaction. If a broker, for instance, buys at a lower or sells at a higher price than one already marked, he might not think it necessary to mark afresh. If Consols, for instance, are already marked $112\frac{3}{4}$, 113 on the board, business done at either of those rates, or at any fraction between them, would fall within the existing markings, so that "112¾, 113" may either mean two transactions at those respective prices or may represent 100 different transactions that have taken place within those limits. It should also be borne in mind that many bargains are not allowed to be marked, even if the broker should be anxious to do so. Up to the price of 30 no bargain may be marked at a smaller fraction than $\frac{1}{16}$, and at 30 or over, no bargain may be marked at a smaller fraction than $\frac{1}{8}$. Hence the thousands of bargains that are transacted at thirty-second prices are entirely excluded, and so are the majority of those at sixteenths. As to the amount of Stock in which business has been done the List affords us no information whatever, and a marking that represents a turnover of £20,000 may come to be sandwiched between two others that stand for less than a tithe of that amount. It is usual, however, to specially distinguish bargains in small bonds, or those in which an exceptional amount has changed hands at special prices. On the New York Stock Exchange, as some of you may have noticed, the number of shares dealt in is officially registered each day, and the magnitude of the daily turnover is an unerring guide to the activity of the market; but here in London, the only indication we possess to help us in that respect is the number of markings. If these are unusually numerous, we know that it has been a busy day in that particular market, but as to whether the dealings have amounted to 1,000 shares or 100,000 we are left quite in the dark. Business may be done either for "Money" or for the "Account"—that is to say, either for prompt settlement or for settlement on the next account day; but the great bulk of the transactions are for the "Account", and the quotation, unless otherwise stated, is to be so understood. There are two settlements per month, one towards the middle and one towards the end, but in Consols there is only one settling day, usually on or about the 3rd. All quotations, except those of Indian rupee paper, of some Indian railway debentures, and perhaps of one or two others, which are regarded as money market securities, include the interest that will have accrued on the security up to selling day. The seller makes the buyer a present of it, so to say. Suppose, for instance, that to-day I had bought £1,000 Argentine 1886 loan, which is quoted in the List at 93½, 94½, and on which the interest is due 1st January, I should have to pay for the stock on settling day—the day after to-morrow—but on the 1st January I receive interest, not from the 15th of December, but from the 1st of last July, so that actually the quotation includes $5\frac{1}{2}$ months' interest at 5 per-cent. To arrive at the real cost of the stock, therefore, I must deduct this accrued interest, and if I wish to be perfectly accurate in my book-keeping, I must take care on the 1st of January not to pass the whole coupon to revenue account, but to book only one-twelfth to income and the remaining eleven-twelfths to the credit of Argentine 1886 Loan, which stock will then stand in my ledger at its true net cost. As a consequence of this practice of including interest in the quotation, prices ought in theory to rise after each settlement (other things being equal) by about the amount of a fortnight's interest, and, when the dividend comes off, ought to undergo a fall of equal extent with its value. When 3 per-cent Local Loans Stock, for instance, is marked $x.\,d.$ you will find that it falls $\frac{3}{4}$ per-cent, while Canadian Government 4 per-cent Guaranteed Bonds, on which the dividend is payable half-yearly, fall 2 per-cent when marked $x.\,d.$, and so does the Turkish 1855 loan. In those exceptional cases—and they are very exceptional—in which interest is not included in the quotation, the buyer gives the seller, in addition to the market price, the interest accrued from the date of the last dividend-payment to the date on which he pays for the stock; and the quotation, so far as interest is concerned, need never vary. In one very important instance, however, which stands alone, this usage produces a somewhat remarkable effect. For Stock Exchange purposes the enfaced promissory notes of the Indian Government which are expressed as payable (both principal and interest) in rupees, and which go by the name of Rupee Paper, are quoted at so much per-cent in sterling, the rupee being calculated at the fixed conventional exchange of $2s.$ (that is to say, "Rupee Paper, 60" means £60 for 1,000 rupees) and the accrued interest, which has to be paid by the buyer, is also taken at the same rate of $2s.$ a rupee. Now the annual interest at $3\frac{1}{2}$ per-cent on 1,000 rupees is 35 rupees, equal to about 3 per month, so that if I buy £100 Rupee Paper a month after the interest was paid I shall have to give the seller, in addition to the price, three rupees, or $6s.$ for the accrued interest. But the rupee for which I am paying the seller $2s.$ is really only worth 1*s*. 3*d*., so that I lose 9*d*. per rupee, and that makes, you will find, about ⅛ per-cent per month. Consequently, so long as the Indian exchange stands at 1*s*. 3*d*., Rupee Paper will be worth ⅛ per-cent less for every month's interest that the buyer has to pay, and if it stood say at 61 the day the dividend came off, we should expect to see it a month afterwards at 60⅞; four months after at 60½, and so on. Instead, therefore, of the price remaining stationary, or of its rising from settlement to settlement, as is the case with other securities, and falling back again when the interest is paid, the price gradually declines (assuming the exchange to be steady at 1*s*. 3*d*., and other things being equal) at the rate of ⅛ per-cent per month, and the day it is marked *x. d.* goes up again to starting point. I must tax your patience a little longer upon this subject of accrued interest. In order to arrive at the actual cost of a stock purchase, it is necessary, as I said, to deduct from its price the interest that has been accumulating since the last dividend was received, and this is a fact we must carefully bear in mind whenever we have occasion to compare the yield of different investments. Thus, a 4 per-cent stock at 101, the dividends on which are due January and July, is not really so dear to-day as a 4 per-cent stock at par on which the dividends are due in June and December, because, of course, the price of the former includes 5 months' more interest, equal to 1⅔ per-cent, than that of the latter. Then, again, the question of interest must be carefully considered if you should have occasion to compare the foreign price of a security with the London price, or, what is much the same thing, if you should have to work out the cost of any stock from a foreign quotation; and as I have little doubt that insurance companies with huge funds to dispose of will sooner or later find it repay them to scrutinize the Continental Stock Exchange Lists in search of suitable investments, I hope you will not consider that I am wasting your time if I go into this matter rather more fully than might otherwise appear necessary. In the case of stocks quoted both in London and abroad a comparison of the respective prices constitutes what is called an "arbitrage" calculation, and the object of such calculations, when treated as a special business, is to take advantage of existing differences in value by buying in the cheapest and selling in the dearest market. Suppose, for instance, we know the price of a stock at A and the exchange between A and B, we can by a simple calculation ascertain the corresponding price of the stock at B. In like manner, if we knew the price at B and the rate of exchange, we can work out the price at A. This is called the "arbitrated" price or parity. Then, again, if we know the price at A and the price at B, we can, by a comparison of those prices, ascertain the rate of exchange between A and B, as established by these prices. This is called the "arbitrated par of exchange", and is arrived at, as you see, by buying the stock in one place and selling it in another. In actual practice the arbitrated par of exchange is very rarely considered, but in theory it plays an important part. As an example of calculations of arbitrated prices, let us take a simple case. If, for instance, Chartered shares are quoted at £3 in London, and the exchange between London and Paris is 25.25, what is the arbitrated price in Paris?

$$\begin{array}{r} \text{Francs ?} = 1 \text{ Chartered share.} \\ 1 = 3 \text{ £} \\ 1 = 25.25 \text{ francs.} \\ \hline 75.75 \text{ francs.} \end{array}$$

The arbitrated price is 75¾, and if the shares stand higher in Paris (allowing for all expenses of transmission) it will pay to buy them in London and sell them in Paris; if they are lower than 75¾, it will pay to buy them in Paris and sell them in London.

Or we may state the equation from the Paris point of view: that is to say, if Chartereds stand there at 75¾, and the cheque rate is 25.25, what is the arbitrated price in London?

$$\begin{array}{r} \text{£?} = 1 \text{ share.} \\ 1 = 75.75 \text{ francs} \\ 25.25 = 1 \text{ £} \\ \hline 3 \text{ £} \end{array}$$

Here, again, if the London price is so much above £3 as to leave a profit after covering expenses, it will pay to buy in Paris and sell simultaneously in London; or, if lower, to reverse the operation.

Lastly, suppose we have to remit to Paris, and it occurs to us to ask whether it would be cheaper to send Chartered shares than to buy a cheque. What exchange will Chartered shares give if we buy them here at £3 and sell them in Paris at 75¾?

$$\text{Francs ?} = £1.$$
$$£3 = 1 \text{ share}.$$
$$1 = 75.75 \text{ francs}.$$

$$\overline{25.25 \text{ francs}.}$$

This is the arbitrated par of exchange as arrived at from a comparison of the respective prices of Chartered shares, but, as I have already said, an arbitrated par is valueless in practice, owing to the expenses that such an operation would entail.

So far as the theory of arbitrage goes, these three examples present the whole of it; but when we attempt to apply its principles to the prices of stocks quoted abroad *as well as in London*, we encounter at the outset a slight difficulty. The interest on the majority of such stocks is payable abroad, and whenever the interest on a stock is payable abroad the capital, you will find, is expressed in foreign currency.

Take an American railway bond, for instance; if the coupon is payable in London, the bond is expressed in sterling; if in London and New York, the bond is in both sterling and dollars; if in New York only, the bond is in dollars only. Again, the interest on Austrian silver rente is payable in Vienna, and the capital is in florins; on Dutch rente in Amsterdam, and the capital is in guilders; on French rente in Paris, and the capital is in francs; and so on.

But observe. If a bond or stock, the capital of which is expressed in a foreign currency, is dealt in or quoted in London, it is the custom of the Stock Exchange to buy and sell in sterling, and to convert the foreign money into pounds at a fixed conventional exchange, which, though not in each instance stated in the List (on page 2 a number of these stocks with "coupons payable abroad" are grouped together), is well known to all who have dealings in such securities. The Austrian florin, for instance, is taken at 2*s*., while the Dutch florin, which has about the same value, is only taken at 1*s*. 8*d*.; the franc is reckoned at 25 to the £; the mark at 1*s*. each; the American dollar at 4*s*. each, and so on.

A moment's consideration will convince you of the advantage of this plan, which is a custom of the Bourses all over the world. As things are, buyer and seller haggle over the price, and as soon as they arrive at an understanding on that point, the bargain can be concluded; but if the exchange were not fixed, they would have to haggle over the rate of exchange as well, and it would take just twice as long to do the business. Whether the fixed exchange is for or against the buyer does not really matter in the least, because any difference is taken into account in the price. But the fixed exchange is not the only difficulty we shall have to contend with. Another, and to the novice a more perplexing one, is that of interest. In London, as we have seen, the accrued interest is included in the price of the stock, and the same practice obtains in Paris and in New York. London, Paris, and New York quote net prices, but on almost all the foreign Bourses—Amsterdam, Berlin, Antwerp, Brussels, Copenhagen, St. Petersburg, Vienna, Hamburg, &c.,—the interest which has accrued on the stock since the payment of the last coupon is added to the price quoted in the List. This interest is always taken on the nominal amount of the stock, and is charged at the rate which the stock actually bears, but in the case of shares, with varying dividends, it is taken at a conventional rate (in Germany generally at 4 per-cent), which is usually stated in the foreign Lists side by side with the quotation. Now, let us see whether we can turn our information to any practical use.

I propose to take the prices of a few illustrative stocks from the foreign telegrams in to-day's *Times*, and to state the equations for you, but shall leave you to work out the parities for yourselves, and to compare them with the actual London prices in the List.

FRENCH $3\frac{1}{2}$ PER-CENT RENTE. PARIS PRICE, $106\frac{3}{4}$.

The interest on this stock is payable abroad, and the capital is expressed in francs, which are taken here at 25 to the £. The actual exchange for cheques on Paris is $25.18\frac{1}{2}$.

$$£ ? = 100 £ \text{ stock,}$$
If £ stock $1 = 25$ francs stock,
if francs stock $100 = 106.75$ francs,
and francs $25.185 = 1 £$.

CHESAPEAKE AND OHIO 4½ PER-CENT BONDS.
NEW YORK PRICE, 81.

Interest payable New York. Capital expressed in dollars. Fixed exchange, $5 = £1. Actual exchange $4.86 = £1.

$$£\ ?\ =\ 100\ £\ \text{stock}.$$
$$\text{If }£\text{ stock}\quad 1 = \quad 5\ \$\text{ stock}.$$
$$\text{If }\$\text{ stock}\ 100 = \quad 81\ \$.$$
$$\text{If }\$\qquad\ 4.86 = \quad 1\ £.$$

PRUSSIAN 3 PER-CENT CONSOLS. BERLIN PRICE, 97.40.

Interest payable Berlin on 1 April and 1 October (not included in the price). Capital expressed in Reichsmarks. Fixed exchange m. 20 = £1. Actual exchange, 20.37½.

N.B.—In Germany and on the Continent generally, the year is taken in interest calculations at 360 days, and the month at 30 days.

$$£\ ?\ =\ 100\ £\ \text{stock}.$$
$$\text{If }£\text{ stock}\quad 1 = \quad 20\ \text{m. stock}.$$
$$\text{If m. stock}\ 100 = \ *98.02\tfrac{1}{2}\ \text{m}.$$
$$\text{If m.}\quad 20.37\tfrac{1}{2} = \quad 1\ £.$$

* 98.02½ is the price (97.40), plus 2½ months' accrued interest (1 October to 15 December), at 3 per-cent.

MEXICAN 6 PER-CENT 1888 LOAN. BERLIN PRICE, 96.60.

Interest payable quarterly in London. Capital expressed in sterling. Fixed exchange in Berlin, £1 = m. 20. Actual exchange, 20.37½.

$$£\ ?\ =\ 100\ £\ \text{stock}.$$
$$\text{If }£\text{ stock}\quad 1 = \quad 20\ \text{m. stock}.$$
$$\text{If m. stock}\ 100 = \ *97.85\ \text{m}.$$
$$\text{If m.}\quad 20.37\tfrac{1}{2} = \quad 1\ £.$$

* 97.85 is the price (96.60), plus 2½ months' accrued interest (1 October to 15 December) at 6 per-cent.

ITALIAN 5 PER-CENT RENTE. BERLIN PRICE, 95.10.

Interest payable Paris on 1 January and 1 July, less 20 per-cent Italian tax. Capital expressed in francs. Fixed exchange in Berlin fcs. 100 = m. 80; Fixed exchange in London, fcs. 25 = £1. Actual exchange, Berlin on London, 20.37½.

$$£\,? = 100\ £\ \text{stock.}$$
If £ stock   1 = 25 francs stock.
If francs stock 100 = 80 m. stock.
If m. stock 100 = *96.88 m.
If m.   20.37½ = 1 £.

* 96.88 is the price (95.10), plus 5¼ months' accrued interest (1 July to 15 December), at 4 per-cent.

AUSTRIAN SILVER RENTE. VIENNA PRICE, 101¼.

Interest payable Vienna, less 16 per-cent tax. Capital expressed in florins. Fixed exchange, fl. 10 = £1. Actual exchange, 12.07.

$$£\,? = 100\ £\ \text{stock.}$$
If £ stock . 1 = 10 florins stock.
If fl. stock 100 = *103.42 florins.
If fl.   12.07 = 1 £.

* 103.42 is the price (101.50), plus 5¼ months' accrued interest (1 July to 15 December), 4¼ per-cent.

In the case of stocks not quoted in London, and in which the question of the fixed exchange does not arise, the foreign price, plus interest, if divided by the sight-exchange, gives the cost in London, to which must be added the expense of getting the stock over.

Those of you who may have studied the subject of the foreign Exchanges will probably remember to have read that a rising rate is frequently held in check, and prevented from reaching gold point by arbitrage operations in stocks, and you will now be better able to understand what that statement means. The point is this: the higher the exchange rises, the less it costs to remit from this side, and the less the remittance costs, the cheaper the stock works out.

Thus, if Chartered shares stand at £3 in London, and at 75.30 in Paris, when the exchange is at 25.10, the price would be the same on both sides; but if the exchange rose to 25.22½, the parity would work out ½ per-cent cheaper, and it might then pay to buy the shares in Paris, and sell them in London. If such operations were carried out on a large scale, it is easily seen that the increased supply of London paper in Paris (or the increased demand for Paris paper in London) would stay the further rise in the exchange until the price of the shares adjusted themselves to the changed conditions of supply and demand by rising a fraction in Paris and falling a fraction in London.

THE

LONDON DAILY STOCK AND SHARE LIST.

SECOND LECTURE.

[*Delivered 10 January 1898.*]

AT our last session we discussed the history and composition of the Official List, and we now proceed to examine its contents. It starts well, you will see, for in the first group we have the pick of the basket. It begins by setting out those securities which constitute an *absolute first charge* on the wealth and industry of the richest kingdom of the world, and of its greatest dependency. Under the superscription of British Funds, &c., we find all the Parliamentary Stocks and Government Securities of the United Kingdom: all those securities, the interest on which is guaranteed by Parliament, the stocks of the Bank of England and Ireland, and those forming the debt of India; the all-round high quality of this little assortment being attested by the fact that it is lawful for a trustee, unless expressly forbidden by the instrument creating the trust, to invest any trust funds in his hands in every one of them, except Rupee Paper. The leading items in the group are, of course, those which make up the National Debt, and this it will be well to consider as a whole, before we proceed to examine its separate parts.

Our National Debt, like that of most other Great Powers, is in the main a war debt; but though it was in the reign of William the Third that the practice of borrowing money to carry on war was first introduced together with its corollary, the Funding system, it would be a mistake to imagine that the device of meeting the exigencies of the State by loans was imported into our Island by William's Dutch advisers. The expedient of anticipating revenue by borrowing at short date was of great antiquity, and in times when the system of tax collection was far less prompt than it is now was unavoidable. It is one, moreover, that prevails in a familiar shape to this day, for in every quarter when there is a deficiency in the means to meet the charges upon the Consolidated Fund, advances to the required amount are obtained from the Bank of England (or the Bank of Ireland), which are paid off from the accruing revenue of the ensuing quarter and which constitute, therefore, a loan in anticipation of revenue. In the Exchequer and Audit Department Act of 1866, you find it enacted that "At the close of each of the "quarters ending on the 31st day of March, the 30th day of " June, the 30th day of September, and the 31st day of " December in every year, the Treasury shall prepare an " account of the income and charge of the Consolidated Fund " in Great Britain and in Ireland for such quarter, and the " charges for the Public Debt, due on the 5th day of April, " the 5th day of July, the 10th day of October, and the 5th " day of January, shall be included in the accounts of the said " charge for the quarters ending on the days preceding the " latter dates; and a copy of such account shall forthwith be " transmitted by the Treasury to the Comptroller and Auditor- " General; and if it shall appear by such account that the " income of the Consolidated Fund in Great Britain or in " Ireland for the quarter is not sufficient to defray the charge " upon it, the Comptroller and Auditor-General, if satisfied of " the correctness of the deficiency, shall certify the amount " thereof to the Bank of England or to the Bank of Ireland, " as the case may be, and upon such certificates the said Banks " shall be authorized to make advances from time to time " during the succeeding quarter, on the application of the " Treasury, by writing in a form to be from time to time " determined by them to an amount not exceeding in the " aggregate the sums specified in such certificates; and all " such advances shall be placed to the credit of the Exchequer " Acounts at the said Banks and be available to satisfy the " Orders for Credits granted, or to be granted, upon the said " accounts by the Comptroller and Auditor-General; and the "principal and interest of all such advances shall be paid out "of the growing produce of the Consolidated Fund in the "said succeeding quarter." The Government cannot borrow without express permission, and the Act was passed to give them that permission. What really dates from the Revolution, as Macaulay points out, is not the system of borrowing but the system of funding. Merely to contract debts was no novelty, but the system introduced by William the Third, of honestly paying them, was a genuine innovation. The origin of our indebtedness as a nation may be traced to a piece of chicanery on the part of Charles the Second. After the Restoration, the London goldsmiths, who were bankers as well as dealers in the precious metals, lent the Government about £1,300,000, which had been deposited with them by their customers. This money the King appropiated to himself in 1672 by suddenly shutting up the Exchequer, and informing the lenders that, though it was not convenient to let them have the principal, he should be pleased to go on paying them interest. Many years afterwards, in 1701, the half of this sum was formally acknowledged by Parliament as a national obligation, so that in point of origin it forms the oldest part of the public debt. During the war waged by King William against the French allies of his father-in-law, it was found impracticable to meet the excessive expenditure by revenue raised within the year, and recourse was therefore had to loans. At first the Government felt its way cautiously; it borrowed only for short periods, promised to repay by instalments, and pledged particular taxes to secure the return of the principal and interest. These taxes were to be levied only for a limited number of years, and it was expected that their produce would discharge the debt within the period for which they were granted. In 1692, for instance, a law was passed imposing certain new duties on beer and other liquors, and it was ordered that these duties should be kept in the exchequer separate from all other receipts, and that they should form a *fund*, on the credit of which a million was to be raised by life annuities. Had the war quickly terminated, this and similar arrangements would probably have been adhered to; but its long duration, and the new emergencies to which it gave rise, rendered it necessary to put the redemption off to a future day. The loans had to be renewed, and the taxes continued; the pretence of repayment was gradually abandoned; and the country was at last committed to the plan of paying interest only, and of allowing the principal to stand over as a permanent liability. Once fairly entered upon, this system of permanent borrowing went steadily on from year to year, and under one administration after another, until, at the termination of the long struggle which ended in 1815, the debt, funded and unfunded, reached its highest point of nine hundred millions (in this sum I include the value of the terminable annuities which at that time were not reckoned part of the debt), having thus attained its maximum in the short space of about a century and a quarter. Whether those who incurred that liability had the right to cast so large a share of its burden upon posterity is a question to which there are two sides. The annual charge for interest and sinking fund is so large an item of our national expenditure, that its extinction would create a revolution in our finances, and it would be very agreeable, no doubt, if we could awake one morning to find ourselves free of the six hundred millions of debt contracted by Mr. Pitt and his successors—it would be very agreeable, that is to say, if we could be rid of it without otherwise altering our circumstances. But would our circumstances be the same? Is it not likely, as the late Lord Iddesleigh, who gave considerable attention to the subject, appears to have thought, that if that money had been raised by excessive taxation, the load would have been too great for the springs of industry and commerce to bear, and hence that our national resources at the present time would be far more seriously crippled than they actually are by the burden of the debt? After all, it may possibly be better for us that Mr. Pitt allowed the money to fructify in the hands of our great-grandfathers, instead of forcing it out of their possession by taxation. It is generally admitted too, as an abstract principle, that the money cost of a struggle for national existence may, with justice and propriety, be left for succeeding generations to liquidate. The cost in blood and tears must be borne at the time, but the mere debit balance in the national ledger may be left for settlement in the future. I speak now, of course, of those great wars in which a nation fights for its life and liberty. As to the little wars which every generation has to engage in, which confer only a temporary benefit, and which are essentially the evils of a day, their cost, it is clear, is a charge against revenue and not against capital, and the Government that undertakes them, and which gains in popularity thereby, ought undoubtedly to settle the bill.

The public debt is of two descriptions. In addition to that greater portion which has solidified into a permanent shape, and which is known as the funded debt, there always exists a varying amount of indebtedness of a less degree of fixity known as the unfunded or floating debt. This consists of loans raised for short periods and for temporary purposes. It represents money borrowed from time to time to meet national expenses for which no provision has been made, or for which the provision made has either proved insufficient or not forthcoming at the time when wanted. Our credit as a nation, it is to be observed, is committed to the due payment of interest on both classes of obligation alike; but while on the former the State contracts to pay interest only, it undertakes, in regard to the latter, to discharge the principal as well as the interest. In other words, the State promises to pay off the unfunded debt on certain specified dates, but the funded debt it need never pay at all. The securities representing unfunded debt are, or rather were until recently, of three denominations, namely, Exchequer Bills, Exchequer Bonds, and Treasury Bills. For the invention of the Exchequer Bill we are indebted to the fertile genius of Charles Montague, William the Third's renowned Chancellor of the Exchequer. During the great re-coinage undertaken in that reign, the withdrawal of the old money appears to have proceeded more rapidly than the issue of the new, and the country fell into great distress for want of the currency needed to conduct its business. In order to fill the void, a clause was inserted at Montague's instance in the Ways and Means Bill of 1696, empowering the issue of interest-bearing Government paper, based on the security of the revenue, and in July of that year the first Exchequer Bills appeared. The success of the issue was great, and though intended merely as a temporary substitute for the new money then in course of manufacture, the country took to the Bills so kindly, even after the immediate necessity had passed away, that the Government decided on their permanent adoption, and they continued in use down to the present year. A newly-issued Bill bore interest coupons running for five years, but as the holder might claim repayment of the principal on any anniversary of the date of the Bill, it was practically twelve months' paper. To ensure convertibility, they were made receivable in payment of customs, excise, or other duties, at any time in the last six months of every year from the date of the Bill, and the interest due on them at the time of presentation was allowed in the payment. They were issued at two periods only, March and June, and the interest, which might not exceed 5½ per cent., was fixed half-yearly, and always at such a rate so as to keep the Bill at a slight premium. There was a very good reason for this practice. In case of an emergency, the Chancellor of the Exchequer might have had need to raise a few millions as quickly as possible, and by keeping the Exchequer Bill at a trifling premium, he could always be sure that a new issue at par would be eagerly taken up. Until the introduction of the Treasury Bill, the theory held with regard to the Exchequer Bill was that it provided a security of which not only was the repayment at par assured, but which, by bearing a variable interest, adjustable to the circumstances of the money market, should always preserve a fixed value, and hence be a suitable investment for floating money. In practice, however, the theory was never fully carried out, because the interest, instead of being adjusted from week to week, or even from month to month—as it would require to have been if the value of the principal was never to vary—was fixed for half a year in advance, during which period there was always the possibility, owing to unforeseen changes in the money market, of the Bill falling to a discount, as it frequently did. But apart from this drawback, the Exchequer Bill, it had long been evident, had had its day. It belonged to a time when the rate of interest on short loans did not fluctuate so often as it does now, and when the system of holding vast sums of money ready for short investment was unknown. The expedient, too, of permitting them to be used in payment of duties grew antiquated, and did not accord with modern ideas. Gradually the issue grew smaller, and finally, in 1897, it dwindled away altogether. In his Budget speech in April last, the Chancellor of the Exchequer, referring to this subject, said: "The unfunded debt, besides being reduced, has been " greatly simplified. It now consists solely of Treasury Bills. " The remnant of Exchequer Bonds borrowed by the First " Lord of the Admiralty to pay off the holders of consols, has " been paid off during the past year. Exchequer Bills have " ceased. That security which was invented 200 years ago

" by one of the greatest of my predecessors, Mr. Charles
" Montague, in order to effect a great re-coinage for the
" benefit of the country, has often stood the Treasury in good
" stead, and never more so than during the great war early in
" this century. But these Bills, issued as they were for terms
" of five years, the interest on them being fixed half-yearly
" by the Treasury, have become inconvenient. Certainly it
" was an invidious task to fix the interest on Exchequer Bills.
" You might fix it too high, and if you did, there was a loss
" to the Exchequer; if you fixed it too low, the holders of the
" Bills had a right to present them at certain periods in
" payment of duty. And in these days Treasury Bills issued
" for periods of not more than 12 months at a rate fixed by
" the competition of the market, are far more convenient, and
" a better form of security." The Exchequer Bond to which
the Chancellor of the Exchequer refers, was another form of
security invented by Mr. Gladstone in 1853. Bonds to bearer
are of course common enough now, but at that time they were
little known. The interest on the Exchequer Bond was to be
payable by coupon, and Mr. Gladstone thought that foreign
buyers of our investments would be likely to give the
preference to one of which the actual security itself would be
in their possession, and of which they could encash the interest
in whatever part of the world they might be by simply cutting
off and selling a coupon. For some reason or another the
Exchequer Bond was not a success, and for many years the public
heard no more of them, the few that came out at intervals
being issued to the National Debt Commissioners against
advances made out of the funds under their control. In 1889,
however, Mr. Goschen decided to resuscitate them, and a new
form of bond was prepared to meet modern requirements, but
these also were paid off last year, and now it is very likely
that we have seen the last of them. The third and last
division of the unfunded debt, and now in fact the only one,
is that of Treasury Bills. These are Money Market securities,
and, as they are not dealt in on the Stock Exchange, you will
not find them in the Official List; but that need not prevent us
from bestowing a little attention on them. I think I am
right in saying that the first conception of the Treasury
Bill is contained in a suggestion put forward by the late
Mr. Walter Bagehot, who, in an article in the *Economist* of 1876,
asked the very apposite question, " Why not issue Exchequer

Bills at short dates"? Up to that time, whenever it was the duty of the Chancellor of the Exchequer to raise money for temporary purposes, he had to choose between the Exchequer Bond and the 12 months' Exchequer Bill. On the former he could never hope to borrow at much less than 3 per-cent, and on the latter, although backed up by the finest credit in the world, the Government had just announced the rate to be 2 per-cent, while a private individual could, on the same day, have taken a three months' Bank Bill into the market and have borrowed on it at just half that rate. The fault, said Mr. Bagehot, lies in the present form of Exchequer Bill. It runs too long, and it is too clumsy. If the Government wish to take advantage of the tempting cheapness of the money available for this class of investment, let them issue a more handy and more negotiable security. For a three months' bill the market would be found willing to pay the best price, and the Government ought to study its wants. The wisdom of the advice was recognized in the proper quarter, and early in the following year the Chancellor of the Exchequer, Sir Stafford Northcote, introduced a Bill providing for the issue of a new form of floating debt obligation, to be known as a Treasury Bill. The Act imposed no restrictions on the Treasury in respect of the rate which it might pay—the rate on Exchequer Bills was limited to $5\frac{1}{2}$ per-cent—but the term of the Bill was not to exceed 12 months. Immediately afterwards, in March 1877, tenders were invited for the first emission under the new plan, and to the gratification of those concerned, the Government succeeded in obtaining the best market rate. Being new and strange, however, the Treasury Bills were for some time looked upon rather shyly, but during the City of Glasgow Bank crisis, which occurred in 1878, French bankers manifested so strong a predilection for such perfectly A 1 paper as to give them the character of an international Bill, and from that time they have taken their proper place as the highest class of paper known to the market. From the point of view of the Chancellor of the Exchequer, Treasury Bills possess another excellent quality in addition to that of enabling him to borrow cheaply; they also enable him to spread the liabilility over the whole year. There was no legal reason why an Exchequer Bill should not bear date on any date that the Treasury might appoint, but the peculiarity of the interest conditions appeared to render it convenient to issue only twice a year, so that the danger of having to take them up was concentrated on two days only, whereas the three months' Treasury Bills are arranged in such a manner as to fall due about twice a month all the year round, and, at the worst, the Government could only have a small proportion thrown on its hands at one time. As the Treasury Bill bears no interest, the buyer pays the amount, less discount. In tendering for them, "the tenders must specify the net amount per-cent which will be given"; that is to say, instead of offering to take a 12 months' bill at $2\frac{1}{2}$ per-cent, you bid £97. 10s. per-cent for it. Perhaps I need hardly mention that, as this is bankers' discount, and not true discount, the buyer at that price really obtains rather more than $2\frac{1}{2}$ per-cent on his money.

Let us revert now for a moment to the loan that I spoke of as being raised in 1692. Its repayment, I told you, was secured by the hypothecation of certain fresh duties which were simultaneously imposed to an amount sufficient both to meet the interest and to redeem the principal by instalments. The borrowing system, of course, was then in its infancy, and the national credit consisted of little else than good intentions. The Stuarts had just been driven from the country, and the Government of William was far from firmly established. It was very natural, under these circumstances, that provision for paying back the money borrowed should be deemed an essential part of the scheme. To have attempted, indeed, to borrow, with the avowed intention of never repaying, would only have excited ridicule. Duties or taxes so assigned and set apart, as in this instance, were said to form a *fund*, and his claim upon some such specified *fund* constituted the lender's security.

This practice of the hypothecation of a specific branch of the revenue is a very common practice in the case of countries of inferior credit. The law authorizing the Argentine 1886 Loan, for instance, contains the following clause—"The "service of the loan shall be provided by the general "revenues of the country, the Custom House receipts remain- "ing specially appropriated to the necessary extent for the "annual service." A first-class State, such as England, Germany, France, Holland, &c., borrows, of course, upon its general credit; only a State which cannot do this proposes to mortgage a particular revenue. Security of that kind, even at its best, is very superficial, for if the country which mortgages its customs finds it impossible, or says it finds it impossible to pay, where is the imagined security? In order to realize it, the bondholder would have to usurp the government of the country, which is out of the question. Duties and taxes so assigned and set apart were described, I repeat, as a *fund*, and his *claim* upon some such specified fund constituted the lender's security. Gradually, however, by that process of contraction, which is the offspring of frequent repetition, dealing in *claims* on the funds, came to be spoken of as dealings in "the funds" simply, until, in course of time, the word "funds" almost lost its original signification of the security on which the loans were based, and acquired the new meaning, which it still retains, of the principal of the loans themselves. The use of "funds" in the sense of public debt is, therefore, a survival of the primitive practice. At the outset, again, funding a loan meant, as we have just seen, the provision of resources to extinguish the capital as well as cover the interest, and when the Government first began to contract permanent loans, and to charge the fund with the payment of interest only, this latter process was distinguished as *perpetual* funding; but the "perpetual" appears to have soon dropped away, and we are left with plain "funding" in the altered sense of appropriating revenue for the perpetual payment of interest alone. What we now mean when we speak of our "funded" debt is permanent debt, of which the interest is a perpetual charge on the Consolidated Fund. In modern times the meaning has undergone even further modification, for whereas the word originally indicated that the service of the loan was secured by a fund, and then that the service was secured, and the loan permanent or of long duration, we now either take the security for granted or treat it as a separate matter, and a so-called "funding operation," in many cases, signifies little more than the conversion of an immediate or a short-term debt into a long term or a perpetual debt.

The primitive practice of keeping a separate account of each loan, and of the taxes levied for its service, lasted only a few years. Some of the taxes left a deficit, while others produced a surplus; and the multiplicity of funds complicated the book-keeping. It was therefore decided, about 1715, to collect the various branches of revenue into three large groups, known as the General, the Aggregate, and the South Sea Funds, each of which was charged with the payment of certain specific annuities. This arrangement, though still involving a separate calculation at the Custom House for each of the different subsidies, was a distinct improvement over the former system, and for some time worked well enough; but long before the end of the century the country had outgrown it, and further simplification was urgently called for. In 1787, accordingly, Mr. Pitt pointed out to the fundholders that, as the credit of the country was committed to the fulfilment of all its obligations alike, the comparative priority of the various loans was more imaginary than real; and, on obtaining their consent to an amalgamation of the security, he abolished a distinction that had become practically valueless and established one single fund, to which he carried the whole of the permanent revenue, and to which he gave the name of "The Consolidated Fund." The principal and interest of the Unfunded Debt, and the whole of the perpetual annuities payable in respect of the Funded Debt, form a first charge upon and are payable out of this Consolidated Fund of the United Kingdom, without distinction or priority.

That greater portion of our national indebtedness, which is repayable only at the option of the Government, and not at the option of the annuitant, is called the Funded Debt, and is composed of the following stocks: Two-and-a-Half per-cent Annuities; Two-and-Three-quarters per-cent Annuities; and Two-and-Three-quarters per-cent Consolidated Stock, as well as the book-debts owing to the Banks of England and Ireland. To discover its first beginnings, we must look to the negotiations that led to the incorporation of the Bank of England. There can be little doubt that the Government then contemplated the contraction, for the first time, of a permanent debt; for though the Charter was made terminable in 1706, it is not to be supposed that the Government had any intention of withdrawing it after twelve years, or the Bank of asking for repayment. The advance by the Bank to the public of £1,200,000 in 1694 was therefore the foundation stone of our Funded Debt; and Bank of England Stock is the patriarch of the official List. The stock that takes the lead in our schedule—Two-and-a-Half per-cents—owes its origin, indirectly, to the discoveries of gold, between 1848 and 1851, in

California and Australia. As a consequence of those discoveries, which occasioned a great influx of the metal to this country, the belief was strongly entertained 45 years ago, that we were on the eve of a great and permanent reduction in the value of money. In February, 1853, the rate of interest on Exchequer Bills was cut down from $1\frac{1}{2}d.$ to $1d.$ per day, but not one Bill was sent in for repayment, and they still stood at a premium; and Consols were quoted at par. Rumours of a projected reduction of interest on the Debt got abroad, and, as the nation appeared to have fully prepared itself for a conversion, Mr. Gladstone decided not to disappoint it. His scheme, which was produced in March, had a two-fold object. His minor aim, in which he succeeded, was to sweep away a few remnants of old stocks connected with the South Sea Company, that still encumbered the List; but his great purpose was to lay the foundation of the stock of the future—of a permanent form of irredeemable public debt (irredeemable, that is to say, at the option of the holder), bearing interest at $2\frac{1}{2}$ per-cent. To this end he offered to give, in exchange for each £100 of Three per-cent Stock, yielding 60s. per-cent, either £110 of Two-and-a-Half per-cent Stock, yielding 55s. per-cent, or £82½ of Three-and-a-Half per-cent Stock, yielding a rather better income, namely, 57s. 9d. per-cent. In both cases he guaranteed the holder against further interference until 1894. The latter stock (the Three-and-a-Half per-cent.) was created with a view to the convenience of those who might prefer a larger present payment at the sacrifice of part of their future capital, but as less than a quarter of a million was applied for, it would seem that very few such people existed. At any rate, the stock was a dead failure, and in 1894 it was paid off and abolished. As to the Two-and-a-Half per-cents, Mr. Gladstone's stock of the future, the only fault Parliament could find with it was that it was a great deal too cheap, and everyone confidently predicted that it would be taken with avidity. The Opposition even professed great alarm at the enormous increase of fifty millions in the capital of the debt which would ensue if the holders of the existing five hundred millions of Consols and Reduced Threes assented in a body, as the City said they would, and to appease their fears, Mr. Gladstone promised to allot only thirty millions to begin with, and to extinguish the increase of capital by applying the annual saving of $\frac{1}{4}$ per-cent interest to a sinking fund. To cut the story short, the end of this much-belauded plan was that only *three millions* of the new stock were applied for. Before it could be fairly launched on the market, the political horizon had begun to cloud over and the coming event of the Russian war was casting its first shadow over the minds of far-seeing statesmen and capitalists. The year that had opened so auspiciously with bank rate at 2 per-cent and Consols at par, closed with money at 5 per-cent and Consols at 92½, and amid the general depression, the great conversion scheme of 1853 —the only prominent financial failure with which Mr. Gladstone's name is connected—suffered complete shipwreck. Over a quarter of a century was to pass away before a new generation of business men were to see Consols once more at par. It was not until November, 1880, that they again crept up to three figures, and that investors again began to ask themselves how soon the Government would feel itself bound, as guardian of the public purse, to make a fresh attempt at the inevitable reduction. If the credit of the country was now such as to enable it to borrow at less than 3 per-cent, it was, of course, incumbent on the Chancellor of the Exchequer to reconsider the terms of the bargain between the national debtor and the national creditor, and if possible to ease the burden of the taxes by inducing the fund-holder to accept a little less, or, if he proved obdurate, by borrowing elsewhere on lower terms and gradually paying him off; but it was not until 1884 that Mr. Childers made the anticipated proposal. This consisted of an offer to the holders of the Three-per-cents to exchange each £100 of stock yielding 60*s.* per-cent, into either £108 of Two-and-a-Half per-cent stock yielding 54*s.* per-cent, or £102 of a new Two-and-Three-quarters per-cent stock yielding 56*s.* 1*d.* per-cent. In this case, both stocks were made irredeemable until 1905, and, as in the case of Mr. Gladstone's conversion of 1853, the increase of capital in the case of the Two-and-a-Half per-cent Stock to be paid off by a sinking fund. The Two-and-a-Half per-cent Stock was Mr. Gladstone's old creation, which had meanwhile been increased by sundry operations to fourteen millions, but Mr. Childers extended the period during which it was irredeemable from 1894 to 1905. That the terms were very liberal was agreed on all hands, and it was generally expected that the response to the invitation would be practically unanimous. The general expectation, however, was again falsified; for the option was only taken advantage of to the extent of nineteen-and-a-quarter millions of the old Two-and-a-Half per-cents, nearly thirteen millions of which were applied for by Government departments, and four-and-a-half millions of the new Two-and-Three-quarter per-cents, so that another small stock was thus added to the List. Politics could not be blamed this time for the want of success, yet there was evidently a miscalculation somewhere. The mistake, it would appear, was that of offering alternative stocks, instead of proposing a general and progressive reduction of interest in the existing stock. Like the proverbial bundles of hay, the two alternatives only served to render the investor undecided, and in the end to prevent him from accepting either, besides which, they also produced the more serious effect of causing the bankers to hold back. Why the latter should have refrained, as a body, from supporting the scheme was perfectly clear; they disliked seeing a great stock, such as consols was, split into halves, and, moreover, if they were to be forced into conversion, they at least wished to make sure, before committing themselves, which of the alternative stocks would command the wider market. They wanted, as Mr. Pickwick once advised, to shout with the largest crowd, and immediately it became evident that the fund-holders generally meant to hold on as long as possible to their beloved Three per-cents, all hope of a voluntary surrender on the part of the banks was at an end. The net result of the two conversions that we have been discussing, was the addition to the List of two new stocks, one of which is so small in amount that any inference drawn from a comparison between its price movements and those of Consols would hardly be reliable, but the other—the Two-and-a-Half per-cents—has on two occasions, when Consols were over par, served a most useful purpose. It has acted as a gauge, or testing machine, by which to ascertain the true value of the public credit, and, as the point is interesting, we will step aside for a moment to examine it. Consols, as we have seen, touched par in November 1880, but to save the trouble of deducting accrued dividend, we will compare the prices of the 6th January 1881, which are free of interest. The quotations were: 82 for the Two-and-a-Half per-cents, and $98\frac{7}{8}$ for Consols. Now, if a Two-and-a-Half per-cent stock is worth 82, a Three per-cent stock, which is based on precisely the same security, and the price of which is governed by the same considerations, ought to be worth one-fifth more, or $98\frac{2}{5}$, but as Consols were in rather better demand at the time than the Two-and-a-Half per-cents, they were quoted a little higher, at $98\frac{7}{8}$, which, however, is quite near enough. Three years afterwards, in January 1884, on looking again at the price of the Two-and-a-Half per-cents, we find it has improved to $90\frac{3}{8}$, and we naturally expect that the same flowing tide will have carried Consols up in a like proportion to $108\frac{1}{4}$. But, as a matter of fact, Consols only stood at $101\frac{1}{4}$; the reason of the check being that, as they were redeemable at par at any time after twelve months' notice, the buyer ran the risk of soon losing whatever premium he paid, and consequently felt it unsafe to go more than a point or two beyond par. We begin now to see the advantage of a reference to the Two-and-a-Half per-cents quotation. If Consols had been the only stock to go by, it would have been reasonable to infer from the current price that a Perpetual Government Annuity of £3 was worth no more than £$101\frac{1}{4}$, whereas the real value, as made manifest by the price of the Two-and-a-Half per-cents, was over £108. For the time being, in fact, the price of the latter alone correctly gauged the actual value of the national credit, and deductions drawn from the price of consols were fallacious. In the speech introducing the conversion scheme of 1888, Mr. Goschen also took occasion to point out that while the Two-and-a-Half per-cents, which enjoyed an immunity from conversion for many years, were then quoted at 96, Consols, with this imminent danger hanging over them, were no higher than 102, and that under the circumstances the former were the genuine indicators of the real value of Government security.

We now come to Consols, " the historical stock of this country—the champion stock of the world", as Mr. Goschen enthusiastically termed it. There appears to exist a popular notion that Consols is a sort of generic name for all the Government stocks forming the Funded Debt, and that the separate headings in the schedule only serve to distinguish between the different species; but, strictly speaking, the term only applies, of course, to Consols proper, which is a stock that was formed in 1752, by *consolidating* into one, or, as we should now call it, unifying, a number of small stocks, all bearing 3 per-cent interest. The unified stock was entitled " Three per-cent Consolidated Annuities ", from which to plain

"Consols" was an easy transition. Other consolidated annuities, of higher denominations, afterwards appeared in the schedule, but the Three per-cents always retained their distinctive designation of "Consols", both because they came first in point of time, and because they took the lead in the matter of magnitude. Owing to a change made in the system of funding about the year 1781, this particular stock was one that grew rapidly. Before that year the sound principle had been adhered to of varying the amount of the annuity according to circumstances, but of never selling it below par; but in 1781, as the difficulty of raising money increased, the practice grew up of keeping the annuity invariable, and selling it for what it would fetch. The difference was this—under the old system, if it was required to raise £100 when the rate was 6 per-cent, the Government would have sold £100 6 per-cent stock at par. Under the new system it sold £200 3 per-cent stock at 50. Upon the capital of the Debt the consequences were deplorable. From the beginning of the American War to the end of the French War we borrowed 417 millions in money, but created 589 millions in stock, thus increasing the debt by 172 millions more than was necessary. In defence of this practice, it was maintained that the issue of loans at par at a time when the value of the national credit rose with every victory, and declined with every reverse, would have meant a sub-division of the debt into stock at all sorts of awkward and unmanageable rates, besides which, if stock had been created to a greater amount than the cash really received, what did it matter after all? The Government was not bound to pay it off at par, but could always go into the market like anyone else and buy it at the price of the day, and if the price of the day should be higher than the price of issue, it only showed that the credit of the nation had improved, which would be a matter to rejoice over and not to cavil at; as the stock, moreover, was held in England by Englishmen, its redemption at a higher rate was, to a certain extent, but a transference from one pocket to another, and was no loss to the country as a whole. It would be beside our purpose to follow this argument any further, and I only referred to it in order to explain the growth of Consols, for as it was in the Three per-cents, that most of the loans raised at the time were funded, the stock increased in the 30 years between 1776 and 1805 from 38 millions to 390 millions, or at the rate of over 11 millions a year. Great reductions were afterwards made, but it still amounted in 1888 to 323 millions. In that year the famous stock which had endured for 136 years, and which had triumphantly withstood the assaults of Mr. Gladstone and Mr. Childers, finally succumbed to the determined attack of Mr. Goschen, and the "sweet simplicity of the Three percents" is now a thing of the past.

THE

LONDON DAILY STOCK AND SHARE LIST.

THIRD LECTURE.

[*Delivered 24 January 1898.*]

I HAVE already had occasion to mention that the old Three per-cent Consols reached par thrice during the last half-century, and that on each occasion the guardian of our public purse had felt it his duty to try and drive a somewhat harder bargain with the national creditor. Two of these attempts—the conversions of 1853 and 1880—ended, as we know, in failure, Mr. Gladstone being defeated by unfavourable politics, and Mr. Childers by the opposition of the city; but the scheme put forward by Mr. Goschen in 1888 met with general acceptance and was triumphantly carried through. His plan was simplicity itself. He offered the holders of the Three per-cents (New, Reduced, and Consols), a new stock, at par, bearing 3 per-cent for one year and $2\frac{3}{4}$ per-cent for 14 years, until April 1903; after which the rate fell automatically to $2\frac{1}{2}$ per-cent, but was guaranteed against any further reduction until 1923. (It may be remarked in passing, that, in comparing the price with others, it will be found simpler to regard the new Consols as a Two-and-a-Half per-cent stock, and to deduct the present value of the $\frac{1}{4}$ per-cent bonus from the price. Thus, if you deduct $1\frac{1}{4}$, the approximate present value of a five years' bonus of $\frac{1}{4}$ per-cent from to-day's quotation of $112\frac{3}{4}$, you get $111\frac{1}{2}$ as the price of a Two-and-a-Half per-cent stock).

The phenomenal success of the conversion is to be ascribed to the favour with which it was received by the banking interest, who, knowing that the reduction was bound to come sooner or later, and finding on examination that the scheme contained all the good points, and none of the bad ones, of its predecessors, consented to lead the way, and were followed by the public. In the first place, instead of contracting the market by splitting up existing stocks, Mr. Goschen proposed to enlarge it by merging the whole of the Three per-cents into one great and homogeneous stock, which would amount to between five and six hundred millions; secondly, there were no alternatives to puzzle the investor, or arouse his suspicion—one stock alone was offered, and he must either take that or his money; thirdly, no book-keeping complications were created by disturbance of capital—£100 old stock exchanged for £100 new stock, neither more nor less; and lastly, Mr. Goschen proposed to retain the time-honoured name of Consols by giving his new creation the title of Two-and-Three-quarters per-cent *Consolidated* Stock. As to the first point—the preference shown for a large, instead of a small, stock,—I may explain that the banker looks on Consols from a point of view somewhat different from that of the ordinary investor, who is attracted mainly by their absolute safety. The security they offer—that of a first mortgage on the whole of the national assets—is, of course, the best conceivable. No promise or obligation whatever is, or can be, so good as the bond of a great, wealthy, and honourable nation. Railway Debentures and Corporation Stocks rank next in order; but it is quite conceivable that railways may some day be ruined by the invention of a new mode of locomotion, whilst a great conflagration or the collapse of some particular industry might render the bond of a city almost worthless. But the taxability of the British nation is all but inexhaustible. We can augment the national income, if need be, in a manner and to an extent which no other community or corporation possibly can, and on that income the service of the debt is the first charge. In addition, however, to this indispensable quality of perfect security, the banker requires something else. He also requires the scarcely less valuable attribute of convertibility—of convertibility, that is to say, without delay, and at a minimum of expense or loss. Next to cash in his reserves, he ranks such securities as are immediately realizable in time of difficulty or pressure, and repeated experience has shown him that, in this respect, Consols stand first and alone, because owing to their magnitude they offer at all times a free market, and a market, moreover, in which the dealer's "turn" and the broker's commission are cut down to the very lowest figures. As you see from the quotation, the "turn of the market" is only $\frac{1}{8}$ per-cent, and is the lowest of any stock in the List. As a matter of fact, the jobbers in that market will always make you a $\frac{1}{8}$ price, and under pressure, might even quote a $\frac{1}{16}$ price, and as Consols are changing hands daily and hourly in all imaginable sums, they constitute a stock which the banker can get in and out of both easily and cheaply. There is but one article known to commerce of which we are able to say positively that at all times and under all circumstances you can be certain of instantly turning it into cash in London, and that is—gold; but next to gold in the quality of ready saleability comes Consols, and it is no exaggeration to say that on a day of panic it would be easier to sell half-a-million of them than it would be to find a buyer for fifty thousand pounds' worth of Indian or Colonial Stock, or of Railway Debentures. Another prepossessing feature of the new stock was, as I mentioned, its name. Care had to be taken that the appellation should not clash with that of Mr. Childers' Two-and-Three-quarters per-cents, and in bestowing on it the title of Consolidated Stock, Mr. Goschen expressed a hope that, after the extinction of the Three per-cents, the public would transfer to it the old and familiar abbreviation of "Consols." That hope was fulfilled; but Mr. Goschen had a very narrow escape from being immortalized, for in the neck-and-neck struggle that ensued between "Consols" and "Goschens" for popular favour, it certainly looked for a time as though the latter were to be the winner. There appears to be no previous instance of the word "stock" being employed in the official designation of any part of the Funded Debt, and, to a certain extent, it is a misnomer. The root is that of the verb "stick", and the primary notion is that of something which is stuck in and remains fast. The fund contributed by those who took shares in the first public companies, such as the East India Company, the Bank of England, the South Sea Company, &c., was called the "Capital *Stock*", probably because the money when once put in could not be taken out again, and the term appears to have been applied by analogy to the imaginary capital of the Government Annuities. This view of the case appears to have been taken by Richardson in his New English Dictionary (1844), where he describes stocks as "the public funds where the money of unhappy persons is now fixed." Our finances were at a very low ebb in 1844, and that might explain the definition. The profit, too, that was periodically divided by such companies was called the "dividend"; and by carrying the analogy a step further, the instalments periodically paid by Government on account of the Perpetual Annuities were also called dividends.

Having just referred to the principal sum, in respect of which the Perpetual Annuities are payable, as an "imaginary capital", it would, perhaps, be well to be a little more explicit. The National Debt divides, as we have seen, into two branches, between which it is now necessary to draw a very sharp distinction. The one—the Unfunded or Floating Debt—actually *is* debt, being made up of obligations to pay certain definite sums of money on certain fixed days; but the other, the so-called Funded Debt, is really no debt at all. That um of five hundred and odd millions which you see standings in the List as the present amount of Consols, was never borrowed by the Government; the money is not owing to anybody; and the State has never promised to pay it to anybody. What happened was this. The Government, wishing on various occasions to raise money for certain purposes, created Perpetual Annuities of £3 each, and *sold* them, at the best price obtainable, in sufficient quantity to realize the sum required. The thing sold was a perpetual annuity; that is to say, an unending series of future annual payments of £3 each; and the price given for it was a lump sum of money down, which, whether £100, or whether only £50, was, all things considered, of equal value at the time of payment. Strictly speaking, there was no question of a loan in the transaction at all, but only of a purchase and sale. If I were to buy a £5 life annuity from an insurance company for £100, I presume you would regard it as nonsense to say that the company *owed* me £100; and, in like manner, it is irrational to suppose, because I buy a Perpetual Government Annuity of 55*s*., that the Government actually owes me £100, on which it has undertaken to pay me $2\frac{3}{4}$ per-cent interest. The only engagement it enters into is an engagement to pay me a specific annuity, and, so long as that annuity is duly forthcoming, it does not owe me a penny. I have not told you quite the whole of the bargain, however. As the State might, some day, wish to pay off the annuitant, it always took care to stipulate that, after a certain date, and after giving a certain notice, it should have the right to buy back the annuity at the fixed price of £100. The price the Government got for it made no matter; whether they had sold it cheap just before Waterloo, or sold it dear just after, was all one; if they ever wanted to dispossess the holder of it against his will, they undertook to give him £100. Mr. Goschen made precisely the same stipulation nine years ago. Here is what he said in "The National Debt (Conversion) Act, 1888": "The new stock shall " not be redeemable until the fifth day of April, one thousand " nine hundred and twenty-three, but on and after that day " shall be redeemable by Parliament on such notice, at such " time or times, and either in one sum, or in such sums or " proportions, and in such order and manner as Parliament " may direct, at the rate of one hundred pounds sterling for " every one hundred pounds of the capital sums in respect of " which the annuities constituting the stock are payable." While all else about the redemption has been left to the future discretion of Parliament, the price at which it shall take place is definite and unmistakeable. What we are to understand by the statement in the List that the present amount of Consolidated Stock is £525,000,000 is now growing clearer. That sum is not debt; for Consolidated Stock is merely the name given to a huge mass of perpetual annuities, and so long as the quarterly instalments are punctually met, there can be nothing owing. It is simply the maximum redemption-value—the outside limit of the sum we may be called upon to pay in case the holder of the annuity refuses to part with it until he is forced. But, in addition, there also attaches to it a conventional signification, based, not on principle, but on general agreement and custom. Whether you regard £2. 15s. as the amount of an annuity, pure and simple, or whether, for convenience in book-keeping and to avoid a troublesome circumlocution, you choose to consider it as the annual interest on a hypothetical principal of £100, makes little difference when once you are quite clear as to the true nature of the bargain; and, as a matter of fact, it has been found extremely convenient, both by the State and the annuitant, to adopt the latter supposition. The old consols were not called annuities of £3 each, but annuities of £3 *per-cent* each, and the "per-cent" referred to an imaginary capital of £100 which the Government assigned to each of them, with a view, no doubt, to simplify the keeping of the accounts. It was not necessary to do so; and the French Consols (Rentes) which resemble ours, make no mention at all of a principal. A certificate of French Rente states the amount of the annual payment to which the bearer is entitled, but says nothing about a capital sum. Yet, even the French are illogical; for, though they studiously avoid all mention of a capital sum, they, at the same time, entitle the stock Three *per-cent* Rente. The Government, I said, assigned a hypothetical principal of £100 to each annuity; and when we speak of buying or selling £100 Consols, we really mean the annuity corresponding to an imaginary capital of £100 stock. I trust you will now understand, therefore, that "Funded *Debt*", "borrowing", or "raising a loan" (as applied to a fresh issue of consols), and such like expressions, though sanctioned by ordinary usage, must be taken strictly in a conventional, and not in too literal a sense.

Let us now turn our attention to "The National Debt Act, 1870", which regulates the transfer and dividend arrangements of all the Funds, and which, being a consolidation of the various enactments relating to the perpetual annuities that had been making their appearance on the Statute Book at greater or less intervals ever since the end of the seventeenth century, presents matter of interest that we cannot afford to overlook. It was passed, of course, before the Two-and-Three-quarters per-cents, and the new Consols were created, but the Acts of 1884 and 1888 both incorporate its provisions by reference. The first section that appears to call for special comment is No. 7, which says—"The annuities and dividends aforesaid " shall continue to be free from all taxes, charges, and im- " positions, in like manner as heretofore." Now, I think it probable that if I were to ask any one of you to put your own rational construction on that clause, and to tell me what it meant, you would be inclined to reply that it was so clearly expressed in plain English as to need no interpretation, and that it just meant what it distinctly said, namely, that the dividends on consols and on the other perpetual annuities shall be payable free from all taxes, as hitherto. But, if that be the true meaning, how comes it that the dividends are not actually paid free from all taxes? How comes it that the Bank of England deducts income tax; and that, if your quarterly dividend be £10, the Bank keeps back 6*s.* 8*d.*, and only gives you £9. 13*s.* 4*d.* To the legal mind there may appear to be no inconsistency in that deduction, but to us, who have not had the benefit of a legal training, it certainly seems to call for explanation; and, in order that we may view the matter in a right light, we will ask, firstly, with what object that clause could have been incorporated in the original Loan Acts, and secondly, whether the imposition of income tax on the dividends is, or is not, consistent with the spirit and purpose of the exemption. As to its purpose there can be little doubt. It was meant to protect the fundholder from sharp practice on the part of the Government. The lender of money to the State had in view the possibility that, at some time or other an unwise or unscrupulous Minister might attempt to trick him out of part of his money under the pretext of taxation; and he therefore stipulated that payment of the full annuity, without deduction, should be one of the terms of the bargain. The other question is more difficult to answer. To judge whether or no the imposition of income tax is a violation of contract we shall have to glance at the circumstances under which it was originally levied. The first Income Tax Act was passed in 1799, a few years after we had entered into the great war. The impost was sanctioned because there was no help for it. Money had to be raised by hook or by crook, and however obnoxious a tax of such an oppressive and inquisitorial nature might be, no other way could be found of raising it. *All* income, from whatever source it might be derived, was made chargeable, and whether the taxpayer obtained his revenue from trading or from a profession, from landed property or from funded property, made no difference. In one case as in another it was income, and as such had to pay; and though no special mention was made in the Act of the public funds, yet as all the dividends formed part of somebody's receipts they, of course, contributed in common with other income. Shortly afterwards, on the renewal of the tax, a change was made in the manner of its collection, the principle being adopted, which we still adhere to, of charging incomes *at their source*, that is to say, of charging them when in the hands of the first possessor, instead of in the hands of the ultimate proprietor.

The tax on rent, for instance, was to be collected from the occupier instead of the landlord; the tax on interest, from the borrower instead of the lender; and the tax on income derived from the funds, instead of being gathered from the fundholder himself, was to be collected from the Bank of England, which was authorised to deduct it from the dividends. All at once the fundholder discovered that his annuity was no longer payable free from all taxes. "You have broken faith with me," he cried. "You pledged your "solemn word to pay me without deduction, and now you "begin to violate the compact!" "Nothing of the sort!" indignantly retorted Mr. Pitt. "I only promised that no tax "should be imposed on the stockholder, separately and "distinctly. I only promised that no impost should be "levelled directly at the fundholder, as such, and I still "uphold that promise in its integrity. The engagement was "sacred, and whatever happens, we will stand by it. We "tax the dividend, *not as dividend, but as income;* and so long "as we subject it to no special tax, but treat it only like all "other income, we maintain that your exemption remains "inviolate." Now, who was right? Was the fundholder or was Mr. Pitt? I express no opinion; but simply tell you how the imposition was justified. Mark, however, the result of setting a bad example. Section 71 of our Act says—"No "stamp duty shall be payable in respect of any dividend "warrant, transfer of stock, stock certificate, or coupon," which is language as unequivocal as it well can be. Nevertheless, in 1831, Lord Althorp proposed to levy a duty of ½ per-cent on all transfers of stock, and when the astonished House reminded him of this express provision in all the Loan Acts, calmly asserted that his proposal could not possibly be construed into a breach of faith, inasmuch as he intended charging *all* transfers, and not transfers of the funds alone, which, to his mind, appeared precisely on all fours with the precedent set by Mr. Pitt. So great, however, was the outburst of anger which the scheme provoked that it was at once withdrawn. Then again, in 1852 Mr. Disraeli proposed to tax income from the funds at a higher rate than other income, which likewise would have been a clear violation of principle. Immediately the war was over the tax had to be taken off, and I may mention, as an interesting scrap of history, that, in order to be rid of the detested impost once for all, the

House ordered the assessment papers and the records of the Commissioners' proceedings to be destroyed, and was very near falling in with Mr. Brougham's serio-jocular suggestion that they should be publicly burnt by the common hangman. After that, though successive administrations cast many a longing look on the forbidden tax, over a quarter of a century passed before any minister could summon up sufficient courage to propose its re-imposition, and it was only under a very grave sense of the disaster threatening our national finances that Sir Robert Peel dared to do so in 1842. Desperate diseases justify desperate remedies; but the remedy in this case, I am sorry to say, overstepped the limits of national probity. During the former continuance of the income tax, Mr. Pitt had carefully laid down and maintained one great distinction, which he justly considered essential to public faith, namely, the exemption from its incidence of foreign fundholders residing abroad, who, as they were not represented in Parliament, could not be said to have accepted the tax through the vote of their spokesman, as might have been argued in the case of the British fundholder. Foreigners residing in this country, and enjoying the protection of its government and laws, are bound to pay their share of the expense of keeping up that protection, but, as there exists neither the power nor the right to impose British taxes on foreigners residing outside our dominions, it is clear that, if taxed at all, they are taxed as fundholders, and as fundholders only. But Mr. Pitt contended that he was not taxing the fundholder, as such, and, as a logical sequence of that contention, he exempted the foreign holder. Sir Robert Peel, on the other hand, decided not to exempt him; and, it is difficult to arrive at any other conclusion but that, in so doing, he committed a breach of good faith. The chief reason alleged for the departure from precedent was that exemption might open the door to fraud, by inducing British subjects to register their stock in foreign names, but even if evasion of the tax had been an established fact, instead of a mere assumption, it would have been no justification for paying the foreigner less than we had promised to pay him, or, in other words, for partial repudiation. To defend the imposition is, in short, tantamount to asserting that those who have borrowed money shall be at liberty to tax the lenders at their own discretion, which is preposterous. The only extenuating circumstance—

and a lame excuse it is—that we can now plead for neglecting to reverse Sir Robert Peel's decision, is that all aliens who, at the present time, hold British funds, have acquired them subject to that condition. The course taken by Sir Robert Peel was not only a violation of contract, it was also a blunder. It was pointed out to him that the national obligations of many countries were almost entirely in the hands of foreigners —principally Englishmen—and that if England once set the fashion of taxing debt, it would be difficult to blame them for imitating us, as they assuredly would. That warning we have since had reason to remember, and may have again. Italy, for instance, takes toll from all holders of her Rente, and India taxes the dividend on rupee paper, and a few years ago I remember noticing that a prominent colonial statesman had been advocating the imposition of income tax on New Zealand stocks. The British bondholder, he argued, had a direct interest in the maintenance of order and good government in the colony, and might help to pay for them. I daresay you will think I am treating this question with an unwarrantable degree of prolixity, but as there is an important principle involved in its consideration, I wished to place it before you as clearly as I could. Returning now to our Clause No. 7, we can make sense of it by mentally adding "except income tax", or by reading it in conjunction with No. 36, which openly recognizes the deduction. The greater part of the rest of the Act is made up of regulations concerning the management of the Debt. The arrangements respecting such matters as the payment of dividends, the transfer of stock from one person to another, the preparation of certificates, and so forth, are not settled by voluntary agreement between the Government and the Bank, as might be supposed, but are prescribed by statute. The law provides, for instance, that all the dividends shall be payable at the Bank of England—so that, if the Chancellor of the Exchequer wanted to make part of them payable elsewhere, he would have to get a special Act of Parliament passed to authorize it—and it also provides (Sec. 72) that the Bank of England shall continue a corporation as long as any part of the Debt remains unpaid. It is, of course, infinitely more convenient to the fundholder to be able to draw his dividend or transfer his stock in the very heart of the City than it would be to have to go to the Treasury or to Somerset House for that purpose, but the original reason for bringing in the name of the Bank was probably to convince the public that everything was straightforward about the loan, just as at the present day its name inspires confidence in, and gives a fillip to, a Colonial or Corporation issue, and that of Rothschild to a foreign one. The Act also imposes upon the Government the duty of paying over to the Chief Cashier of the Bank, out of the Consolidated Fund, sufficient money to meet the dividends as they fall due; and, if there should not be enough standing to its credit at the time, it is empowered by the Exchequer and Audit Act of 1866 to borrow the difference from the Bank, on condition of repaying it from the first accruing revenue of the next quarter. The operation of these provisions is to make the dividends on the Public Debt, when they become due, a charge upon the moneys in the Exchequer in priority to all other claims; and, in the event of the sum being insufficient, a prior charge is created upon the first receipts of revenue thereafter. As to Part IV., which deals with the subject of transfer, it is obvious that, as the Debt is only repayable at the option of the Government, and that, as the stockholder's title consists simply of an entry in the books of the Bank, and not of a document (the so-called stock receipt which the purchaser receives, merely proves that a transfer in his name was effected on a certain day, beyond which it has no actual value, and is not evidence of title) capitalists would be unwilling to lend, unless there existed an easy, cheap, and speedy means of transferring their claim to someone else who was willing to buy it from them; and the Act therefore makes arrangements to that effect. The fund-holder may transfer his holding to as many people as he chooses, and the Bank will prepare the documents and make all the necessary entries without charging him a farthing for its labour, and without putting him to any trouble beyond asking him, if not personally known to them, to show that he is the party he represents himself to be (which he usually proves by getting his broker or solicitor to identify him.) No limit is imposed as to the amount that may be transferred, for as it is a great advantage to a nation that its public debt should be as much divided among the population as possible —the greater the number of State creditors, the greater being also the number of those who have a direct interest in upholding the Government—accounts may be opened for any amount from a penny upwards. I am not aware that there is any instance of an account being opened for a penny, but I believe there are cases where people have transferred nearly the whole of their stock and carelessly left a trifle over, so that there are accounts standing over in the Bank's books for a few pence. And now we will leave the Act.

The best of all instruments, it has sometimes been said, for the discovery of truth in political economy, is a reference to like circumstances or to similar transactions in private life; and one of the applications of this principle supples a favourite argument to debt reformers. "What should we think," they ask, "of the moral courage of a private individual who, in " bad years, or whenever he had exceptional expenditure to " meet, made a practice of borrowing money on the mortgage " of his estate; but who, instead of striving in good years to " clear off the encumbrance, allowed his opportunities to slip " by, and accustomed himself to regard the burden as a " dispensation of Providence, which it was useless to struggle " against. If such conduct would be contemptible in the " individual, how can it be otherwise than reprehensible in the " case of that aggregate of individuals which we call a nation." It is quite conceivable, they admit, that, if the estate were undergoing development, it might be good policy to let the mortgage stand and to lay out all the money that could be spared in improvements, which, in after years, might return ten-fold; but, when once its productive powers are fully evolved, and when the annual yield becomes greater than the amount that can be wisely spent again upon it, then prudence and common sense dictate that the proprietor should address himself seriously to the task of paying off the mortgage. That is one side of the question; now let us hear what can be argued on the other. In the first place, it is maintained that, as the public creditor is our fellow-citizen, and that, as a debt owing by one part of the community to another is, in a national sense, no debt at all, it is just as absurd to be alarmed at the magnitude of the sum owing by the public debtor as it would be to take fright at the total of, let us say, our banking deposits, which are also money owing by one part of the community to another. The interest paid on the debt is national expenditure, and has to be provided for by taxation, true!—but it is also national income, and helps to pay that taxation; and though the Chancellor of the Exchequer takes money from us with one hand to meet the debt charge, yet he gives it back with the other in the shape of the quarterly dividends. If the National Debt, in fact, were paid off to-morrow, the nation would not be a penny the richer, except as regards the smaller portion of it held by foreigners, and, indeed, if anything, it would even be poorer, for a part of the dislodged capital would inevitably be exchanged for some of the rubbish of the stock and share market, and its owners never see it back. This, in the main is true ; and, at any rate, there is no gainsaying the fact that the weight of a debt held at home, as consols and French rentes are, and of which the interest is spent at home, is not nearly so much felt as that of a debt held abroad, and the interest upon which has to be sent out of the country. Nevertheless, even an internal debt is an evil, and that for at least three reasons : (1) A great deal of money is wasted over the operation of raising the interest, the nation having to support an army of tax-gatherers, many of whom, if the debt were extinguished, could be better employed otherwise; (2) The interest, added to our necessary expenditure, tends to use up the good and fair taxes, and to leave us, in case of war, with only the unjust and irritating taxes to fall back upon; (3) While the whole community, from A to Z, must contribute to make up the interest, only a small portion of it, only A, B, and C, receive that interest. Another argument against redemption is that the national creditors, as a body, do not ask or wish to be paid, but on the contrary, strenuously object. Whenever a holder, here or there, wants to have his money back, there is always someone else ready to buy him out, and step into his place. Then, again, the funds are the one investment that is absolutely safe, and that requires no looking after ; the one investment which widows and orphans, and all those who are incapable of the business-like management of property, may put their money into, and sleep in peace, and the one investment into which bankers can place their reserves with the certainty of being able to realize whenever necessary. Lastly, the money to repay debt must in part—not all, but in part—be withdrawn from profitable occupation. Whilst the debt subsists, the public creditor is virtually advancing capital to the public debtor at a little over $2\frac{1}{2}$ per-cent, or including all expenses of collection and management, at say 3 per-cent, and the latter can employ that capital to yield him double or treble as much. By redeeming its indebtedness, therefore, the nation ceases to pay interest on the amount discharged, but ceases also to receive profit on the money so applied, or rather, on that portion of the money so applied which was previously laid out to advantage. In spite, however, of these and such like plausible and ingenious arguments, the general opinion—and certainly the opinion of those whose judgment is entitled to the greatest respect—is that a generation whose taxes are light, productive, and unimpeding, ought undoubtedly to do something to ease the burden of coming generations, which can hardly be much better off than we are and may be a great deal worse off. Our children and our children's children will have their own exigencies to provide for, and it is our plain duty, in time of national well-being and prosperity, to work off a part of our great mortgage, and not to hand down to them difficulties which it is in our power to alleviate. We must remember, too, that the faster we pay off debt the better our credit, and that our credit is what we rely upon for help in time of trouble. If England should again become involved in a great and protracted struggle—and who shall say that we may not? —it is no exaggeration to say that two or three years of war expenditure on the modern scale would probably suffice to re-add to the debt the reductions of a century.

The first Minister to establish a fund for the redemption of the Debt, and the first Minister, also, to lay violent hands on the accumulation, as soon as it became worth the stealing, was Sir Robert Walpole; but the Sinking Fund which is best remembered is that established by Pitt in 1786. This was based practically on the amazing principle, that if the nation lent itself money, charged itself interest, and continually invested and re-invested that interest in fresh loans to itself, it would, in course of time, grow so rich that the Debt could be paid off with the utmost ease, and yet nobody be a penny the poorer. The House and the country were delighted with the plan, and it passed by acclamation. Some stupid people —people of that sort who always try to pick holes in what they cannot understand—said it was repugnant to common sense to suppose that the nation could gain riches by lending to itself, any more than a shopkeeper could make money by buying his own stock; but it was explained to them how a certain Dr. Price had calculated that if one penny had been put out at our Saviour's birth at five per-cent compound interest, it would, by the year 1781, have increased to a greater sum than would be contained in two hundred million globes, the size of the earth, all of solid gold, while, at simple interest, it would in the same time have amounted to no more than seven shillings and sixpence. "Well", said the disbelievers, " and what of that"? "Why, simply this", was the triumphant reply. "Let the Chancellor of the Exchequer *borrow* a million a year at *simple* interest, and *lend* a million a year at *compound* interest, and—there you are"! This arithmetical puzzle deluded the nation for years, and throughout the whole of the French war we kept up the farce of annually paying off large sums of debt, though we always borrowed the money with which to pay it, and a great deal more besides. Mr. Pitt himself was not deceived. There is no doubt that he really meant to redeem the debt out of savings; but that, finding this impossible, and having to choose between either a fictitious Sinking Fund, or none at all, he deliberately adopted the former alternative, in the hope that, by educating the country to regard reduction of debt as a bounden duty, he might be able, when better times came round, to change pretence into reality. Eventually, however, the nation saw its folly, and, in 1829, the whole of the previous legislation affecting the Sinking Fund was swept away. In its stead was instituted the sound and solid principle that the *actual surplus* of income over expenditure in every financial year shall be paid over to the National Debt Commissioners, and by them be applied in immediate cancellation of debt. This system, which has remained in operation down to the present day, is known as the *Old* Sinking Fund, and it may be well to point out with regard to it that the *actual* surplus in question is not to be confounded with the *estimated* surplus, which the Chancellor of the Exchequer is, now-a-days, expected to provide, and make us a present of, on Budget night. If, I repeat, there should remain, at the end of the financial year, a genuine balance to the good—not of hypothetical figures, but of actual cash—that money must, by Act of Parliament, be laid out in the payment of debt; and, as it was formerly the practice of our Finance Ministers not to count their chickens before they were hatched, by anticipating the normal growth of revenue, the Old Sinking Fund has served to effect a genuine cancellation of indebtedness to the amount, at the end of 1896, of seventy-nine millions. Until twenty-three years ago, the revenue estimates of the coming year were based strictly on the actual receipts of the previous year, without one sixpence of allowance for the augmentation that might reasonably be anticipated as a natural outcome of the growth of population; but the system came to a sudden end, under curious circumstances, in 1874, coincidently with the fall of the Liberal administration. In his appeal to the country, in the early part of that year, Mr. Gladstone had held out the bribe of a total repeal of the income tax, and had demonstrated the possibility of its abolition by a sort of *pro-formâ* Budget statement, in which he took into account the full normal expansion of revenue; but, though the electors refused to take Mr. Gladstone back, they hungered after the surplus which he had dangled before their eyes, and when the Conservatives took office, they deemed it expedient not to disappoint the country in that respect, but to adopt the estimates of their predecessors. In this way the system was initiated, which has ever since prevailed, of discounting the elasticity of the revenue by estimates which are drawn up with scientific precision, and which aim at the closest possible approach to perfect accuracy. If we make estimates at all, it is, doubtless, better that they should be true ones; but, for all that, financial reformers look back with regret to the years 1865 to 1874, during which, by wilfully under-estimating our income, we were able to wipe off debt to the amount of many millions. Having deprived the "Old Sinking Fund" of its virtue, Sir Stafford Northcote was bound, in common decency, to take other measures for the liquidation of debt, as it was quite obvious that popular pressure for the reduction of inconvenient taxation would never allow him to put aside an *estimated* surplus for that purpose. We may be very virtuous and very sincere in our professions; but whenever the Chancellor of the Exchequer has money over, and asks what he shall do with it, we invariably discover that it would be a pity to waste it in paying debts. In 1875, accordingly, Sir Stafford Northcote brought forward a proposal for a "*New* Sinking Fund", which was to operate in conjunction with the existing scheme. His plan, which was simplicity itself, was to take the debt charge in the estimate of expenditure at a fixed sum, somewhat in excess of the amount actually required, and to apply the surplus each year in the purchase of consols, &c. This permanent annual charge now amounts to £25,000,000; of which about £8,000,000 represent capital, and £17,000,000 interest and cost of management. If not tampered with, it will necessarily become more effective every year. A third way—perhaps the best of all—of paying off the debt still remains; and that is, by the gradual conversion of perpetual annuities into terminable annuities. So long as we go on paying interest only, we make little progress; but, if we could add the principal to the interest, and pay the two together by means of fixed annual instalments extending over a term of years, the time would eventually come when both would disappear. This plan was always open to us; but the objection to it was its costliness, as people could not be induced to buy terminable annuities, unless the price was disproportionately low. They were disliked for several reasons. The proper way to deal with them is to re-invest each year a certain part of the annual income, so that, at the termination of the annuity you may have entire the sum you spent in buying it; but most persons do not know how to make the necessary calculations, and the ordinary investor—if he is wise—avoids what he cannot understand. Then, again, as the tendency of Government stock is to rise, and as the amount to be paid for a terminable annuity was always based on the current price of consols at the time of the sale, there was ever a possibility that the annual re-investment would prove insufficient to replace the capital. Lastly, income tax had to be paid on the full amount of the annuity—both on the capital and interest—and, if the tax went up, the holder might find himself a good deal out in his estimate. The consequence was that, though the system of terminable annuities (or long annuities, as we formerly called them) has been in existence even longer than the Funded Debt—the first loan on this basis having been issued in 1692—they were never a favourite form of investment, and those in existence up to 1860 had, in most cases, been forced out by the custom of the Government, when raising money, of granting, in addition to the stock created, bonuses in the form of terminable annuities. Shortly after the establishment of the Post Office Savings' Bank in 1861, it occurred, however, to Mr. Gladstone, that if he created large blocks of annuities in his capacity of Chancellor of the Exchequer, he might himself purchase them in his capacity of custodian of the poor man's savings. It occurred to him that, as he was the largest fundholder on the books, he might, from time to time, commute portions of the stock held by him against Savings

Banks' funds into terminable annuities, and, by thus increasing the present burden of the nation, diminish its future burden. The plan worked, and has continued to work, admirably. In 1883, no less than £70,000,000 of Consols, £30,000,000 of which belonged to the Savings Banks' Fund, and £40,000,000 to the Chancery Paymaster, were in this way cancelled, and terminable annuities set up to replace the Stock. Let me explain again what the scheme is. The Chancellor of the Exchequer sent, we will suppose, for the Paymaster-General of the Court of Chancery, and said: "I want to make a "proposal to you. I find that you are the holder of "£40,000,000 of stock, which you hold as an investment, "and which you will, no doubt, continue to hold for the next "twenty years. If you will hand that stock over to me to be "cancelled, I will give you, in exchange, a twenty years' "annuity of £2,666,000. Of this amount, £1,200,000 repre- "sents the interest you have hitherto been receiving, so "that, as far as that item goes, you are just in the same "position as though you kept the stock, and the remaining "£1,466,000 represents return of capital, which, if annually "invested by you in Consols, and allowed to accumulate, will, "in twenty years' time, reinstate you in possession of your "£40,000,000 of stock." These terminable annuities are, at present, automatically paying off upwards of £4,500,000 a-year, and, in case of emergency, we always have the convenient option of re-converting them into an equivalent amount of stock—a process which, though it amounts to the same thing as suspension of the sinking fund, does not sound quite so alarming. The total amount paid off by the sinking fund system is continually on the increase, and, at the present time, is about £8,000,000 a-year. Assuming that the State can borrow at 2½ per-cent (it can actually borrow at much less), that sum would pay the interest on a capital of £320,000,000 ; so that, by simply suspending the sinking fund, England could raise a war loan of £300,000,000 without adding a single shilling to the taxation of the country. Other nations, who boast of *their* war-chests, might mark that fact with advantage. Now, as it is obvious, on consideration, that every mode of alleviating the burden of debt must resolve itself, under whatever name it may be known, into the appro- priation, to that end, of *actual surplus revenue*, and nothing more, the question suggests itself—Why should it be necessary to hide away so plain a process behind all this hocus-pocus of sinking funds and terminable annuities, as though they were ashamed of it? Why cannot Sir M. Hicks-Beach come down to the House next April and say, in a straightforward way, that our actual expenses for next year will amount to, let us say, £100,000,000, but that he means to make us pay £108,000,000, and to use the difference in writing down our liabilities for the benefit of posterity? Well, if he did, I suppose he would render himself the most unpopular man in the country. The "unemployed" would burn him in effigy, I dare say, and he would probably need police protection. The fact is that, in matters of this sort, it is expedient—nay, more than expedient, it is necessary—to hoodwink the country. Experience has proved, beyond all question, that Parliament cannot be trusted to deliberately vote large specific annual sums towards the repayment of debt; but that, on the other hand, if it once consents to devote a certain sum to the setting up of an annuity, it can be relied upon to keep its word, and not to be for ever tampering with the arrangement; and the more so, because, as the true nature of the operation is concealed from public view, members need not go in fear of their constituents. The complicated machinery of terminable annuities is preferable, therefore, to other methods of debt reduction, because it enables the Chancellor of the Exchequer to make sure that our efforts to lighten the load that presses on the industry of the nation will be steady and unremitting in their application, and increasingly beneficial in their result. A few words with reference to the price-movements of consols will exhaust what is still left to say about them. Without going into details, I think it is possible to enunciate a general principle that will account for all their fluctuations. The law appears to be no more than this; that, if the disturbing influence of politics could be eliminated, the steady application of the New Sinking Fund, the operation of the terminable annuities, and the unceasing absorption of the stock into other channels where such holdings are a necessity, must inevitably cause a continuous upward movement. Supply being limited, the ever-present demand cannot fail, when other influences are in abeyance, to produce a perpetual enhancement of value. But consols are a *political* security; and a political occurrence of real magnitude might, as has happened before, bring down the price with startling rapidity.

Holders of the national stock appear to lose their heads over events which would hardly cause possessors of Metropolitans or of railway debenture stocks to turn a hair, and the reason is not far to seek. It is not because our credit begins to totter immediately a war-cloud is seen on the horizon; on the contrary, our credit is stability itself; and, since 1815, no public annuitant has ever, for an instant, doubted the safety of his investment. It is because Consols are a stock the quantity of which is liable to indefinite and absolutely incalculable expansion. In the event of our becoming involved in a first-class war, the quantity forced on the market might reckon, not by millions, but by scores—even hundreds—of millions; and the greater the augmentation of supply, the greater the depreciation of value. That is why "bulls" of the stock are in such a hurry to scuttle out whenever politics take an unfavourable turn, and why the public also, if matters look really serious, become anxious to part with their holdings at a small present loss, in order to avoid the possibility of a greater future sacrifice.

THE

LONDON DAILY STOCK AND SHARE LIST.

FOURTH LECTURE.

[*Delivered 7 February 1898.*]

WHEN speaking the other evening of the Two-and-a-half per-cent Stock originally created by Mr. Gladstone in 1854, I mentioned the fact that both Mr. Childers and Mr. Goschen had referred to its importance as a testing machine by which to ascertain the true value of the public credit, and it has since occurred to me that it would be of interest to further elucidate this point, by instituting a comparison between the present prices and the yield of Consols, Local Loans Stock, and the Two-and-a-half per-cents, all of which, being based on exactly the same security, ought, after allowance is made for the difference in the dates of redemption, to give about the same return. Consols are redeemable in 1923, Local Loans Stock in 1912, and the Two-and-a-half per-cents in 1905, and we shall assume, in each instance, that the holder will be paid off at par at these respective dates, which is the worst that can happen to him. In each case we must, of course, deduct accrued interest from the price, and, as all the stocks stand over par, we must also in each case, set up an annuity which, if allowed to accumulate at $2\frac{1}{2}$ per-cent until the date of redemption, will, by that time, restore the premium which the buyer at to-day's price would otherwise lose.

Price of Consols				£112	12	6
Less 2 months' accrued interest			...	0	9	2
				£112	3	4
Less the present value of a 5 years' annuity of 5s., deducted in order to reduce the stock to a 2½ per-cent basis				1	3	4
Net price			...	£111	0	0
Gross yield...	£2	10	0			
Less amount of annual sinking fund necessary to replace the premium of £11 at end of 25 years	0	6	5			
Net yield ...	£2	3	7			
If £111 yield	2	3	7			
£100 will yield				1	19	3

Price of Local Loans Stock ...			...	£113	10	0
Less 2 months' accrued interest			...	0	10	0
				£113	0	0
Gross yield...	£3	0	0			
Less annual sinking fund to replace £13 at end of 14 years	0	15	9			
Net yield ...	£2	4	3			
If £113 yield	2	4	3			
£100 will yield				1	19	2

Price of Two-and-a-half per-cents				£106	0	0
Less 2 months' accrued interest				0	8	4
				£105	11	8
Gross yield...	£2	10	0			
Less annual sinking fund to replace £5 11 8 at end of 7 years ...	0	14	9			
Net yield ...	£1	15	3			
If £105 11 8 yield	1	15	3			
£100 will yield				1	13	5

This remarkable result can only be explained by the supposition that the cost of the Two-and-a-half per-cents "looks cheap" as compared with that of Consols and Local Loans Stock, and has induced buyers to pay what is, really, an extravagant price. If we reject this explanation, the only inference open to us is, that the true value of British credit is less than $1\frac{3}{4}$ per-cent. We have now disposed of all the stocks constituting the National Debt, and the next item on the Official List is Local Loans Stock, the capital of which, amounting to forty-one millions, represent advances made by the State, for sundry purposes, to local authorities. The principle of lending public money to municipalities, and other corporate bodies, can be traced back for upwards of a hundred years; but, as a definite system, it took shape in 1817, when, owing to the disorganization of the labour market, caused by the great influx of disbanded soldiers and sailors on the close of the great war, it was found necessary to start relief-works for the alleviation of distress. The system took firm root, and since that time the Government has been in the habit of making advances, through the agency of commissioners, for almost every conceivable purpose—for sanitary and water works; for schools, free libraries, and artizans' dwellings; for harbours and lighthouses; for markets and fairs; and so forth—the object in view being to assist small communities who desire to carry out really useful works, but who, although they may have fairly good security to offer, could hardly borrow in the open market without great disadvantage, because the amounts they require are so small. During the past thirty or forty years in particular, great extension has been given to this plan of borrowing from the State by numerous Acts of Parliament, which expressly authorize and encourage it. Some of these have been local Acts, passed for the purpose of enabling a particular borough to raise money for a specific object, but others, especially "The Artizans' Dwelling Act", "The Elementary Education Act", and "The Public Health Acts", have bestowed such powers on local bodies all over the country. As the objects for which such bodies are invited to incur debt are mostly matters of Imperial concern, and have been enforced by Imperial legislation, it is but just and proper that the Imperial authority should, by interposing its own credit, enable the local authority to raise the necessary funds on the best terms.

The applications for loans have to be made to certain commissioners (in England, the Public Works Loan Commissioners; in Ireland, the Board of Works and the Land Commissioners), whose business it is to ascertain whether the applicants have power to borrow, whether they have complied with the statutory provisions in regard to the loan, and whether they have sufficient security to offer. If satisfied on these points, they decide how much they will lend, and on what terms. From a recent report of the Public Works Loan Board, it appears that most of the advances have been made at $3\frac{1}{2}$ per-cent, and are repayable within thirty years; also, that fourteen millions of money are represented by balances standing at the debit of no less than 2,500 School Boards in England and Scotland, while another eight millions have been borrowed by about 1,000 Boards of Health and other sanitary authorities. Until 1887, the funds required for these advances were supplied by the Treasury, which provided the money in whatever way happened to be most convenient at the time when it was wanted. If there was plenty of cash at the bank, it simply lent from its balance; if not, it raised the means by an issue of Exchequer or Treasury Bills. As no distinction was ever made, however, between the money it borrowed to spend and that which it borrowed to lend, the National Debt had, for very many years, included a varying sum, against which there was a set-off on the other side of the account, and the Chancellor of the Exchequer used to have to explain that the debt appeared to be greater than it really was, because there were so-and-so many millions owing to the nation by local authorities which ought to be deducted. To this unsatisfactory style of book-keeping, Mr. Goschen determined, in 1887, to put an end; and he did what a merchant would have done if he found that his cashier had been lending people money against their I O U's, charging it to expenses, and re-crediting the account with it when paid back; that is to say, he ordered the general expenditure account to be entirely cleared of these items, and a separate page to be opened for them in the national ledger, in order that the country might always know exactly how it stood. The amount was thirty-seven millions, and, as a matter of course, if those millions had never been lent, the National Debt would have been that much the smaller. To complete the operation, therefore, Mr. Goschen created a new stock to the amount of thirty-seven millions, and allotted the whole of it to himself, as National Debt Commissioner, in exchange for a like total of funded and unfunded debt, which he held against savings banks' funds, and which he immediately cancelled. He also laid down the business-like principle that, whenever the local authorities wanted more money, the State was not, in future, to lend it out of its own pocket, but, if the repayments from old loans were not sufficient to meet new loans, was to *borrow* it for them; or, what came to the same thing, the State might let them have the money at once, but was invariably to recoup itself, sooner or later, by creating and selling additional issues of the new stock, to which he gave the descriptive title of Local Loans Stock. The stock was to bear 3 per-cent interest, and the difference between 3 per-cent and the rate to be charged to the local borrowers, was meant to cover expenses of management, and to provide a sinking fund for bad debts; but the money has been lent so carefully that bad debts are unknown. As regards security and exemption from stamp duty, Local Loans Stock is on precisely the same footing as Consols. Though primarily a charge on the Local Loans Fund, which consists of the interest and repayments received from the local borrowers, it is expressly provided by the Act of 1887 that any deficiency of interest shall be charged on the Consolidated Fund, and that, in default of payment by a borrower, the deficiency of capital, if any, shall be made good by Parliament. We now come to a stock which, though classed under the head of "British Funds, &c.", is in no sense a liability, either direct or indirect, of the British Government. The reason why the capital-stock of the Bank of England stands here, instead of among those of other banks, is, presumably, because "Debt due to the Bank of England" has figured as a national liability ever since we owned a funded debt, and also because bank stock for many years enjoyed the pre-eminence of being the only security, outside consols and East India stocks, in which trust funds might be invested. There is, no doubt, a very general impression that the capital of the Bank and the Government debt of eleven millions are in some way connected; and it has frequently been urged, by those who undertake the easy task of pointing out the numerous anomalies and inconsistencies of the English money market, that the State ought no longer to allow its name to appear on the list of debtors of a trading corporation. When the debt was originally incurred, they say, the Government was poor, and glad to borrow, and the bank, in return for the loan of its capital, acquired a valuable monopoly; but, as the Government is now rich, and as the bank has long ago been deprived of its exclusive privileges, it is illogical and undignified to let the money still be owing. Set free her capital, they argue, and let the bank invest it in bills, and you will then see that she will have no difficulty in rendering her control over the market as effectual and as complete as it ought to be. Now, this argument, plausible as it sounds, would appear to be based on an entire misconception of the existing facts; and those who reason in this way forget that the debt was virtually paid off over fifty years ago. Until the Act of 1844 came into operation, the holder of bank stock had a right to say that the Government owed him money, for here is how the chief cashier used to make up his balance sheet (this being the last return issued in the old form):

LIABILITIES.	ASSETS.
Circulation, £21·3 millions	Securities, £22·9 millions
Deposits ... 14·1 ,,	Bullion ... 15·6 ,,
£35·4 ,,	£38·5 ,,

Only the liabilities to the public were shown, and the assets held against them. The liabilities to the proprietors were:

Capital	...	...	£14·6 millions
Rest ...	...	...	3·1 ,,
			£17·7 ,,

and, as the Bank's other assets consisted of—

Securities	...	£3·6 millions
Government Debt		11·0 ,,
		£14·6 ,,

it is clear that the stock-holders regarded the loan to the Government as an investment of their own money, and not of that of the public. But the effect of the Act was to deprive the bank of the privilege of issuing notes on its own credit, and to convert it from a bank of issue and deposit into a bank of deposit only. For 150 years the bank had been able to earn a large profit by issuing as many notes as it pleased against just so much cash as it pleased—and now the power to coin its credit was taken away. All notes were, henceforth, to emanate from a new Government office, called the Issue Department, the management of which was, for practical reasons, placed in the hands of the bank directors, who were, in that capacity, to act as agents of the State; and in the process of establishing that Issue Department, the Government, to all intents and purposes, discharged its debt to the bank. "You owe the note-holder twenty-one millions", said the Chancellor of the Exchequer to the directors, "and Parlia-"ment insists that you pay him off at once. I will tell you "how to do it. You have already given me eleven millions; "now, give me ten millions more, and I will pay him off for "you, and then we can cry quits." And the bank did so. It gave the Issue Department three millions in securities, and seven millions in gold and silver, and thus got rid of its liability on the circulation. And the result was, that the eleven millions, which the Government had hitherto owed to the holders of bank stock, was henceforth to be considered as owing to the holders of issue-department notes, whom it undertakes to settle up with whenever they may feel inclined to ask for their money. Immediately afterwards, the Issue Department drew up its first balance-sheet, which was as follows :

AN ACCOUNT FOR THE WEEK ENDING 7 SEPTEMBER 1844.

Issue Department.

Notes issued £28·4 millions.	Government debt	£11·0 millions
	Other securities	3·0 ,,
	Gold coin & bullion	12·7 ,,
	Silver bullion	1·7 ,,
£28·4 ,,		£28·4 ,,

This is the first account issued by the bank after the passing of the Bank Act. You will notice that the notes have increased. They were twenty-one millions in the last account, and they have increased to twenty-eight millions, because the bank itself, for its own purposes, took seven millions of the new notes. Practically, that is much the same as the account at the present day. If all these notes were presented to the bank for payment, the Government would have to intervene, because eleven millions of them are issued against the Government debt. It is clear, therefore, from this return, and from every return that has been issued subsequently, that the Government debt is really due to the note-holder, and not, as is commonly supposed, to the Governor and Company of the Bank of England, with whose trading capital it no longer has any connection whatever.

Last, though not least, of the stocks forming this group, comes the debt of our Indian Empire, the division of which into India stock and India rupee paper invites enquiry into the distinction that exists between an external and an internal loan. The essential difference between the two is, that the interest on an internal loan is payable at home, while that on an external loan has to be remitted abroad. Internal loans are those, such as consols and French rente, which a State raises in its own currency among its own subjects. External loans, on the other hand, are those which it raises in foreign currency among the inhabitants of other countries, and the interest upon which is, for the convenience of the lender, made receivable abroad. There is no reason why the native capitalist should not invest in the external debt, if he likes it better, or why the foreigner, if so inclined, should not give the preference to the obligations manufactured expressly for home consumption; but if the Calcutta merchant buys India stock, he will have to put up with the inconvenience of a certificate, the coupons attached to which are payable in London in gold, and if the London merchant buys rupee paper, he finds that the interest is payable by a draft or coupon on Calcutta for so-and-so many silver rupees. In both cases the transaction would, under present circumstances, savour more of the nature of an exchange speculation than of an investment. Another distinction is usually drawn between home and foreign loans. The one, it is said, is liable to taxation; the other not. It is held, with regard to the latter, that the borrower is bound to abide by the strict letter of his bargain, and that the terms which he imposes upon himself in the prospectus, and on the strength of which the money is advanced to him, cannot afterwards be modified, unless and until he obtains the consent of the lender. Without that consent, modification is repudiation, and, as such, may entail the condign punishment of being "warned off" by the committee of the Stock Exchange. In the case of an internal loan, however, it seems to be supposed that the Government of the country is justified, seeing that it represents, at one and the same time, both fund-holder and taxpayer, in dealing with the debt in such manner as the exigencies of the State may render necessary; and that it is at full liberty to tax it, or to reduce the interest, at its own absolute discretion. But this is surely a mistake. A State which borrows money at home and then withholds from its creditors part of that which it has agreed to pay them, must be just as wanting in integrity as the State which borrows abroad and repudiates. England, it is true, taxes her home debt, and so does India; but this is explained away as a tax on income, which all pay alike; and the fact of its being universal is held to be a safeguard against injustice. In both cases, however, it is injudicious, to say the least of it, to tax the foreign holder, and, so far as India is concerned, this liability to taxation helps to explain the disparity of value between its internal and external debt obligation. If, however, instead of being an impartial tax on income derived from every source, it were a tax on income derived from the funds alone, the imposition would clearly amount to repudiation, and to repudiation in its meanest and most dangerous form. Until the year 1858, when the Government of India was transferred, after the suppression of the mutiny, from the East India Company to the Crown, rupee paper was scarcely known at all to English investors. The company had power to raise loans in this country on obtaining the sanction of Parliament; but it had usually preferred to pay a higher rate and borrow on its own authority in India, where it had contracted by far the greater part of its debt. In addition to the greater convenience and less expense of effecting interest payments on the spot, there were political reasons for the preference. The company held the wise opinion that those who had much to lose by the subversion of its power, would desire to see that power maintained; and as that astute prince, the Rajah of Chutneypore, deemed it expedient to secure the fidelity of his Sepoys by keeping their pay two or three years in arrear, so the company, on the principle that a native was a native, whether sepoy or prince, took measures to ensure the passive goodwill of His Highness by inviting him politely, but firmly, to subscribe a good round sum to their new loan. That principle still holds good in India. The home debt was practically in the shape of promissory notes, which were not capable of being held out of the country, because it was necessary to present them at the Indian Treasuries to encash the interest as it fell due. With a view to improve its credit by the removal of this obstacle, the Indian Government decided, in November 1858, to pay the interest in London by means of sight drafts on India, and issued the following notification: "When holders of notes in Calcutta desire that " the interest thereon should be made payable by bills issued " in London, they must present their notes at the office of the " Accountant-General to the Government of India, where an " enfacement* will be made on each of the notes in question, " as follows: ' Interest payable in London by draft on Calcutta " ' (or Madras, as the case may be).'" The measure was not adopted without some misgivings, as it was feared that, if the European capitalist stepped in, the native capitalist might step out, and the Indian Government thus lose its hold over the self-interest of the moneyed classes. In the result, however, the fear proved unfounded. The demand that immediately sprang up on this side for rupee paper, which returned the buyer 5 per-cent, as against 4 per-cent yielded by India stock, not only enhanced its value to the native holder, but also proved that the English themselves had full confidence in the stability of the Indian Government, and were quite ready to back their opinion with their money—a fact which the natives had been much inclined to doubt; and from that time onward the Indian capitalist lent much more freely than ever he had done before. "Enfaced" rupee paper—the portion, that is to say, which is held in Europe—amounts, at the present time, to about a third of the whole issue, and is a favourite investment, or, rather, a favourite speculation with those who believe that silver still has a future before it. The

---

* "Enfacement" is the antonym of *endorsement*, which obviously suggested it. This seems to be its first appearance in public, and it was, doubtless, coined for the occasion to express a form of words written, printed, or stamped on the face of a bill, note, or other document. Though a useful addition to the language, it has never come into general use, except in "enfaced rupee paper", and has escaped the notice of nearly every lexicographer.

comparative expediency of raising money in England or in India depends, now-a-days, on several considerations. The advantage of borrowing in India is two-fold. On political grounds it is advisable that the native should be encouraged to hold a stake in the country; and, on financial grounds, it is advisable both that the debt should be incurred in silver, the metal in which the revenue is received, and that the country should have the benefit of the fund-holder's expenditure. The disadvantages are, firstly, that on silver loans raised in India a higher rate of interest must be paid than on gold loans negotiated here; and, secondly, that there is difficulty in obtaining the amount required, and obtaining it quickly, as the Government has never yet succeeded in attracting the petty savings of the people, who prefer either to lay out their money in ornaments, or to employ it in usury. To borrowing in the London market, where money is abundant and cheap, the one great drawback is, that the interest must be met in gold, and that the Government hazards a serious loss in converting its silver. Thus, if India borrows £1,000 here at $2\frac{1}{2}$ per-cent when the exchange is at 1s. 3d., she receives Rs.1,600, and has to pay £25 interest, which is provided by selling a council draft for 400 rupees. If the exchange now rises to 1s. 4d., the £25 interest will cost her only 375 rupees; but if, on the contrary, it were to fall to, say 1s., the interest would amount to 500 rupees. The point to be determined, therefore, is whether the difference of interest does, or does not, counterbalance the risk of loss in exchange. In other words, if the Indian Government can borrow 25 per-cent cheaper in London than it can in Calcutta—that is to say, at $2\frac{1}{2}$ per-cent as against $3\frac{1}{2}$ per-cent—is 25 per-cent a sufficient premium to cover the risk of a future fall in silver? Taking the rupee at the conventional rate of two shillings, the total debt of India amounted, on 31 March 1896, to—

In England	£115,903,732
In India ...	103,188,928

and is, therefore, pretty equally divided between internal and external loans. A peculiar feature in connection with the external debt is, that India has to obtain the permission of Parliament before issuing a loan here. No other Government has to do so. Our self-governing colonies are at full liberty to borrow as much as they please in London on their own responsibility, and so are all foreign States. If the king of Patagonia, for example, likes to go to the expense of printing and advertising a prospectus, he may publicly invite subscriptions to his 10 per-cent Government Loan of five millions at 60, and need ask leave of no one. But if the Secretary of State for India wants to buy a railway with English capital, he has first to convince Parliament that the proposed outlay is legitimate and necessary, and is not allowed to raise the money until an Act has been passed authorizing him to do so. The origin of the practice is curious. The East India Company, in its first beginnings, was a chartered association of adventurers, possessing certain exclusive privileges of trade (like the African companies of to-day), and it was only by accident that, in course of time, it acquired its sovereign governing authority. Being no more, at the outset, than a simple trading company, its borrowing powers were limited by Parliament, just as at the present time the borrowing powers of railway companies are limited. When it eventually developed into a great political body, and dropped its mercantile functions, the directors took the opinion of counsel as to whether there was any legal obstacle to their contracting funded debt in this country, and were advised that there existed no hindrance to their so doing; but when, in 1858, it was found necessary to resort to the London market for assistance, and the directors contemplated testing their right, the Government thought, and represented to them, that, inasmuch as it had been the invariable practice for Parliament to authorize them to borrow on bonds in this country, it would not be expedient to act on the opinion expressed by counsel, and that it would be more respectful to Parliament to apply for express permission, as had always been done before. Application was, therefore, made in the usual way, and an Act was passed (21 Vict., c. III), the preamble of which recites that, " In consequence of the disturbances in India, it is expedient " that the East India Company should be enabled to raise " money in the United Kingdom on the credit of the revenues " of India." This was in March 1858, and before six months were over, the East India Company—the most famous joint-stock association of which there is any record—had ceased to exist; but the course taken by it in asking for power to enable it to borrow here, was regarded as a precedent by the new India Council, which took over all the company's responsibilities, and when, in the following year, more money was required, the same step was again taken of requesting Parliament to sanction the loan. Another Act (22 Vict., c. XI) was accordingly passed, which, *mutatis mutandis*, was almost a copy of the statute of the previous year, and which stated in the preamble that, "In consequence of the recent disturb-" ances in India, it is expedient that *the Secretary of State in* " *Council of India* should be enabled to raise money in the " United Kingdom on the credit of the revenues of India"; and from that day to this the same practice of asking leave to borrow has been invariably pursued. There is one other topic to be considered before we leave the subject of the Debt of India, and that is the question whether England, in authorizing India to borrow, virtually assumes the responsibility of seeing that India's creditors shall be paid in full, and thus creates a contingent charge on her own revenue. No one supposes that any legal liability rests on the Imperial Exchequer. On that point the law is as plain and clear as it well can be. Every India Loan Bill contains a clause enacting that the principal and interest thereby secured "shall be " charged on, and payable out of, the revenues of India, in " like manner as other liabilities incurred on account of the " government of the said territories"; and there is no word that can be construed into a guarantee on the part of this country. It was, in fact, with a view to completely settle all controversy that the Government first introduced that clause in 1858, and, so far as the contract is concerned, the terms are too distinct to admit of any doubt that the holder of Indian funds lends his money on the security of the Indian revenue, and on that security alone. It is not on the ground of right, however, that doubts arise, but on the ground of policy. Having assumed the responsibility of governing India, can we dissociate from that responsibility the obligation of meeting the engagements chargeable on Indian revenue? Looking at the fact that upwards of a hundred millions have been lent to India by European capitalists, would it be morally possible for this country to altogether repudiate the Indian Debt without seriously endangering its own credit? This is a question which—as Lord Stanley said, in 1859, in words that to-day, in presence of the ominous aspect of the silver problem, have a prophetic sound—"will recur again and "again, and which will have to be considered *in the future* as "well as in the present." Many other eminent men have also questioned the feasibility of our being able to answer that we "decline to intervene" if ever the creditor of India should have to present his protested bill to us, "in case of need." "Depend upon it", said Sir Robert Peel, when Prime Minister, in 1842, "if the credit of India should become disordered, if "some great exertion should become necessary, then the credit "of England must be brought forward to its support." Again, "It is idle", said Mr. Disraeli, when Chancellor of the Exchequer, in 1858, "any longer to distinguish between "Indian and English finance. If the President of the India "Council—a Queen's Minister in Downing Street—should "find it necessary to raise money by public loan to pay "Her Majesty's troops in India, it will be idle, when the "dividends are due on that loan, to pretend to assert that he "will be able to say, if the means are not at hand, the "exchequer of India is empty, and the revenue of India is "alone liable." I might cite further instances, but these will suffice to show that, notwithstanding the absence of a specific guarantee, many of our leading statesmen have been of opinion that a refusal to help India in case of emergency, would neither be generous nor wise. Moreover, there are good grounds for asserting that it would not even be practicable. The fund-holder's charge on Indian revenue is a first charge, which he can enforce, if necessary, by suing the Secretary for India, and if, after paying him, the revenue proved insufficient to meet the cost of the civil and military establishments, we should either have to maintain the Governor-General and the army at our own expense, or leave India without administration and without defence. On the other side of the question it has been argued, that if we were once to admit responsibility in the case of India, we should have to apply the same rule to Canada and Australia, which also raise money on the security of their own revenues. But the cases are quite dissimilar. The colonies govern themselves; they have representative institutions; they determine upon their own policy, contract their own debts, and impose their own taxes. India, on the other hand, is under a regulated despotism, and its people have no voice, either in their government or in their

taxation. Besides which, colonial debt has been contracted for colonial purposes only, while a great part of the expenditure charged against India has been incurred in fighting to maintain our supremacy. On this question of guarantee, there appeared in the *Times*, last August, a letter from Mr. Benjamin Cohen, a well-known authority on finance, which states the matter so well that I think I will read it to you. He says:
" I suggest once more, as I did in the House of Commons in
" 1895, that the money raised by loan by the Indian Govern-
" ment should be raised, in future, with the Imperial guarantee.
" It is true such a step as I advocate would not secure for the
" Indian Government, now, anything like the saving that
" would have resulted had it been taken in former years.
" The credit of the Indian Government is now, and deserves
" to be, almost as good as that of the home Government.
" But that, surely, is an argument in favour of, and not against,
" my proposal, while it is certain that there never has been a
" moment when such a policy would have more political
" effect on the loyal population of India, as well as on the
" insignificant, but still not to be ignored, disloyal portion of
" the native population. While, therefore, it appears to me
" there is everything to be gained by such a guarantee
" being given, and given specially at this moment, there is
" absolutely nothing to be lost. The relations between the
" home and the Indian Governments are different from those
" subsisting between the executive Government at home and
" any other part of Her Majesty's dominions. India is not a
" self-governing nor a Crown colony. All her finance, all her
" fiscal arrangements are subject to the approval of the
" Secretary of State in Council. She can neither take off nor
" impose a single tax, nor raise a rupee by loan, without the
" sanction of the Government at home. She would be
" responsible, as now, for every penny raised, and would be
" able, as now, to meet her engagements. Of this, I suppose,
" no one has any doubt, and certainly none is entertained in
" the City, as is shown by the level at which her credit
" stands", &c. One proposal made at the time when the subject was under discussion, was, that India should borrow from the home Government, paying just the same rate as she would have had to give in the open market, and that the home Government should apply the difference of 1 per-cent

between the rate paid for the money by India, and the rate at which she herself could borrow, to a sinking fund, which, in fifty years, or less, would extinguish the debt. To this excellent suggestion the chief objection appears to have been that it might encourage India to be extravagant, and that she would never exert herself to pay her own way, unless we gave her clearly to understand that she must depend on herself alone. I think the objection very weak indeed, and it is a great pity that the idea was never carried out, as the sinking fund, by this time, would have wiped out a great portion of the debt. The final outcome of the controversy was, that a middle course was adopted. While positively refusing to admit the principle that this country could, in any event, be held answerable for the debts contracted by our protégé, Parliament, at the same time, came to the conclusion that it would be well, for the future, to keep a more watchful eye over Indian finance; and, since 1858, it has not only subjected Indian expenditure to close scrutiny, and taken care that no unnecessary charge should be imposed on Indian revenue, but has also insisted on full explanations being given whenever it has been proposed to increase the external debt. So far we have been discussing the position of the bond-holder in case of India's insolvency. What his position might be, in the very improbable event of our giving up India, or, in the still more improbable event of our being driven out of India, are cases that fall outside the range of practical possibilities, and which it would be unprofitable to waste time over.

Our examination of the stocks forming the first group in the official List is now at an end, and as it would be inexpedient, at this advanced stage, to broach the subject of Corporation Stocks, which stand next in order for consideration, I purpose directing your attention, in the few minutes that remain at our disposal, to the subject of Trust Investments. When Mr. Goschen introduced his conversion scheme in 1888, it was represented to the Government that the reduction of interest would operate very harshly in the case of stock held by trustees, the interest derived from which was, in many instances, all that widows and orphans had to depend upon, and that to suddenly deprive a helpless class of people, who usually have no means of earning a livelihood, of a part of their small fixed incomes for the benefit of the taxpayer, would be to inflict upon them a grave injustice. As there was really no reason, it was also said, why the beneficiary of a trust should not be allowed as full an enjoyment of the produce of the fund as was consistent with the safety of the capital—this latter being always the paramount consideration—it was suggested, as a remedy, that the limited range of investment, to which the trustee's choice had hitherto been restricted by law, should be extended, in order to include such other securities as would, while equally safe, yield a somewhat better return. Though Mr. Goschen did not appear to like the proposal—seeming to consider it desirable that trust-money should be employed to support the credit of the State—he, nevertheless, promised to think the matter over, and in the following year a Trust Investment Act was passed, which, in addition to consolidating the existing law on the subject, gave trustees much wider powers of selection than they had up to that time possessed. Until that Bill became law, the securities in which trustees might invest—failing express directions in the trust deed—were only to be ascertained by searching through a number of Acts. The first of these, passed in 1859 (before which year the trustee might have incurred personal liability if he had purchased anything but consols or other Government securities), authorized investment in Bank Stock and East India Stock; in 1867, the authority was extended to any stock, the interest on which was guaranteed by Parliament; in 1871, to Metropolitan Consols; and in 1882, to first-class railway debenture stocks. The necessity for all this piecemeal legislation was of a two-fold nature; on the one hand there had been an enormous increase in the amount of trust funds, which were growing, as proved by the yield of the death duties, at the rate of millions a year, and which are believed to amount, at the present time, to something like £200,000,000, and on the other, there was a concurrent decrease in the available supply of Government securities, which were being steadily absorbed, both by the operation of the sinking fund, and by the purchases of the Court of Chancery and of the Savings' Bank authorities. The policy pursued by Parliament with regard to the successive additions to the authorized list, had been to select only from among such securities as were subject to the jurisdiction of the British courts, and also, as far as possible, from these over which it might be said to exercise control to the extent of determining to what amount they should be issued; and this, you will find, was the guiding principle that was also followed in drawing up the Trust Investment Act of 1889.

THE
LONDON DAILY STOCK AND SHARE LIST.

FIFTH LECTURE.

[*Delivered 21 February 1898.*]

You will remember that, when discussing the obligations which represent our indebtedness as a nation, I had occasion to point out, as a matter of congratulation, that, in compliance with the general wish of all political parties, and thanks to our enjoyment of a prolonged period of peace and prosperity, continuous efforts had been made for many years past to lighten the pressure of our huge incumbrance, and had been attended with so great a measure of success that, from its highest point of £900,000,000, which the National Debt attained at the close of the great war, the total had now shrunk to less than £650,000,000. So far as it goes, this is, of course, eminently satisfactory; but a glance at the next item in the Official List, that of Corporation Stocks, is calculated to arouse some misgiving as to whether a bald statement that the Public Debt has been reduced by upwards of £250,000,000 conveys the whole of the truth; and, on turning to the Local Taxation Returns, our doubts are confirmed, for we are there brought face to face with the unpleasant and, at first sight, startling fact that the diminution of one description of national indebtedness has been accompanied by the creation and growth of another, and that practically the whole of the money so laboriously scraped together by the Imperial authority for the benefit of its creditors has been re-borrowed by our local authorities, who, at the end of March 1895—the date of the latest available return—had piled up a liability amounting to no less than £235,000,000. The first year for which the Local Taxation Returns give the amount of the Local Debt is 1874–75.

In that year it is stated to have been	£92,820,100
And the National Debt was ...	755,619,537
	£848,439,637
In 1880–81 the respective figures were :	
Local Debt	£144,203,299
National Debt	734,670,016
	£878,873,315
And in 1894–95 :	
Local Debt	£235,335,049
National Debt	656,998,941
	£892,333,990

The decrease of the one has, therefore, in the last twenty years, been more than counterbalanced by the increase of the other. Taking the two classes of indebtedness together, moreover, our national obligations, at the present time, are almost as onerous as ever they were. It may be objected, however, with some sort of plausibility, that this presentment of the case brings into conjunction, and places an unfair construction upon, facts which are entirely disconnected, and that no useful purpose can be served by linking the National with the Local Debt, inasmuch as the two are of essentially different natures. The National Debt, it is commonly said, is the heritage of costly and mostly useless wars; and all that we have to show for it— apart from warships, telegraph lines, government buildings, and the Suez Canal shares—is an indefinite amount of prestige and glory. The Local Debt, on the other hand, has been incurred in providing for the requirements of a higher civilization, and for a great portion of it we are able to point to tangible and realizable assets, in the shape of valuable, and in many instances reproductive, property, acquired and held for the enjoyment of the public for ever. If full justice is to be done to the subject of Corporation Stocks, which we are about to enter upon, it will be necessary to discuss the growth and development of this Local Debt in some detail, as well as to ask whether the expenditure of so large a sum of borrowed money has been justified by the benefits received from it, and whether local indebtedness has now reached its approximate limit, or is likely to continue growing until it finally becomes as great as, or even greater than, the National Debt itself. To discover the beginnings of Local Debt, we must go back as far as 1792, in which year the system originated of advancing public money to local bodies in furtherance of objects approved of by Parliament. The usual purpose for which assistance was given was the carrying on of relief works for the alleviation of distress; but, in some instances, loans were also granted for the promotion of important public works, such as land drainage, river embankments, &c., the execution of which, though of acknowledged necessity, did not fall within the scope of Government operations. It is unnecessary to go further into the history of these State loans, as we went over the same ground in connection with the subject of Local Loans Stock; but I may mention that the practice of borrowing from Government—though now chiefly confined to small communities who require sums too trivial to be worth asking for in the open market—still exists, and has been extended to numerous objects. For upwards of half-a-century the growth of the debt was a matter of insignificance, and it is only when we come to the present reign, and to the new era of reformed corporations, inaugurated by the Municipal Reform Act of 1835, that it begins to assume importance. Up to that time the privilege of incorporation had been either granted to serve political ends or acquired by purchase, and as it so happened that the governing councils nominated by most of the early charters were given the right to appoint their own successors, there had gradually grown up in our great towns exclusive and independent corporations, which had succeeded in monopolizing privileges belonging to the borough as a whole, and had in many cases even assumed to themselves the sole right of returning members to Parliament. Owing to the notorious jobbery and corruption to which this system gave rise, the inhabitants of incorporated towns had long manifested a general and just dissatisfaction with their municipal institutions, and one of the first duties of the reformed Parliament of 1832, was the appointment of a Commission to enquire into the constitution and privileges of civic corporations. The

Commissioners discovered disgraceful abuses, and reported that "the existing municipal corporations of England and Wales "neither possess nor deserve public confidence or respect, and "that a thorough reform must be effected before they can "become, what they ought to be, useful and efficient instruments "of local government." The outcome of their recommendations was the great charter of English municipal liberties, the Municipal Corporations Act of 1835, which enlarged the basis of local representation, put an end to the abuses exposed by the Commissioners, and provided a uniform constitution for all boroughs to which it applied. It also provided for the creation by charter of new municipalities. If the inhabitants of an unincorporated town deem themselves worthy of the dignity of a mayor and corporation, they may petition for a charter, which on their convincing the Privy Council of their fitness to be entrusted with the privilege, will be granted them, unless good cause appears for withholding it. What we call a town, it may be well to explain, has no legal existence as such, and its name is no more than a geographical expression, identifying a certain collection of houses larger than a village. The law may recognize a parish, or a sanitary district of that name, but knows not the town until it is incorporated, and has been scheduled as one of the boroughs to which the Act applies. Its government thereafter rests in the hands of a local representative body, the Town Council, and, as a municipal corporation, it becomes endowed with a perpetual succession —that is to say, however the members may fluctuate, the corporate body never ceases to exist—and with the power of holding lands in mortmain. The Act of 1835 was amended by numerous subsequent enactments, and was eventually superseded by "The Municipal Corporations Act, 1882", which consolidated the whole of the law on the subject.

The success that attended the first great experiment in local self-government, as manifested in the growth of a municipal administration far more vigorous and intelligent than had been possible during the era of close corporations, speedily led to a great extension in the powers conferred upon towns of managing their own affairs; and the legislation of the last fifty years has cast upon local authorities a constant succession of new duties and new responsibilities. In the attempt to cope with the multiform and ever-increasing wants of society, their labours have grown with the growth of their capacity; and were it but generally realized how greatly the internal welfare of the community,—its health, and its safety, its pleasures and its comforts,—depends on the wisdom and foresight displayed by our local administrators, the subject of local administration would surely meet with the attention it deserves. To them is confided the relief of the distressed poor, the maintenance of elementary schools, the control of the police, and the management of numerous endowments. They provide baths and wash-houses for the poor, hospitals for the sick, workhouses for the destitute, asylums for the lunatic, and graves for all. Under one group of Acts, they cleanse, drain, repair and light our streets. Another bids them erect healthy dwellings for the poor, and keep an eye on common lodging-houses. We look to them to regulate the traffic, to give us libraries and public parks, and even to see that the so-called comic song of the music-hall pays due regard to the conventionalities of public decorum. They register our coming into the world, and, if necessary, vaccinate and educate us; they record our departure from it, and, if need be, bury us. Of all their functions, the most important, however, is the care of the public health. The present reign witnessed the first serious attempts that have ever been made to solve the hygienic problems that spring from the crowding together in great towns of dense masses of human beings, and systematic sanitary legislation may be said to begin with the Public Health Act of 1848. Water supply, food analysis, the maintenance of sewers and drains, measures to arrest the spread of infection, the inspection and prevention of nuisances, and such like, have been the chief subjects of this legislation, which has necessarily applied more to towns than to the country. The dweller in rural districts still sinks his own well and digs his own cesspool, but in towns the householder is absolutely dependent on the cistern and the dust-cart. Another Public Health Act came into force in 1875. It effected little actual change, however, in the existing sanitary law, but, by codifying the large number of statutes relating to it, rendered it simpler and more intelligible. The long catalogue of offices undertaken by local authorities is even yet not exhausted. Provincial municipalities have shown an increasing disposition, for many years past, to supplant private enterprise by joint action in the supply of such public conveniences or necessities as are of the nature of monopolies, and by including the sale of gas and water, and of cemetery lots, within the sphere of their activity, have been able to apply a considerable margin of profit towards the relief of local rates. Latterly, too, they have been turning their attention to electric lighting, and to the acquisition of tramways, while one great corporation—that of Manchester—has been investing money in a ship canal, and talks now of establishing a municipal theatre. It is not to be supposed, of course, that duties so numerous and so varied can all be performed by one class of authority. Nor is such the case. In addition to County Councils, District Councils and Parish Councils, to Boards of Guardians and Boards of Health, we find Local Boards, School Boards, Highway Boards, Burial Boards, Harbour Boards, Vestries, Commissioners, and a dozen others. But if the ratepayer attempts to discover which is which of these bodies, to trace out their relations to each other, to distinguish between their functions, to map out their administrative areas, and, in short, to find out for himself how, and by whom, he is rated and governed, the complexity of the subject will strike terror to his soul. It would almost appear that, whenever it has become necessary to legislate for a new social want, Parliament has made provision for it, quite regardless of existing machinery and existing areas. We have parishes and unions; we have urban and rural sanitary districts; we have school board areas, highway districts, and what not; almost all independent of each other, and, as often as not, interlacing and overlapping. "For almost every new " administrative function the Legislature has provided a new " area containing a new constituency, who, by a new method of " election, choose candidates who satisfy a new qualification, to " sit upon a new board, during a new term, to levy a new rate, " and to spend a good deal of the new revenues in paying new " officers, and erecting new buildings. Thus there has been " created, not a system, but a chaos; a chaos of areas, a chaos of " elections, a chaos of authorities, a chaos of rates, a chaos of " returns." The consequence is, that not one householder in a thousand understands the construction and working of the machinery of local government; in fact, the great majority of us scarcely know even as much as the names of the motley crowd of public authorities by whom the local business of the district is carried on, and by whom our money is spent. The system defies criticism, simply because so few of us can spare the time and trouble to find out what it is and what it does.

All we know for certain is, that the rates grow heavier year by year, and that they must be paid; and we pay and grumble.

To all who have paid the least attention to matters of finance, it is perfectly well known that the cost of public works of any magnitude is rarely, if ever, defrayed out of current revenue. In the first place, it is obvious that, if a work is of permanent utility, it would be most unfair to make those who happen to be residing in the district at the time of its construction pay for that which will last long after they may have removed or died. Then, again, when it has been once decided that certain work must be done—a main sewer constructed, or a town hall built—it is best that the work should proceed quickly, and without interruption. It would be quite possible, of course, to build gradually, spending as much each year as the ordinary revenue allowed, and then suspending operations until additional funds accumulated; but, in most cases, the certain consequence of delay would be damage to the work already done, and it is the common experience in such matters that waste of time is waste of money. Generally speaking, therefore, it is essential, before beginning any important undertaking, that there should be sufficient money at command to ensure its completion, and the principle is, nowadays, firmly established of borrowing the requisite capital, and of spreading the repayment of principal and interest over a term of years. Now, a corporation or other local authority cannot, any more than an individual, borrow a large sum of money without giving security for its repayment; and it cannot give security—that is to say, it cannot legally pledge the rates—without express statutory authority. Being a creation of the law, it is possessed only of such rights and privileges as the law bestows upon it. Until 1848, however, the facilities which are now so common for deferring to a future day the greater part of the payment for local improvements had only been granted by Parliament in some exceptional cases, where special application had been made; and, as a consequence, our towns had shown themselves extremely unwilling to lay out money on such unremunerative objects as drainage, sewerage, and paving, because the ratepayers objected to being saddled with the whole of the cost. As this neglect of sanitary measures was costing the country thousands of lives each year, and undermining the health of the whole urban population, it became necessary to overcome their reluctance by removing its cause, and in the Public Health Act of that year, which enforced a heavy expenditure, Parliament not only authorized all local authorities administering the statute to levy a new rate for improvements, but also empowered them to raise capital by mortgaging the said rate, and to pay back by instalments. The snow-ball of local debt was thus fairly set rolling; and before many years had passed, its growth was fostered and encouraged by a variety of subsequent acts, which aimed at improving the social condition and general health of the people, and which invariably conferred fresh powers of borrowing. At the outset, and for a long time afterwards, almost all these loans were obtained from the State, through the medium of the Public Works Loan Commissioners, but the great inconvenience which this system occasioned to the Treasury, from the fact of frequently having to honour large drafts when funds were low and money dear, led the Government, in 1875, to introduce a Local Loans Act, with a view to encourage local authorities to go to the open market for what they wanted. To some extent they had already done so, having borrowed considerable sums by private arrangement, from solicitors and insurance companies, &c., as they still do, but the security which they were able to offer—that of a mortgage deed, charging a specified rate—besides being inconvenient and expensive, was not readily negotiable, and appealed only to a special and limited class of investor. Thinking that facilities for issuing a a more marketable form of security might induce the municipalities to try their luck in the money market, instead of coming with a petition to Downing Street, the Government gave them liberty, by means of the Local Loans Act, to create debentures, debenture stock, or annuity certificates; and, in order to tempt the appetite of the ordinary investor, made provision for the official sanction of their loans by the Local Government Board, such sanction to be conclusive evidence that the borrower had power to issue the security, and that the same was in conformity with the Act, thus rendering it indisputable. Though the Act was a distinct step in advance, inasmuch as it clearly recognized the principle that the form given to an acknowledgment of debt is an important element in the success of its issue, yet it met with very little favour, and is practically a dead letter. The mistake made was that of requiring that the debenture, or debenture stock, should be a specific charge on a particular local rate or property, a condition, the result of which would be to split up the debt of a town into a number of small divisions—one issue of stock being secured, let us say, on the district rate, and another on the poor rate; one batch of debentures charged on the markets, another on the gas works, another on the town hall, and so forth. But as the marketability of a security depends on its quantity as well as on its quality, that is to say, on the fact of its existing in sufficient bulk to render buying or selling easy within narrow limits, the effect of sub-division is to detract from its value; and this objection proved fatal. Besides which, the corporations had other ideas. The phenomenal success of a daring experiment attempted a year or two previously by the Metropolitan Board of Works, had set them thinking of a new departure in their system of finance. Formerly, the Board of Works had raised money, like other borrowers, by the cumbrous method of mortgaging the rates; but, having exhausted its credit in that direction, it had obtained permission in 1869 to make a direct appeal to capitalists by the issue of a Consolidated Three-and-a-Half per-cent Stock, the service of which was made a first charge on the whole of its property and revenues. The advantage of this plan was that, in lieu of renewable mortgages at various rates of interest, differing in priority and charged upon different securities, the entire debt became merged into one homogeneous class of obligation, which was simple, uniform, and intelligible in all its conditions, and which was secured on the whole body of the assets without distinction. Though a stock based upon rates, instead of on taxes, was a distinct novelty to investors, it had grown greatly in favour since its attributes came to be better understood—so much so, indeed, that an issue of £2,600,000 offered in 1874 at 94½ had been subscribed for eight times over, and, before the Local Loans Bill became law, the stock had risen to 102. It needed little insight on the part of the local authorities to discover that the true solution of the problem "how to borrow cheaply, quickly, and conveniently", had now been found, and, turning their backs on the facilities placed at their disposal by the Local Loans Act, they were soon busily at work drafting private Bills, which should bestow also upon them the coveted right and privilege of issuing the new-fashioned Corporation Stock.

The borrowing powers of corporations are derived either

from the general law, or from private Bills. Under the former they may borrow with the sanction of a Government Department, in virtue of the authority conferred by the Public Health Acts, the Elementary Education Act, the Artisans' Dwellings Act, and numerous others, for the purposes authorized by the respective statutes; but, under the latter, they may borrow for any purpose that Parliament can be induced to approve of. Under the former, again, they may borrow either from the State or from the public; under the latter, from the public only. When borrowing from the public under the general law they had formerly to choose between issuing a mortgage-deed, or adopting one of the methods authorized by the Local Loans Act; but in private Bills they almost invariably asked for authority to issue Corporation Stock. Until quite recently the power to create Stock, other than Debenture Stock, could only be obtained by a special Act, and, as the expense of promoting a private Bill is very considerable, the smaller corporations were practically debarred from issuing it. In 1890, however, an Act was passed—"The Public Health Acts Amendment Act"—which authorizes its creation by all urban sanitary authorities. The enabling clause, s. 52, is as follows: "Where any " authority, whether a municipal corporation, local board, or " improvement commissioners, which is an urban authority, have " for the time being, either in their capacity as urban authority, " or in any other capacity, any power to borrow money, they " may, with the consent of the Local Government Board, exercise " such power by the creation of stock, to be created, issued, " transferred, dealt with, and redeemed in such manner, and in " accordance with such regulations as the Local Government " Board may from time to time prescribe." This Act has been very freely taken advantage of, and, since 1890, many small towns have been able to borrow by issuing stock at 3 per-cent, while if they had applied to the Public Works Loan Commissioners they would probably have had to pay $3\frac{1}{2}$ per-cent for the money. Such control as is exercised over the borrowing powers of Corporations rests almost entirely in the hands of the Local Government Board. This Board, the duties of which extend far and wide, and which is the mainspring of the sanitary organization of the country, was established in 1871, with the object of concentrating in one department of the Government the supervision, which till then had been shared between the Home Secretary, the Privy Council, and the Board of Trade, of the laws relating to the public health, to the relief of the poor, and to local government. No loan can be raised by a sanitary authority under the general law without its express sanction, which is only given after enquiry to show that the money is required for a proper purpose, that the works proposed are sufficient for their object, and will, without doubt, last good for at least as long a time as that limited for the repayment of the loan, and that the estimates, of which full details must be supplied, are fair and reasonable. This enquiry is held in the district concerned by one of the Local Board inspectors, and public notice is given of it, in order that the ratepayers and other persons interested may have the opportunity of expressing any objection they may entertain to the scheme. If land should be required for the proposed works, the purchase of which is hindered by the caprice of its owners, the Board may also grant a Provisional Order for its compulsory acquisition; but the Order only becomes operative after its confirmation by Parliament. In the case of private Acts that comprise borrowing powers, a copy of the Bill must be lodged with the Board, which reports upon it to the Select Committee of the House appointed to hear the evidence on the subject. Its recommendations always have great weight, even if they are not invariably adopted. Borrowers under private Acts are also required to furnish the Board with annual returns showing the exact position of their loan accounts. It is hardly necessary to say that local Acts never confer unlimited borrowing powers. The corporation must specify the amount it requires and prove its estimates before the committee. As already mentioned, it is an axiom with the Local Government Board that the time allowed for the repayment of a loan should be regulated by the probable duration of the work to be constructed, so that the burden of the expenditure may be borne by the generation that chiefly benefits by it; but, with regard to private Bills, Parliament appears, for many years, to have observed no fixed principle in its practice, and cases were not uncommon in which local authorities were allowed as much as a full century in which to pay back the money borrowed for gas and water works. There can be little doubt, in fact, that the expectation of obtaining a longer term for the repayment of their loans under private Bills than would have been permitted them under the general law, operated as a strong inducement to some of the local authorities to include in their local Acts powers of borrowing for the execution of works which ought, in strictness, to have been carried out under public Acts, and that the laxity displayed by Parliament in this respect led to much money being spent on objects which might very well have waited a few years longer. It will hardly be disputed that the ease with which the Governments of civilized and semi-civilized States have been able during the past thirty or forty years to contract permanent, or quasi-permanent, debt, and to bequeath to posterity the fetters forged by their folly, or their misfortune, has been a fatal facility, and in too many instances has proved to be an abiding curse. There is all the more reason, therefore, why, with this experience before us, our local authorities should be restrained from drawing at too long a date on the ratepayer of the future. That unfortunate individual will have quite enough to do to provide for his own wants and requirements, without having to repay money in the expenditure of which he had no voice, and which, for any benefit that he may derive from it, need very likely never have been spent at all. Besides, the very fact of being able to incur debts for others to settle opens the door to extravagance and jobbery. With borrowing rendered so easy that it is but to ask and have, and repayment so easy that the money will scarcely be missed, it is hardly to be wondered at that local authorities should shrink from the hard and thankless task of opposing expenditure on betterments and embellishments which, whether justifiable or not, are always popular and plausible. That "Borrowing dulls the edge of husbandry" is as true now as in the days of Polonius. Then, again, to have the handling and disposal of these enormous sums means the wielding of great power and influence, and, in more ways than one, must be a very agreeable thing; so that it would be irrational to suppose that Town Councils will ever be found over-jealous in their advocacy of a wise and prudent economy. One hundred years is, in fact, much too long a time to keep open any municipal liability, and, for all practical purposes, is little better than no term of repayment at all. Even in the case of water works, which are perhaps the most durable of the purposes for which long loans have been granted, it is doubtful whether they can be constructed to last for a century without extensive and costly repairs; while as to gas works it is obvious, in view of the growing competition of the electric light, that the cost ought to be written off at a far more rapid rate. In 1882, the attention of Parliament was directed to the urgent need of checking this great evil, and the House of Commons determined, by a new Standing Order (No. 173a), that the extreme limit for the repayment of loans to be henceforth authorized by local Acts should be sixty years. For the future, therefore, fresh borrowing powers for a longer period than sixty years can only be given by the suspension of the Standing Order, which ran as follows: "In the case of any Bill promoted by "or conferring powers on a Municipal Corporation or Local "Board, Improvement Commissioners, or other local authority, "the Committee on the Bill are to consider the clauses of the "Bill with reference to the following matters: *(a)* Whether "the Bill gives powers relating to police or sanitary regulations "in conflict with, deviation from, or excess of the provisions or "powers of the general law. *(b)* Whether the Bill gives "powers which may be obtained by means of bye-laws made "subject to the restrictions of general Acts already existing. "*(c)* Whether the Bill assigns a period for repayment of any "loans under the Bill exceeding the term of sixty years, which "term the Committee are not in any case to allow to be "exceeded, or any period disproportionate to the duration of "the works to be executed, or other objects of the loan. "*(d)* Whether the Bill gives borrowing powers for purposes "for which such powers already exist, or may be obtained "under general Acts without subjecting the exercise of the "powers under the Bill to approval from time to time by the "proper Government Department. The Committee are to "report specially to the House in what manner any clauses "relating to the several matters aforesaid have been dealt with "by them; and whether any Report from any Government "Department relative to the Bill has been referred to the "Committee; and, if so, in what manner the recommendations "in that Report have been dealt with by the Committee, and "any other circumstances of which, in the opinion of the "Committee, it is desirable that the House should be informed; "and the Report of the Committee is to be printed and "circulated with the Votes." Sixty years, it may be mentioned, is the period fixed by the Metropolitan Board of Works Loan Acts, as well as for loans under the Public Health Act. The term cannot be regarded as a hardship by corporations, seeing that it only entails an annual sinking fund of $\frac{5}{8}$ per-cent (invested at 3 per-cent) to pay off the debt.

Notwithstanding the fact that the considerations advanced by those who oppose the creation of long-term local debts have gained acceptance to the extent of influencing legislation, it would be a mistake to infer that nothing remains to be said on the other side of the question. It has been maintained, for instance, that, though it may be right to insist on the early repayment of debts created for local improvements or other unremunerative purposes, the reasoning that leads to this conclusion does not apply with equal force to loans raised for the acquisition of water works, tramways, &c., which stand on an entirely different footing. Outlay of this description being essentially an investment of municipal capital in co-operative business enterprise, it is held that the treatment of the capital account ought to be governed by the usual commercial principles that would obtain in the case of a well-managed joint-stock concern of similar nature. The capital of an ordinary water or tramway company is represented by the plant in which it has been invested, and, so long as the original good order and condition are strictly kept up out of revenue, it is not expected that the cost of the property should be systematically redeemed, though it is, of course, wise to set up a reserve fund as provision against contingencies. Without going so far as to assert that a corporation should be allowed to issue perpetual stock against its investments in trading undertakings, it has been submitted that these grounds justify much longer terms of repayment than are now usually granted. That is not the only argument, however. At the present time another and far more serious contention is being urged, which threatens to become one of the burning questions of the day. It is contended, namely, that the incidence of local taxation is grossly unfair, and that, until it has been re-adjusted on a proper basis, the ratepayer ought not to be burdened with heavier repayments than are absolutely necessary. By local taxation is meant the charges levied on defined localities for supposed local purposes. Its principle is that the cost of such matters as concern only the dwellers in a particular neighbourhood, and not the nation at large, ought to be borne by the district affected; and the grievances to which it has given rise are that personalty does not bear its share, that the division of rates between occupier and owner is unequal, and that ground rents almost escape. It originates with the poor rate imposed on occupiers in the reign of Queen Elizabeth, at which time, and for long afterwards, the number of occupying owners was very large. The property of these occupying owners was the natural and obvious quarry of local levies; but owing to the comparative rarity of the tenant farmer class, the question of a division of the rate between owner, as such, and occupier, as such, was not raised, or if raised was disregarded. At first, relief of destitution was almost the only purpose for which a charge was made on occupancy; but in course of time other imposts came to be levied on the same assessment, and still continued to be exacted from occupiers, though these, in the great majority of cases, had ceased to be owners, and were now tenants. How anomalous the incidence of local taxes has become strikes one forcibly on contrasting it with that of the national taxes. In both cases the true principle is that all classes should contribute in proportion to their means. To this end the Chancellor of the Exchequer spreads his net as widely as possible, and always makes at least the pretence of distributing his attentions equally over the community, taxing both directly and indirectly, and taking tribute as well from real as from personal property. But the whole burden of rates falls on a particular class. Personal property has nothing to fear from them; but the moment capital is invested in landed property it falls a victim, and, though there is no doubt that a large part of the local outgoings directly affects and benefits houses and land, it cannot be claimed that any gain is derived from the expenditure on such matters as poor relief or elementary education. Hence, owners of real property complain of the injustice to which they are subject, and call for contributions from personalty. Then there is also the great wrong that, when owner and occupier are different persons, the occupier, and not the owner, is taxed. Thus, if money is borrowed for, let us say, necessary sewage works, the whole cost of paying the interest and extinguishing the principal is thrown upon householders, who are thereby compelled to improve the estate of the ground landlord at their own expense. The theory is, of course, that the tax ultimately falls upon the owner, because, if it were not imposed, he would be able to charge a higher rent for his house. This may be doubted; but if it be true that the owner pays all the rates in the end, it is a pity he cannot see his way to pay them in the beginning, and thus end the dispute. Certain it is that the discontent resulting from the belief of occupiers that they are made to pay for the improvement of other people's property is growing every day, and that local bodies now hardly dare undertake many useful works, because they dread the indignation that will be aroused by an increase of the rates.

The favour with which investors were from the first inclined to look upon corporation stocks, and of which the absorption within the last twenty years of upwards of £100,000,000 is substantial proof, was confirmed and increased by their inclusion in the list of stocks authorized by the Trust Funds Act of 1889; for, as it was known that the select committee, to whom the Bill was referred, had made searching enquiry into the soundness of local loans, and had satisfied itself that the security they offered was practically unexceptionable, any little doubt that the public may have felt on that score was entirely removed. Unless expressly forbidden by the instrument creating the trust, a trustee may now lawfully invest " *(m)* In nominal or inscribed stock issued, " or to be issued, by the corporation of any municipal borough, " having, according to the returns of the last census prior to " the date of investment, a population exceeding fifty thousand, " or by any county council, under the authority of any Act of " Parliament or Provisional Order;" and the permission has been widely taken advantage of. The clause calls for the remark that, as the stability of a corporation stock does not depend on counting heads, it is not very obvious why a taboo should have been placed on the loans issued by incorporated towns of less than fifty thousand inhabitants, unless on the principle that a line had to be drawn somewhere. Perhaps the most curious result of that exception is the fact that the stock issued last year by the Corporation of the City of London is not a trust stock, simply because the population of the City does not attain the requisite minimum. The security offered by a corporation stock is that of a charge on the rates, which the corporation has power to levy, and on the whole of the revenue arising from its lands, markets, gas works, &c., and all other property for the time being. In case of default, provision is made for the appointment by the Court of Chancery of a receiver, but it need hardly be said that no occasion to exert the power has yet arisen. The assets of the corporations are doubtless of enormous value (the City of Manchester, for instance, appraises its corporate property at upwards of £14,000,000), but the ultimate and real security for the debt is the rateable value of property, and rates form the mainstay of local finance. The total Poor Rate Valuation of England and Wales is upwards of £160,000,000 and, if we assume that property is on the average worth from sixteen to twenty years' purchase of the assessment, it is obvious that the repayment of the debt of £235,000,000 is assured beyond all reasonable doubt. It must also be borne in mind, that, as rates are not limited in amount, a town must become absolutely bankrupt before the security fails. Good as rates may be, however, they are not equal to taxes as a debt security. Only death or emigration to a desert island will relieve the taxpayer of his burden; but the ratepayer can always shake off part of his load by removing to a less heavily rated district. The weak point about rates is, therefore, that if their pressure becomes too severe they inevitably tend to drive trade outside the municipal boundary, thus reducing both the rateable value and the local revenue. As high rates may thus prove to be the forerunners of local decay, their relative amount is a most important element in the prosperity of a borough, and is a point that should always be taken into consideration by the investor in corporation stocks. Another test of comparative value is the ratio which the unproductive portion of the debt—that part which represents money spent and not money invested—bears to the rateable value. To institute a comparison between the rateable value and the entire debt is of every little use, because a borough which has borrowed up to four or five times the amount of its assessment, may possess such lucrative assets as to be in a sounder position than another, the debt of which, though less than its rateable value, may be represented solely by unremunerative expenditure. Money spent in pulling down slums, building board schools, and laying out recreation grounds is money that has been well spent, and which in due season will return an ample yield in the shape of an increase in the health, happiness and intelligence of the people; but from the investor's point of view a mortgage on health and happiness presents an unsubstantial aspect, and he is apt to remember that the entire charge of a debt incurred for such purposes falls solely on the rates. As yet the process of discrimination between the stocks of different corporations can hardly be said to have begun. All are still regarded as about equally good, just as Colonial Stocks used to be not many years ago. But there are signs that it may not be long deferred, and when that time does come—when the investor does at last begin to pick and choose—those towns which have borrowed most largely for unproductive purposes (and especially such among them as may be dependent on the prosperity of one particular industry), are likely to receive a rude reminder that they have long been treading on dangerous ground.

THE

LONDON DAILY STOCK AND SHARE LIST.

SIXTH LECTURE.

[*Delivered 7 March 1891.*]

AT our last meeting I was endeavouring to impress upon your minds the magnitude of the proportions attained by our Local Debt, which, though contracted by urban and rural authorities, solely for what are supposed to be local purposes, constitutes just as much a charge upon the national prosperity as do the Imperial obligations. Two hundred and thirty-five millions would be a large sum to owe, even if we had no National Debt. It means that every child born in England and Wales begins life £7. 16s. 7d. behindhand. It is as large as the Public Debt of India, or as that of all the Australasian Colonies combined, and even exceeds the total of the Public Debts of Germany, Holland, Sweden, Norway and Denmark, all added together. And yet, serious as is the fact of our handicapping the rising generation with so large an additional liability, its rapid growth appears to give rise to very little uneasiness, and notwithstanding the persistent efforts of a few statisticians to direct public attention to it, is regarded with all but complete apathy, being neither followed nor understood. While Imperial finance and taxation seem to be everybody's business, local finance and taxation are nobody's. Let twopence be added to the Income Tax, and we are ready to wreck the Government; let it be added to the rates, and we submit with resignation, because conscious of our abject ignorance and helplessness. Now, large figures such as these cannot be made to yield their true meaning without a certain amount of manipulation. Simply to know that so great a sum has been spent is not enough; we must know how and why it has been spent. We ought also to know which of the purposes are remunerative, and which not, and, with regard to the capital expenditure for non-productive purposes, must ask to what extent it was justifiable. In the Local Taxation Returns for the financial year 1894–95, the outstanding debt in respect of reproductive outlay, so far as it is practicable to identify it, is stated to be as follows:

Water Works ...	£43,970,490
Gas Works ...	16,931,943
Markets	5,771,076
Cemeteries and Burial Grounds	2,718,133
Tramways	1,466,610
Harbours, Piers, Docks, and Quays	32,777,992
Electric Lighting and Supply ...	1,378,818
Total	£105,015,062

These amounts, it is necessary to observe, do not represent the present values of the water works, and gas works, &c., nor yet the original cost, but are merely the balances remaining open under the various heads. In other words, this is simply an analysis and apportionment of the undischarged debt, and does not purport to be the credit side of a balance sheet. A complete statement of the liabilities and assets of all the local authorities would be of inestimable value, if it were possible to procure it. There exists no such thing, however, and from the nature of the case, it does not seem feasible to draw one up. Some of the corporations have, it is true, published a valuation of their possessions, for the information of those who are able to put faith in such estimates; but the great mass of the local bodies make no attempt to issue a balance sheet, and confine their book-keeping to accounts of income and expenditure. So far, however, as these profit-earning assets are concerned, it is quite certain that their actual value enormously exceeds the proportion of the debt by which they are here represented, and some writers have even affirmed that, if such a thing can be imagined as the demunicipalization of the municipal trading undertakings, they would be valued for sale to companies at prices fully equal, in the aggregate, to the entire outstanding total of local indebtedness for all purposes. The first and most unexceptionable items in the table are the debts that have been incurred, with general approval, for the purchase or construction of water works and gas works. That water should be cheap, pure, and plentiful is, for sanitary reasons, of the utmost importance; and those local authorities who have taken the supply into their own hands, instead of leaving the consumer at the mercy of a commercial company, have acted with true wisdom. Gas, also, being almost a necessity, as well as an article in the supply of which competition is inadmissible, may legitimately be included in the scope of municipal socialism. The mode of acquiring such undertakings may be described as an application of the joint stock principle. The townspeople go into partnership, so to say, and the town council, as it has no power to issue shares, provides the necessary capital by borrowing. If the management is honest and efficient, there is no reason whatever why debt so incurred should entail any present or prospective expense on the ratepayer, and, as a matter of fact, most of the corporations can afford, after providing for interest, sinking fund, and working expenses, to apply a substantial sum out of the annual revenue in relief of the general rates. To the consumer, the only difference the transfer makes is that his water or gas bill is payable to the town council instead of to a company. Whether corporations have the right to make profit out of their gas and water supply, without specific powers to do so, is a question that has never been tested, but which is considered doubtful. On economic grounds such profits are open to attack, because, firstly, the consumer is taxed, not according to his means, but according to the extent of his consumption; and secondly, because they constitute a tax on production, in the cost of which gas and water are usually important elements. It may be added that the profit derived from water is much less than that from gas, and that, in many instances, the accounts even show a loss, the service charge having been cut down below cost. As regards the remaining items, markets, cemeteries, and tramways are all concerns that are self-supporting, or that can be made so under proper management; while as to harbours and docks, &c., the majority of the loans are not charged on the rates at all. Of capital expenditure that brings in no revenue, we have in the first place the building debt, consisting of:

Schools	£22,970,555
Poor Law purposes (Workhouses, Infirmaries, &c.)	7,773,504
Public Buildings, Offices, &c.	4,958,954
Lunatic Asylums	4,262,968
Police Stations, Gaols, &c.	1,254,469
Baths and Wash-houses	1,469,628
Hospitals	1,141,654
Fire Brigade Stations	693,736
Libraries and Museums	771,138
Slaughter Houses	154,445
Total	£45,451,051

This class of outlay cannot, of course, be called productive; but if the necessity or the utility of the objects for which these various descriptions of buildings have been erected is once admitted—and it would be difficult to take exception to any one of them—it is impossible to blame the local authorities for having become their own landlords by capitalizing what they would otherwise have had to pay as rent. Then many millions have been spent on other unproductive purposes, such as these:

Highways, Street Improvements, and Turnpike Roads	£30,143,979
Sewerage and Sewage Disposal Works	23,734,738
Bridges and Ferries	4,351,500
Parks, Pleasure Grounds, Commons, and Open Spaces	5,051,092
Artizans' and Labourers' Dwellings Improvements	4,351,532
Land Drainage and Embankment, River Conservancy, and Sea Defences ...	3,014,270
Total	£70,647,111

It is hardly correct, perhaps, to say that the whole of this outlay yields no return. In the case of street improvements, for instance, there is usually the direct advantage of surplus lands, which can be either let or sold, and the indirect advantage of an increase in the rateable value of the property benefited. For the use of bridges and ferries, too, tolls are sometimes charged, and artizans' dwellings are certainly not let rent free. But, with these trifling exceptions, the whole of the expenditure is, in a pecuniary sense, unremunerative, and is represented by assets, most of which are unrealizable and possess no money value. Nevertheless, it cannot be stigmatized as waste. To spend great sums on great objects is often the truest and best economy. The construction of sewers and drains, the widening of streets, the clearance of slums, may be works that produce no income, yet their results, in prolonging human life and in rendering it better worth living, entitle them to our most generous appreciation, and the public gain in health and happiness is, let us hope, an ample set-off against the pressure of the additional rates. At the same time, we must not forget that however beneficial such improvements may be, they are based upon debt, and that borrowing with too great rapidity and on too large a scale can never be judicious, whatever the object be. Sanitary science, too, is progressive. What is held to be right to-day may be proved to be wrong to-morrow. Millions have been spent in collecting the filth of towns, and pouring it into our beautiful rivers, to defile and poison them; millions more may some day have to be spent in getting it out again. On every side, in fact, there are indications that money will have to be borrowed in the future to undo work for the doing of which money is still owing that was borrowed in the past. Hence, expenditure of this class cannot be undertaken too carefully; but there is reason to fear that local authorities have not always gone very cautiously to work in the past, and that they have been apt to embark on ambitious, though well-meant, schemes of improvement without fully counting the cost. If it be asked what the prospects are as to the future growth and eventual proportions of the debt, I think the answer must be that the productive portion seems likely to exhibit a large further increase, but that the unproductive part, from which we have most to fear, has almost attained its maximum. Without borrowing, the local authorities could not have accomplished a tithe of what they have already done for the community; and without still further borrowing they will be unable to discharge the new duties which come with growth of population and with fuller knowledge of the laws of health. But, in most large towns, the heaviest works of this nature—the great main sewers and the network of subsidiary drains—have now been completed, and the amount annually repaid under the operation of the sinking funds ought soon to become greater than the fresh debt. The same is true of the outlay on education: the capital expenditure was greatest in the earlier years, and is now fast diminishing. The productive debt will, as I said, probably go on increasing. There appears every reason to believe that municipalities will not rest satisfied until they have given effect to the principle that no person or persons, except the corporation, shall have any right to interfere with public thoroughfares. Carried to its logical conclusion, this theory implies that all undertakings which meddle with, or claim a partial monopoly of, the streets—such as tramway companies, and all those for the supply of gas, water, hydraulic power, electric light, &c.—will eventually come to be taken over by the local authorities. The aspiration is, perhaps, a laudable one; but its realization, if ever it should come to pass, will mean the addition to local indebtedness of untold millions.

The parent of the prolific family of Corporation Stocks, and the only one of sufficient importance to call for special notice, is the well-known Metropolitan Consolidated Stock, created nearly thirty years ago by the late Board of Works. The Metropolitan Board of Works was originally called into existence by Parliament to cope with the pressing problem of London's drainage, as well as for the prosecution of such other undertakings as the changing circumstances of the metropolis might render necessary. In order to provide a sufficient revenue for this purpose, power was given to levy a rate on the whole of the rateable property within the metropolitan area, as defined by the Metropolis Local Management Act of 1855, but, as might have been expected, it was soon discovered, after getting to work, that heavy capital expenditure could not possibly be met out of current income, and that recourse would have to be had to borrowing. Under these circumstances it was natural, seeing that all the operations of the Board were carried on in obedience to the mandate of Parliament, that the Government should feel itself called upon to assist; and this it was decided to do by lending the credit of the State, to which end the Treasury was authorized to guarantee the repayment of any loans that the Board might find it necessary to contract. Aided by this guarantee, no difficulty was for some years experienced in raising all that was wanted at reasonable rates; but, owing to the fact that the security offered was a bond of entirely unmarketable character, the only lenders, practically speaking, were the Bank of England and the National Debt Commissioners, and, as time passed, it became clear that, sooner or later, other arrangements would have to be made, as these two bodies could not go on lending indefinitely. After a while, too, the Government grew anxious to get rid of its guarantee, as it now perceived that in extending the credit of the State to the metropolis, it had set a bad example to other towns in the kingdom, who might also be soon asking it to act as godfather to their debts. There was no great risk connected with the guarantee, but it formed a bad precedent. By 1869, the Board had run up a debt of eight millions, and, having undertaken works which would require an expenditure of two millions more, it was felt that the time had come to place its finances on a more permanent footing, in order that it might obtain funds with a facility commensurate with the security at its disposal. Accordingly, a Bill was brought in providing for the conversion, with the consent of holders, of all the existing loans into one uniform consolidated stock, the leading feature of which was that it would possess almost every attribute of the public funds, except that, instead of being charged on the Consolidated Fund of the nation, it would be charged on the Consolidated Fund of the metropolis. It also provided that all future loans should be raised in the same way. No actual guarantee was given, but, as the borrowing powers of the Board were placed under the stringent supervision of the Treasury, without whose express sanction no fresh loan could be raised, it might be held that there existed a moral guarantee. The stock was not to be perpetual; in the interests of the future ratepayer it was deemed expedient that the capital should ultimately be extinguished, and it was therefore directed that a sufficient annual instalment should be set aside to redeem all the stock in sixty years from the date of its creation, such sinking fund to be likewise under the control of the Treasury. At the suggestion of the Board, the Bill, as originally presented, gave authority to trustees to invest in the stock, unless expressly prohibited from doing so, but Parliament thought it better to first see how the new security would be received, and therefore struck the clause out. Two years afterwards, however—Metropolitans being then an established success—the clause was re-introduced in a supplementary measure, and was duly passed. To strengthen the parallel with Consols, an Act of 1870 enabled the Board to compound for the stamp duty on transfers, so that since that date the stock has changed hands free of charge. The security consisted of a first charge on all the property possessed by the Board, and on the whole of its revenue from every source. This increases as fast as buildings increase; and as the metropolis of a nation must stand or fall with the nation, its credit is practically the same, provided, of course, that the ratio of metropolitan debt to rateable value is not greater than that of the national debt to the national resources. In any case, it should rank higher than that of any provincial city, though, on the other hand, it must be borne in mind that the metropolitan debt has all been contracted for unremunerative undertakings, while the loans raised by provincial corporations have been partly, and in some instances largely, for productive purposes. The first ten issues of the stock, extending in date from 1869 to 1880, were made identical in their conditions, all bearing interest at $3\frac{1}{2}$ per-cent, and being redeemable in 1929, that is to say, in sixty years from the date of the first issue. It would have been quite feasible to bestow the full term of sixty years on each instalment, but this plan was attended by the drawback that it would have split up the stock into numerous divisions, all of different maturities and of comparatively small amounts, and would thus have injured its marketability, as the balance of advantage between a stock having, say only fifty-two years to run, but forming part of a large issue, and a stock having the full sixty years to run, but of no great amount, would almost invariably be in favour of the former. If carried too far, however, this shortening of the term becomes an injustice, because it burdens the ratepayer with a heavier sinking fund than is necessary; and in 1881, when the Three-and-a-half per-cent Stock had attained the respectable total of £17,000,000, the Board thought it time to make a new departure, both because their improved credit justified a lower rate of interest, and because any fresh addition made to the 1929 stock would have had to be paid off in forty-nine years. Tenders were therefore invited for a Three per-cent Stock, redeemable in 1941, of which the minimum price was fixed at ninety per-cent, and this description of Metropolitan Consols continued to be issued until the Board of Works was superseded by the London County Council. I may here mention, as a fact which is perhaps not generally known, that in 1877, the year in which Treasury Bills were first issued, the Board obtained leave to contract unfunded debt to a limited amount by raising the money needed for temporary purposes on short dated paper, somewhat in the form of the the new floating debt obligations, and repayable like them in not more than twelve months after date, and that the power conferred by the Act of 1877 has been renewed by each successive Annual Money Act, both of the Board and their successors, being kept alive in case it might some day prove useful. The considerations by which the Board of Works were influenced in deciding to lower the rate of interest on their stock in 1881, were equally applicable when their successors, the London County Council, brought out their first issue of £1,000,000 in 1889, and led to a repetition of the former proceeding. Since the introduction of the 3 per-cent stock, of which £10,850,000 had been placed on the market, the improvement in the Board's credit had steadily continued, as shown by the enhanced prices fixed for the successive issues, namely—

1881	90	per-cent minimum.	
1882	96	,,	,,
1883	95½	,,	,,
1884	97½	,,	,,
1885	96½	,,	,,
1886	98	,,	,,
1887	98½	,,	,,

and throughout 1889 the quotation had stood over par. Regard being had to the fact that the Council anticipated many and large future additions to their indebtedness, it was deemed advisable, notwithstanding the obvious disadvantage of having to bring before the public a third description of obligation, to adopt at the outset a form of stock to which it was thought certain, humanly speaking, that the Council would be able to permanently adhere, and a first issue of Two-and-a-half per-cents was therefore announced at the minimum price of 88. In further justification of the course taken by the Council, it was pointed out that the majority of steady investors, and especially trustees, to whom Metropolitan Stock presents great attractions, greatly prefer an investment which is redeemable at a profit, and of which the value must necessarily appreciate, to one that will eventually be paid off below cost, even though the latter be actuarially cheaper, and that they would therefore be more inclined to take a Two-and-a-half per-cent Stock at a discount, than a Three per-cent Stock at a premium. The new Two-and-a-half per-cents— or "Rosebery's" as they were dubbed—now amount to £7,700,000, and have been even a greater success than the Three per-cents. In 1892 the minimum was only $85\frac{1}{2}$; in 1893 it rose to 89; in 1894 to $93\frac{1}{2}$; in 1895 to 101; and in 1896 to 104. The date of redemption is 1949; but the County Council reserve the right to pay them off at par at any time after the 19 March 1920, provided that one year's notice of such repayment shall have been previously given. One feature that distinguishes the debt of the County Council from that of provincial corporations is the fact that a very large proportion of it represents money lent to other bodies. Powers have been given by statute to the London School Board, to the Managers of the Metropolitan Asylums District, and to vestries, district boards, guardians, and other public and local authorities, to borrow from it, and of the total debt of £35,000,000 upwards of one-third has been advanced to outside bodies. You will find on reference to the Official List that the entire stock only shows a diminution from its original amount of £71,686, and it may strike you as strange that the operation of the sinking fund should not bring about a steady-going reduction, such as we are accustomed to in the case of the funds. The reason is that the Council are permitted, instead of buying up their own stock with the annual surplus of income, either to invest it in advances to other bodies, or to employ it in capital expenditure for duly authorized purposes. It is expressly provided, however, that the repayment from such loans shall be hypothecated to the redemption of their own debt, and that no such money shall be so used, unless provision shall be made, in such a manner as the Treasury approve, for repaying the same to the Consolidated Loans Fund at, or before, the date at which Consolidated Stock, redeemable by means of such money, is required to be redeemed at par. In other words, if the funds applicable to the redemption of, say, the 1929 stock are lent out, instead of being used in cancelling the stock, it is essential that the loans should be made repayable before 1929, so that the money may be at hand when wanted. If power to invest the sinking fund in this manner had not been given, the Council would be a heavy loser, as it would have had to buy up its own stock at a heavy premium. Mention has more than once been made of the wide-reaching and constant supervision exercised by the Treasury over the financial arrangements in connection with the Metropolitan Stock. No provincial corporation is under control to anything like the same extent. In fact, beyond having to submit an annual statement of their loans' fund to the Local Government Board, whose suggestions they are expected to treat with due deference, they are left to their own devices. But, in the case of loans raised by the County Council, the fund constituted for paying the dividends and redeeming the principal is under strict supervision, and the Treasury controls the sum which must annually be raised by means of the consolidated rate for the service of the debt.

There still remain one or two minor questions to be noticed in connection with Corporation Stocks. The first is that of redemption. Most of the stocks are described as "Redeemable", and either the date of redemption is tacked on, or the period during which the right to redeem may be exercised. In no instance, it should be noted, is there a premium payable on redemption; the rate is always par. But there are also some stocks marked "Irredeemable," and this designation might lead you to infer that certain of the corporations have been absolved from the duty of repaying, and have been allowed to contract a perpetual debt. All it means is, however, that the stock-holder cannot be paid off against his will; and that, as neither time nor price is fixed for the redemption, the stock can only be cancelled by buying it up in the market at the price of the day. Whether redeemable or not, the borrower must set up a sinking fund, the accumulation of which shall be sufficient to extinguish the stock in a given number of years, as determined by the act authorizing the issue; and the advantage of making it redeemable at a specified time and price is that he knows precisely how much money must be set aside each year in order to meet the obligation at maturity. On the other hand, if the stock be irredeemable, it is not the nominal amount that he must provide for, but the market value, which may be a very different thing. To the citizens of Manchester, for instance, it must be most gratifying to know that their promise to pay £4 per annum is thought so highly of in the market as to be now valued at fifty per-cent premium; but it cannot be equally agreeable to reflect that, owing to their Consolidated Stock not having been made redeemable at par, provision must be made out of the corporate revenues to pay back five-and-a-half millions sterling instead of the three and three-quarter millions, which they borrowed. The objection, therefore, to an irredeemable stock is that every rise in price, after par has once been passed, means a re-adjustment of the sinking fund, and that the borrower is made to suffer for the improvement in his own credit; and this objection has so much force, that power to issue stock of this description is now no longer given by Parliament. Its issue in former years was justified by the supposition that it commanded a better price, but it may be doubted whether any investor would ever distinguish between a stock redeemable at par in fifty or sixty years, and one not subject to redemption at all. Another line of demarcation between corporation stocks is that which separates them into stocks liable to stamp duty and those which are free of the impost. This distinction is of more importance than it looks. The price of a stock depends, to a great extent, on its negotiability, that is to say, on the facility with which the would-be seller can find a would-be buyer, and negotiability is undoubtedly hampered if a tax must be paid every time the stock changes hands. In fact, other things being equal, a stock which is subject to the restriction of transfer-duty will always be at a disadvantage as compared with one that escapes the imposition. The fact that taxation seriously detracts from facility of dealing, and hence from market value, impressed itself strongly upon the Metropolitan Board of Works, very soon after the original issue of their Consolidated Stock, and in 1870, the following year, they obtained powers by a special Act of Parliament to compound for transfer-duty by a single payment of 7s. 6d. per-cent (afterwards raised in 1880 to 12s. 6d. per-cent) on the whole amount of the stock, which at once benefited by the concession. In 1875, as you will remember, the Government brought in a Local Loans Bill, and the provincial corporations, having quite expected that whenever such a measure was introduced they would be offered the same option, experienced some disappointment on finding that such was not the case. "The Metropolitan Board of Works", said Mr. Chamberlain, in opposing the Bill, " has been allowed " to compound for stamp-duty; and until Parliament chooses " to give to provincial corporations the same facilities, it need " not expect that they will take advantage of the Local Loans " Bill." The privilege was extended to them, however, in 1880, and in the Stamp Act of 1891, which is now in force, it is enacted that any county council or corporation may enter into an agreement with the Commissioners of Inland Revenue, if the Commissioners in their discretion think proper, for the composition of the stamp duties chargeable on transfers of their stocks on payment, half-yearly, of 6d. per-cent on the nominal amount. Advantage has been taken of this permission to a great extent, and in the prospectus of almost every new issue you now see it stated that transfers will be effected free of stamp duty or other charges, to be followed a week or two afterwards by a short paragraph in the "money article" to the effect that the Commissioners of Inland Revenue have entered into an agreement with the corporation of so-and-so for the composition of the stamp duties payable on transfers of their stock in accordance with the provisions contained in section 115 of "The Stamp Act, 1891."

In addition to the question of liability or non-liability to stamp duty, there are certain other matters of detail associated with the transfer of corporation stocks which call for remark, but which will be found lacking in interest unless we clearly comprehend the principle involved in such arrangements, and the requirements that they ought to fulfil. When a corporation borrows money in order to meet expenditure, of which it is presumably right and proper that the repayment should be spread over a term of years, it would obviously expose itself to extreme inconvenience if the lenders had the right to call in their loans at short notice, and were to exercise such right at a time when the conditions of the money market were not favourable to fresh borrowing. To avoid this risk the loans are made redeemable at fixed dates, and the lender has no power to claim his money until the expiration of the agreed term, which may be anything from thirty years up to sixty or more. But, if that were the whole extent of the bargain, it is more than likely that capitalists would decline to lend on such conditions, or, at any rate, that only very few would be found willing to place their capital beyond control for so long a period, and it is therefore essential that the lender shall be at full liberty, whenever he wishes to realize, to assign his claim to someone else who is willing to buy it of him. The borrower, moreover, must not only undertake to recognize, and act upon the assignment, but is expected to facilitate it as far as he reasonably can by adopting the most workable arrangement. In fact, the easier, the quicker, and the cheaper the claim can be transferred, the easier, the quicker, and the cheaper will the corporation find it possible to borrow. Now, if our cities were in the habit, as foreign municipalities are, of raising loans on bonds to bearer, the title to which passes by delivery, all troublesome transfer formalities would be avoided; but as investors of the class they appeal to mostly prefer (or, if trustees, are even restricted to) a specialized, and therefore safer form of security, they find it advisable to meet the requirements of the market by issuing what we know as stock. This is of the nature of a book debt, the name of the lender, or stock-holder, and the nominal amount of his loan, or stock, being registered by the corporation in a book, just in the same way that a merchant posts in his ledger the names of his creditors, and the sums for which he is indebted to them. In view of the importance of this record, which constitutes the evidence of the stock-holder's title, the duty of keeping a proper register (by register is meant, of course, the whole set of books necessary in connection with the stock), and of inserting therein the names and holdings of all proprietors, is enforced by law, and forms part of every act in which power to create stock is conferred. There are two ways in which stock may be transferred—either by book or by deed. If transferable by signing an entry made in the register itself, the stock is usually designated "Inscribed;" if transferable by signing a separate document or deed of transfer, it is usually described as "Registered." The distinction is quite an artificial one, as "inscribed" and "registered" mean the same thing. Consols are the type of an inscribed stock, and the manner in which they shall be transferred is set forth in section 22 of "The National Debt Act, 1870." "In the offices "of the respective Accountants-General of the Banks of "England and Ireland, books shall continue to be kept wherein "all transfers of stock shall be entered. Every such entry

"shall be conceived in proper words for the purpose of
"transfer, and shall be signed by the party making the
"transfer, or, if he is absent, by his attorney thereunto
"lawfully authorized by writing under his hand and seal,
"attested by two or more credible witnesses. The person
"to whom a transfer is so made may, if he thinks fit,
"underwrite his acceptance thereof. Except as otherwise
"provided by Act of Parliament, no other mode of transferring
"stock shall be good in law." It is also enacted in section 24
that the banks, before allowing any transfer of stock, "may if
"the circumstances of the case appear to them to make it
"expedient, require evidence of the title of any person claiming
"a right to make the transfer." In "The Colonial Stock Act,
1877", which provides for the inscription of stocks issued by
the Colonies, and which appears to have been the chief means
of bringing inscribed stocks into fashion, we find similar
regulations in Section 4: "Colonial Stock to which this Act
"applies, while inscribed in a register kept in the United
"Kingdom, shall be transferred as follows: (1) The transfer
"shall be made only in the register, and shall be signed by the
"transferor, or, if he is absent, by his attorney thereunto
"lawfully authorized by some writing executed under his hand
"and seal and attested. (2) The transferee may, if he thinks
"fit, underwrite his acceptance of the transfer." Stock
transferable by book is the safest form of security that
ingenuity and experience have found it possible to devise.
There is as much difference, in fact, between bonds to bearer
and inscribed stock, in point of safety, as between a bank
note and a crossed "not negotiable" cheque to order. The
investor who holds bearer bonds or "scrip stocks" as they
are commonly called, besides being exposed to the trouble of
detaching and collecting the coupons, must also put up with
the anxiety and expense attendant on their safe custody; but
in the case of inscribed stock, in addition to the convenience
of having the dividend sent to him by post, or paid direct to
his banker, it appears absolutely impossible to deprive him of
his property without his knowledge. A would-be forger must,
in the first place, attend at the office of the registrar and sign
the register in the presence of an official, under which
circumstances it would require astonishing skill to counterfeit
the shareholder's signature sufficiently well to pass muster;
and, secondly, he must be accompanied by a respectable

stockbroker, or by some one else well known to the registrar, who can answer for his identity. Whether these safeguards are ever overcome is only known to the registrars themselves, but I think I am right in saying that loss by forgery, if it does occur, is never allowed to prejudice the stock-holder. Though the buyer of inscribed stock is not required to attend at the office of the registrar when the transfer into his name is effected, he is at liberty to do so and to sign the register if he thinks fit; and it is certainly advisable that he should be present, in order that a specimen of his signature may at once be on record for comparison. Failing his attendance, the registrar has no apparent means of knowing his signature until it comes in on a dividend warrant. Another precaution by which the safety of inscribed stock is increased is that of giving no certificate. There can be little doubt that the issue of a document containing all particulars of the proprietor's holding must tend to facilitate fraud, if fraud is intended. The distinctive characteristic of inscribed stock is, as I said, the transfer by signature in the register itself, and, as this necessitates the personal attendance of the transferor, or his legally appointed attorney, it would obviously be a great bar to negotiability if the register were kept in an out-of-the-way place. You will, therefore, find that in almost every instance, where stock is transferable in the books, the corporation issuing it has appointed a London banker to act as its agent, and to keep the register on its behalf. It should also be noticed that, practically, the whole of the stocks so domiciled are transferable free of charge and in any amount. This latter proviso is of special convenience to trustees, who, when effecting a change of investment, like to re-invest the exact sum in hand without having a fraction left over. As between inscribed and registered stocks, the great advantage of the former is the rapidity with which a transfer can be effected. The seller's broker, having found a buyer, sends to the bank the particulars necessary for preparing the transfer entry, and, an hour or so afterwards, calls in with his client, who signs the book and also a receipt for the purchase money. This receipt, which is on a form supplied by the bank, is witnessed by the bank clerk, and, on handing it over to the buyer in proof of the transfer having been duly made, payment is effected and the transaction is complete. Compare this procedure with the formalities that must be gone through on transferring property in houses or land, and the perfection to which it has been brought will be better appreciated. Registered stock differs from inscribed stock in the two particulars already indicated, namely, that it is transferable by deed, without attendance, and that a certificate under the seal of the corporation and signed by its authorized official is issued to each stock-holder certifying that he is the registered proprietor of a stated amount of stock. This certificate is not in itself proof of ownership, and the object of granting it is simply to enable the holder to deal more easily with his stock. The only conclusive evidence of title is the entry in the register, the certificate being merely a solemn affirmation under seal that the person named therein actually is on the register as owner of stock to the amount specified. When selling registered stock, a transfer deed is prepared, which must be signed and sealed by both seller and buyer—by the former in token that he transfers, and by the latter in witness that he accepts the transfer. "Sealing" the transfer, which consists in sticking a red paper wafer on a certain spot, is a formality which, nowadays, appears meaningless, but which can be insisted upon. By Stock Exchange custom, the seller—that is to say, the seller's broker—has to make the transfer, and the buyer has to pay the the charges (stamp duty and registration fee, if any). Considerable perplexity, not to say suspicion, is sometimes aroused in the mind of the inexperienced investor, on discovering, when signing a transfer for the sale of stock, that the consideration money named therein does not agree with the sum specified in the contract rendered to him by his broker. If he enquires the reason of the difference, he is referred to a note, which is usually printed at the foot of the deed, and which explains, not so clearly as it might, that "the " consideration money set forth in a transfer may differ from " that which the first seller will receive, owing to sub-sales by " the original buyer; the Stamp Act requires that in such " cases the consideration money paid by the sub-purchaser, " shall be the one inserted in the deed, as regulating the " *ad valorem* duty." Notwithstanding the footnote, however, cases occur in which the transferor undoubtedly considers himself aggrieved in having to sign what appears to be an acknowledgment of a arger sum than he actually receives. The difficulty arises from the fact that stock may change hands again and again before settling day. A. B., the original holder, may, for instance, sell to C. D., at say 99¾; C. D. may re-sell to E. F., at par, and E. F. to G. H. at 100¼. As it would obviously be a waste of time and money to execute a chain of transfers, a clearing system is adopted, which there is not time to explain, but the effect of which is that C. D. and E. F. are eliminated from the transaction on payment to them of the respective differences, and that A. B. is represented as transferring direct to G. H. Then comes the question of the consideration money; A. B. sold for £99. 15*s.*, G. H. bought for £100. 5*s.*; if we insert £99. 15*s.*, the deed must bear a 10*s.* stamp, if £100. 5*s.*, a 12*s.* 6*d.* stamp. To save disputes, the Stamp Act settles the point by deciding that duty must be levied on the amount paid by the transferee. The transfer, therefore, reads: " I, A. B., in consideration of the sum of " one hundred pounds and five shillings, paid by G. H., herein- " after called the said transferee, do hereby bargain, etc.", and A. B. must console himself as best as he can. Registered corporation stocks differ widely in their conditions. Some corporations register transfers free of charge, others exact a fee for doing so; some keep their books open all the year round, others close them for a week or a fortnight at a time to prepare the dividends; some will accept the common form of transfer deed, others require a special form to be used; some will transfer any amount, including shillings and pence, others will only transfer multiples of £10, and so on. The golden rule for the corporations to bear in mind is that the fewer the restrictions the better the stock will be liked, and that, other things being equal, the market is sure, sooner or later, to differentiate in favour of stock which is transferable at all times, in all amounts, and free of all charges.

www.ingramcontent.com/pod-product-compliance
Lightning Source LLC
Chambersburg PA
CBHW021826230426
43669CB00008B/885